WOMEN AND SOCIAL ACTION

TELECLASS STUDY GUIDE

Second Edition

Martha E. Thompson, Ph.D.
Professor of Sociology and Women's Studies
Department of Sociology
College of Arts and Sciences
Northeastern Illinois University
Chicago, Illinois

Sponsored by:
The Board of Governors Universities

Member institutions are:

Chicago State University
Eastern Illinois University
Governors State University
Northeastern Illinois University
Western Illinois University

Produced by:
Governors State University
University Park, Illinois

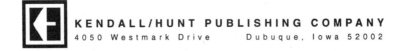

KENDALL/HUNT PUBLISHING COMPANY
4050 Westmark Drive   Dubuque, Iowa 52002

TABLE OF CONTENTS

Introduction .... *i*

Course description; expected student outcomes; required readings; class outlines; how to use this course; opening credits; responses to "Women and Social Action"

Class 1: Social Action and Social Change **1**

Introduction of the course participants, identification of key issues facing women, and an overview of a framework for thinking about social action and social change.
Video interview composite: Irene Campos Carr, Northeastern Illinois University; Helen Um, Korean Self-Help Center; Andrea Smith, Women of All Red Nations; Elaine Stocker, IMPACT Self-Defense for Women; Jean Lachowitz, Genesis House; Paulette Patterson, Council for Disability Rights; Marlene Jackson, The Hopi Tribe; Judy Panko Reis, Health Resource Center for Women with Disabilities
Interview Excerpt: Judy Panko Reis, Health Resource Center for Women with Disabilities

Class 2: Perspectives on Women **9**

Varied perspectives on women and social action. How our experiences shape the development of our perspectives and social actions.
Video interview composite: Pauline Bart, University of Illinois at Chicago; Laura McAlpine, Chicago Women's Health Center; Radhika Sharma, Apna Ghar; Rachel Lucas-Thompson; Ellen Dreyfus, Congregation Beth Sholom; Betty Achinstein, Thurgood Marshall Middle School
Studio guest: Mary Ann Schwartz, Professor of Sociology and Women's Studies, Northeastern Illinois University
Interview Excerpts: Jean Lachowitz, Genesis House; Andrea Smith, Women of All Red Nations; Irene Campos Carr, Northeastern Illinois University

Class 3: Leadership and Social Action **17**

Principles of leadership associated with an empowerment model of social change.
Video interview: Regina Curry, Associate Director, Woodlawn East Community and Neighbors (WE CAN)
Studio guest: Charles Payne, Associate Professor of African-American Studies, Sociology, and Urban Affairs, Northwestern University
Interview Excerpt: Norma Seledon-Telez, Coordinator, Latina Leadership Project, Mujeres Latinas En Accion

Class 4: Commonalities and Differences **25**

Dealing effectively with diversity among women and making connections among diverse issues.
Video interview: Alicia Amador, Youth Outreach Worker and Norma Seledon-Tellez, Coordinator, Latina Leadership Project, Mujeres Latinas En Acción
Studio guest: Yvonne Murry-Ramos, Executive Director, American Indian Economic Development Association (AIEDA)
Interview Excerpt: Theo Pintzuk, Women's Program, Howard Brown Health Center

Class 5: Gender Socialization **33**

Ways women are challenging gender socialization. How gender socialization relates to social action. The intersection of gender socialization with race and class.
Video interview: B.J. Richards, B.J.'s KIDS
Studio Guest: Barbara Scott, Assistant Professor of Sociology and Women's Studies, Northeastern Illinois University
Interview Excerpt: Della Mitchell, Coordinator, Chicago Coalition for the Homeless Empowerment Project for Homeless Women with Children

Class 6: Transforming Knowledge **41**

Gender and the current state of schools. Multi-cultural education and redefining feminist knowledge and pedagogy.
Video interviews: Betty Achinstein, Thurgood Marshall Middle School; Patricia Beardon, Metcalf Elementary School, and Yolanda Simmons, King High School
Studio guest: Wendy Stack, Director, Professional Development Program, University-Schools Project, Chicago Teachers' Center, Northeastern Illinois University

Class 7: Families **49**

Issues facing families. Looking at families in the context of culture and the political economy. Changes in social policies and social practices.
Video interview composite: The Hopi Tribe, Lynn Ables, Marla Dacawyma, Marlene Jackson, Carol James, Lynn Kalectaca, LuAnn Leonard, Nicole Marietta Leonard, Farron Lomakema, Grace Nejman, Beatrice Norton, Thelma Tewahaftewa, Ethelene Tootsie, and Ellen Wadsworth
Studio guest: Harriet Gross, Professor, Humanities and Social Sciences, Governors State University

Class 8: Child Care **55**

The need for child care. Individual, family, community, and societal responsibilities for child care.
Video interview composite: Catherine Moore, Director, Betty Sandifer, teacher, and Doris Thompson, student and teen parent plus other teen parents and children at Orr Community Academy Infant and Family Development Center
Studio guest: Brenda Chock Arksey, Director, Child Education and Development Services, Chinese American Service League
Interview Excerpt: B.J. Richards, B.J.'s KIDS

Class 9: Women and Health **61**

Women's health issues in a social context. Women-centered and community-based health care alternatives.
Video interview composite: Mary McCauley II, Director, Robin Stein, Sandra Steingraber, and Carol Zimmerman, Lesbian Community Cancer Project; Laura McAlpine, Director, and Sharon Powell, Outreach Coordinator, Chicago Women's Health Center
Studio guest: Geri Shangreaux, Dean of Chicago Campus, Native American Educational Services (NAES)
Interview Excerpts: Judy Panko Reis, Health Resource Center for Women with Disabilities, Sandra Steingraber, Lesbian Community Cancer Project

Class 10: Women, Weight, and Food **71**

Effect on women of cultural obsession with body weight and food. Interconnections of gender, sexuality, and power to understand weight and food. Taking our bodies back.
Studio guest: Demetria Iazzetto, contributor to *The New Our Bodies, Ourselves, Updated and Expanded for the '90s.*
Interview Excerpt: Sharon Powell, Outreach Coordinator, Chicago Women's Health Center

Class 11: Pregnancy and Childbirth 77

Issues women face in pregnancy and childbirth. Medical versus midwifery model of pregnancy and childbirth. The power of women's bodies.
Video interview: Judy Panko Reis, Health Resource Center for Women with Disabilities
Studio guest: Margorie Altergott, health educator; Adjunct Faculty, Department of Sociology, Northeastern Illinois University
Interview Excerpt: Melissa Josephs, Policy Associate, Women Employed

Class 12: Motherhood 85

Motherhood as a social institution and a social relationship. Alternative insemination. Challenging limiting models of motherhood and parenting.
Video interview: Jonathon Blumenthal and Amy Blumenthal
Studio guest: Amy Blumenthal, author of "Scrambled eggs and seed daddies: conversations with my son," *Empathy, Gay and Lesbian Advocacy Research Project*

Class 13: Abortion and Reproductive Issues 91

Abortion and reproduction within a socio-historical context. Differential effects on women of legal barriers, funding restrictions, and blocking access to clinics. Relationship of women's control of reproduction to other social justice struggles.
Video composite: Demonstrations at Cook County Hospital and Rev. Cheryl Pero, Crossings Ministry (Lutheran), Harold Washington College Campus Ministry
Studio guest: Aida Giachello, Assistant Professor, Jane Addams College of Social Work, University of Illinois at Chicago
Interview Excerpt: Andrea Smith, Women of All Red Nations

Class 14: Religion 97

Transforming religious practices and beliefs. Religious beliefs and practices as a basis for transforming society.
Video interviews: Rabbi Ellen Dreyfus, Congregation Beth Sholom; Rev. Cheryl Pero, Crossings Ministry, Harold Washington Campus Ministry
Studio guest: Ellen Cannon, Professor of Political Science and Women's Studies, Northeastern Illinois University
Interview Excerpt: Andrea Smith, Women of All Red Nations

Class 15: Work 105

Women's work in a social context. Support systems for resistance and resocialization. Strategies for networking, mentoring, and advocacy.
Video interview: Melissa Josephs, Policy Associate, and Sheila Rogers, Director of Participant Services, Keys to Success Program, Women Employed
Studio guest: Eileen Kreutz, Training Coordinator, Chicago Women in Trades
Interview Excerpt: Hallie Amey, President, Resident Management Council, Wentworth Gardens

Class 16: Sexual Harassment 113

Understanding sexual harassment—history, culture, laws, sex segregation, and power. Simulated exercises and strategies for dealing with sexual harassment.
Video interviews: Randy Gold, attorney with Lawrence, Kamin, Saunders, and Uhlenhop; Mary Mittler, Vice-President for Student Affairs, Oakton Community College
Studio Guest: Joe Connelly, Instructor, Self Empowerment Group
Interview Excerpt: Melissa Josephs, Policy Associate, Women Employed

Class 17: Low-income Resistance **121**

Impact of low income and few resources on women. Women's resistance to stereotypes and barriers. Modest struggles and social change.
Video interview composite: Hallie Amey, President, Resident Management Council, Wentworth Gardens; Beatrice Harris, President, Local Advisory Council and Resident Management Council Board Member, Wentworth Gardens; Andrea Henley, Director, Boys and Girls Club, Wentworth Gardens
Studio guest: Susan Stall, Assistant Professor of Sociology and Women's Studies, Northeastern Illinois University
Interview Excerpt: Sheila Rogers, Director of Participant Services, Keys to Success Program, Women Employed

Class 18: Homelessness **131**

Homelessness of women and children in a social context. Charity versus empowerment. Strategies for empowerment of homeless women with children.
Video composites: Women at Spiritual Beth Israel Shelter; Shelter representatives on the Coordinating Committee of the Chicago Coalition for the Homeless Empowerment Project for Homeless Women with Children
Studio guest: Della Mitchell, Coordinator, Chicago Coalition for the Homeless Empowerment Project for Homeless Women with Children
Interview Excerpt: Dihya Al Kahina and Judy Vaughan, National Coordinating Team, National Assembly of Religious Women (NARW)

Class 19: Connecting the Issues **137**

Exploring ways to connect issues. Choosing issues on which to work. Dealing with multiple issues through social action.
Video interviews: Dihya Al Kahina and Judy Vaughan, National Coordinating Team, National Assembly of Religious Women (NARW)
Studio guest: Maha Jarad, Director of Women in Organizing Project, Women United for a Better Chicago and Program Development Coordinator, Union of Palestinian Women's Association
Interview Excerpt: Irene Campos Carr, Coordinator, Women's Studies Program at Northeastern Illinois University

Class 20: Violence Against Women **145**

Violence as a social issue. Perspectives on violence. Actions to deal with and to challenge violence against women.
Video interview: Stephanie Riger, co-author, *The Female Fear*, Coordinator of Women's Studies, University of Illinois in Chicago
Studio guests: Ranjana Bhargava, Executive Director, and Lee Maglaya, Board Member, Apna Ghar
Interview Excerpts: Pam Wilson, Office Manager, and Radhika Sharma, Legal Advocate and Community Educator, Apna Ghar

Class 21: On the Streets and in the Jails **155**

Women in prostitution and women in jail. The influence of gender, race, and class on prostitution and the criminal justice system. Actions to deal with and challenge women's experience in prostitution and the criminal justice system.
Video interviews: Jean Lachowitz, Executive Director, Genesis House; Leslie Brown, Director, Support Advocates for Women...Both Inside and Outside Prison (SAW)
Studio guest: Shelley Bannister, Illinois Clemency Project for Battered Women and Associate Professor of Criminal Justice and Women's Studies, Northeastern Illinois University
Interview Excerpt: Leslie Brown, Director, Support Advocates for Women...Both Inside and Outside Prison (SAW)

Class 22: Rape and Self-Defense **163**

Effective self-defense. Relationship between self-defense and the anti-violence movement.
Video composite: IMPACT: Self-Defense for Women
Video interview: Pauline Bart, University of Illinois in Chicago, co-author of *Stopping Rape: Successful Survival Strategies*
Studio guest: Nancy Lanoue, Co-director, Thousand Waves: Martial Arts and Self-Defense for Women and Children

Class 23: Perspectives on Social Change **171**

How perspectives on social change influence definitions of problems, identification of causes, and selection of social actions. Community building and empowerment.
Video Interview: Marca Bristo, President, Access Living, A Center for Service, Advocacy and Social Change for People with Disabilities
Studio guest: Renny Golden, Associate Professor of Criminal Justice and Women's Studies, Northeastern Illinois University
Interview Excerpt: Della Mitchell, Coordinator, Chicago Coalition for the Homeless Empowerment Project for Women with Children

Class 24: New Directions **179**

Empowerment, social action and social change. Building community.

Appendix **185**

A —**Scrambled Eggs and Seed Daddies: Conversations with My Son** **185**

B —**Sexual Harassment: A Sociological Perspective** **189**

C —**(Grassroot) Resident Activism in Wentworth Gardens, a Chicago Public Housing Development: A Case Study of Building Community** **192**

D1 —**The Chicago Coalition for the Homeless Women's Empowerment Project** **199**

D2 —**Homeless Families in Chicago** **200**

E —**NCASA Guidelines for Choosing a Self-Defense Course** **202**

Organizations **204**

Acknowledgements **208**

INTRODUCTION TO "WOMEN AND SOCIAL ACTION"

Welcome to "Women and Social Action!" Is this your first teleclass? Is this your first course with a focus on women? Or are you already familiar with both the teleclass process and women's studies? If you have not taken a teleclass before, you should know that you will be the key person to determine the success of the teleclass. To gain the most from the teleclass, you will need to develop a plan for regularly reading the textbooks and additional handouts, reading and working with the Study Guide, watching the videotapes, and completing the requirements for the course. If you are not sure how to get started, ask for guidance from the faculty member supervising the course, talk to others who have taken a teleclass before, or seek advice from people you know who are independent learners.

Even if you are familiar with women's studies and sociology you may be somewhat surprised by the content and format of the telecourse. Don't expect lectures or lots of statistics. "Women and Social Action" emphasizes storytelling and active student participation, both of which are handled very effectively by television.

Hearing people's stories is an effective way to get a sense of the complexities of people's lives as well as to see the commitment, vision, humor, and compassion underlying empowering social actions. "Women and Social Action" captures on videotape the stories of over seventy women and men who are involved in social action as well as the experiences of students in the course. Through people's stories, we gain a richer understanding of barriers women face, varied goals and strategies for social change, and the rewards and challenges of social action.

Another effective method for helping you learn about women and social action is to have you witness others grappling with the ideas, controversies, and challenges inherent in the subject matter. When people have thought about subject matter from both a deeply personal standpoint and in terms of scholarly reading, discussion can be rich and focused. As you watch the tapes, you will find the students' explorations of the readings, discussions of the video interviews, and dialogues with studio guests thoughtful, moving, and ultimately, I hope, involving for you also.

COURSE DESCRIPTION

When thinking about women and social action, people often focus on the advancement of women in politics, business, or the professions. Media portrayals of women and social action often overstate the successes and failures of women to attain equality in traditionally male-dominated fields. Social change is often portrayed as the result of the efforts of a few women at the center of power or on the fringes of society acting in isolation.

Yet, for most women the struggle for change does not begin in the boardroom or the courtroom, but in their homes, communities, places of worship, and workplaces. Though women are challenging gender stereotypes and discrimination in the workplace and in politics, women are also organizing to reduce poverty, violence, homelessness; to enhance health care, family life, education, and religious experience; and to confront limitations based not only on gender, but also on age, class, disability, ethnicity, race, religion, and sexual orientation.

In "Women and Social Action," we focus on ordinary women who are working collectively in diverse social settings for empowerment. As studio guests or in video interviews, more than seventy people contributed their experiences and ideas about social actions. Typically, the women and men you will meet through "Women and Social Action" are committed to people collectively (1) defining their own problems with attention to commonalities and differences within the group, (2) analyzing the sources of their own problems with an understanding of systems of power operating in the larger society, and (3) determining courses of action most appropriate for their own circumstances which move toward a transformation of these systems of power.

EXPECTED STUDENT OUTCOMES

By the end of the course, students will be able to recognize the impact gender stereotypes and barriers have on women's lives and how they intersect with other social systems, such as age, class, disability, ethnicity, race, religion, and sexual orientation. Students will be able to analyze and evaluate whether or not the goals and methods of particular social actions are consistent with an empowerment model of social change.

REQUIRED READINGS

Andersen, Margaret L. 1997. *Thinking About Women: Sociological Perspectives on Sex and Gender,* fourth edition. NY: Allyn and Bacon.

Cantarow, Ellen. 1980. *Moving the Mountain: Women Working for Social Change.* Old Westbury, NY: Feminist Press.

Required readings contained in the Study Guide include:

Amy Blumenthal. "Scrambled eggs and seed daddies: conversations with my son." Reprinted with permission from *Empathy, Gay and Lesbian Advocacy Research Project.*

"The Chicago Coalition for the Homeless Women's Empowerment Project." Reprinted with permission from *Illinois Women's Advocate.*

Feldman, Roberta M. and Susan Stall. "Resident activism in public housing: a case study of women's invisible work of building community." Reprinted with permission of Environmental Design Research Association.

"NCASA Guidelines for Choosing a Self-Defense Course," originally appearing in *Women in the Martial Arts* and reprinted with the encouragement of the National Coalition Against Sexual Assault (NCASA) to distribute this material with attribution to NCASA.

"Sexual harassment: a sociological perspective." Reprinted with permission from the American Sociological Association.

Sperber, Bob. "Homeless families in Chicago." Reprinted with permission from *Chicago Coalition for the Homeless Newsletter.*

CLASS OUTLINE

This teleclass consists of 24 one-hour tapes. The tapes include class discussion, videotaped interviews, and conversations with studio guests. The students' stories, questions, and comments are a vital part of "Women and Social Action." As you watch the videotapes, you will come to know the students by name. Because we often had visitors interested in the topic for the day, you will occasionally see a new face among the students in the studio. I hope as we go along you find that one or more of the students has a viewpoint similar to your own and raises the questions you would ask if you were in the studio.

Studio guests and the video interviews include people who share a commitment to empowerment, but work on many different social issues and vary in age, physical disability, ethnicity, race, religion, sexual orientation, and social class.

The first four class sessions are an introduction to the themes in "Women and Social Action," including: an empowerment model for social change, connections between personal experience and social action, group-centered leadership, strength in diversity, and connections among social issues. In Class 1 the students and I introduce ourselves, students in the course and women interviewed on videotape identify important issues facing women, and I introduce a framework for social action.

In Class 2 we explore varied perspectives on women and social action and the influence of our backgrounds on shaping the development of our perspectives and actions. In Class 3 we discuss principles of leadership associated with an empowerment model for social change. In Class 4 we discuss dealing effectively with diversity and making connections among issues.

In Classes 5 - 22 we explore some of the diverse issues around which women have organized, such as gender socialization, images of women, education, motherhood, families, child care, health care, reproduction, religion, work, sexual harassment, public housing, homelessness, peace, rape, battery, prostitution, and self-defense. Classes 23 and 24 focus on additional elements of an empowerment model of social change and how to integrate this into our own lives. In Class 23 we explore coalition and community building for social change. In Class 24 class members will talk about what they have learned in "Women and Social Action" and the new directions they plan to take in their lives.

HOW TO USE THIS COURSE

Use the Study Guide to orient yourself to each videotape. In each chapter I recommend what to read prior to watching the videotape and a topic to write about. I recommend you keep a personal journal during the course and complete each assignment prior to viewing the videotape. Your prior reading and thinking about the topic will enhance your video viewing and your journal will be a record of your own thinking in the course.

I introduce each topic in the Study Guide to establish a background or context for viewing the videotape. I also provide commentary on each videotape, suggesting ways to think about the class discussion. Following the videotape commentary, I provide a list of review questions which cover both the reading and the videotape. In the Review Questions, I typically start out with questions from the reading and follow with questions from the videotape. Often questions can be answered from both the reading and videotape. For most of the chapters, an interview excerpt follows the review questions. These excerpts are from interviews conducted with people who were interviewed on location. At the end of each chapter, I provide a list of references in case you would like to do additional reading in a topic area and I provide a list of organizations mentioned in the Study Guide or on videotape in case you would like to volunteer or contact the organization.

Do follow the Study Guide and watch each videotape in sequence. I hope this course will be as much of an inspiration to you as it was to those involved in the production of "Women and Social Action."

OPENING CREDITS

At the beginning of each videotape, you will see the opening credits for the course and the faces of eight of the women who were interviewed for Women and Social Action. In order of appearance are Hallie Amey, President, Resident Management Council of Wentworth Gardens; Carol Zimmerman, Lesbian Community Cancer Project; Pam Wilson, Office Manager, Apna Ghar; Paulette Patterson, Information and Referral Specialist, Council for Disability Rights; Norma Seledon-Tellez, Coordinator, Latina Leadership Project, Mujeres Latinas En Acción; Marca Bristo, President, Access Living; Marlene Jackson, The Hopi Tribe; Helen Um, Coordinator of the Women's Program, Korean Self-Help Center.

RESPONSE TO "WOMEN AND SOCIAL ACTION"
After you've completed the telecourse "Women and Social Action," I'd like to hear from you. If you have comments, suggestions, or concerns, let me know. I look forward to hearing from you.

Martha Thompson
Department of Sociology
Northeastern Illinois University
5500 N. St. Louis Avenue
Chicago, IL 60625
umthomps@govst.edu
(773) 794-2722

WOMEN AND SOCIAL ACTION: CLASS 1
Social Action and Social Change

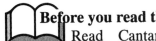 **Before you read this Chapter of the Study Guide**
Read   Cantarow, "Preface"
        Andersen, "Preface"

JOURNAL ASSIGNMENT

Make a list of three issues facing women. Note what you have done about these issues in your own life. Write a brief reflection on how your own background (e.g. family, education, occupation, or historical period in which you grew up) might have influenced the issues you see as important and your involvement or lack of involvement in social action. As you view the tape, note whether or not your issues are included in the list developed by the class.

I. INTRODUCTION

When you envision social action and social change, what do you see? Do you imagine a charismatic speaker inspiring large numbers of people to march in protest? Do you see an elected public official signing a significant piece of legislation into law? Do you see a woman on the Supreme Court, as a State Governor, or in an upper level executive position?

Imagine instead the behind-the-scenes women who put up the posters, made the phone calls, and visited their neighbors to insure a large turnout for the charismatic leader's speech. Imagine the ordinary women who the day after the march began the long and painstaking work of getting people to put their inspiration into action. Imagine the women who wrote letters, visited their legislators, and applied the political pressure to get the legislation drafted and passed. Imagine the women who have worked tirelessly and without recognition to expand educational and occupational opportunities for women, to get team sports for girls in their schools, to improve housing conditions and public services in their neighborhoods, to develop quality child care, to establish shelters for battered women, to enhance health care services for women with disabilities, or to teach self-defense against rape.

As you view Class 1 keep in mind that the media often focus on atypical or dramatic social issues and actions. In Class 1, you will hear about, instead, everyday issues and actions of ordinary women.

II. CLASS THEMES

The purpose of this class session is to introduce participants to the course and to each other. Key themes introduced include:

- The connection between our personal lives and society.
- The value of viewing social action and social change through the experiences of ordinary women.
- The importance of recognizing commonalities and differences in building social actions which contribute to the empowerment of ourselves and others.
- The need for a framework which grounds theories and actions in women's experience.

III. VIDEOTAPE SYNOPSIS

- Overview of the class session
- Introductions of participants
- Video composite of women talking about issues facing women
- Students' brainstorming about additional issues facing women
- A framework for action

IV. VIDEOTAPE COMMENTARY

I suggest you read this section before you watch the videotape. You will find that it will help you organize your thoughts in a more useful way than if you just watch the tape "cold." When you have finished viewing the tape you may want to read this section again.

A. Participants' Introductions

As the students and I introduce ourselves, you will have an opportunity to exercise your socio-logical imagination: How have our ideas, expectations, or experiences been influenced by social, political, or economic structures in society? For example, in my introduction, I recount how my views on social action and social change were influenced by my family background and my experiences at Kent State University with the anti-war movement and the women's liberation movement. Trenace mentions the influence of the African-American community in her life. Debbie mentions how her growing up in the 60s contributed to her feeling that picketing was a normal activity. Janet thinks she might be the skeptic in the class because of her reservations about Kent State and the women's liberation movement. Mary mentions the influence of her organizational and management background on her interest in social change.

Many class members mention the influence their families have had on their beliefs and activism or the influence families have had on their children. For instance, Ada talks about the influence of her mother's strong opinions. Sharon tells us about how her family's commitment to commu-nity work influenced her daughter's choice of a career. Peg states how her longstanding commit-ment to women's issues was influenced by her socially conscious family. Claudia, Debbie, Gunther, Judy, Laura, Janet, Joan, and Virginia mention the influence they have had or hope to have on their children. Listen for other examples of ways individuals have been influenced by their families, communities, or society.

In their introductions, class members also reveal potential commonalities and differences that will likely influence our class discussion. Several members express a deep commitment or interest in women's issues, feminism, or nonsexist education while for others this is new ground. For instance, Carlos was interested in taking this class because he was exposed to neo-Marxist feminists in another class. Claudia and Joe have previously taken women's studies classes and have signed up for another one. Helen has years of commitment to the women's movement and has been the editor of a feminist periodical, *The Creative Woman*. Gail is a women's studies major and has participated in various feminist actions. Debbie raised her daughter in a nonsexist environment and her daughter is now minoring in women's studies. Judy belongs to a women's reading group and has written a paper predicting the status of women in the year 2000. Phyllis and Christine are curious and want to learn more, but this is essentially new material for them. Gunther has never had a women's studies course before and wonders if he is a chauvinist and has raised his daughter in a sexist way.

Class members' introductions also suggest the value of learning about social action and social change through ordinary people's experiences. For example, Mary, Janet, and I express very different reactions to the women's movement of the early 1970s. My life has been profoundly affected by my involvement in the women's movement. Janet was and remains skeptical of the women's movement, but has a commitment to humanism. Until recently, Mary ignored women's issues, but is now rethinking her position. As we go through the course, we will find out more about each member of the class. By listening carefully to our stories and ideas, you can enhance your understanding of what influences your own choices of issues, your own choices of actions, and the perspectives you have on social action and social change.

B. Video Composite of Issues Facing Women

This is the first video clip for this course. As I mention in introducing it, we have much to learn about social action and social change from women who are actively committed to empowerment of themselves and their communities. The names of the women do not appear on the videotape; their names and affiliations are listed below in the order they appear on the tape. As you view the clip, make a list of the issues each identifies.

Irene Campos Carr, Coordinator, Women's Studies Program, Northeastern Illinois University, Chicago

Helen Um, Coordinator, Women's Program, Korean Self-Help Center, Chicago

Andrea Smith, Women of all Red Nations, Chicago

Elaine Stocker, student, IMPACT Self-defense for Women, Chicago

Jean Lachowitz, Executive Director, Genesis House, Chicago

Paulette Patterson, Information and Referral Specialist, Council for Disability Rights, Chicago

Marlene Jackson, The Hopi Tribe, Keams Canyon, Arizona

Judy Panko Reis, Health Resource Center for Women with Disabilities, Chicago

C. Class discussion

Following the composite interviews, students brainstormed additional issues. Add below any other issues you have listed in your reflection or that have come to you as you watched the videotape.

Through the video interviews and brainstorming with students, we see again the strength of diverse perspectives when trying to grasp the scope of the issues facing women. Now that we have a beginning notion of the considerable issues women face, we need to figure out a way to approach them. The purpose of action in the framework below is empowerment, that is, changing the conditions of women's experience so that women control their own lives (Morgen and Bookman, 1988; Rappaport, 1981).

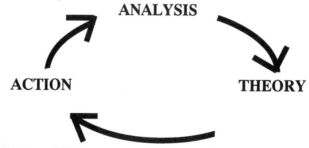

E. Class Discussion

Joan and Ada volunteer stories of situations in which they had felt demeaned, limited, or invisible. When analyzing their stories, we find that they both were in situations in which an employer asked them to do custodial and/or personal tasks outside their job description. Both talk about the deeply negative effects this situation had on their feelings about themselves. Suggesting a theoretical framework, Helen characterized the relationship between male employers and female employees as one of domination. Gunther disagreed with this characterization suggesting that the employer and employees in these circumstances had superior and inferior positions relative to each other. These different characterizations of Joan's and Ada's experiences suggest different foci for action. Helen's concept of domination suggests challenging patterns of male domination and female subordination, a large scale and long term endeavor. Gunther's comments about superior and inferior positions focus on the employer-employee relationship not male-female relationships. His idea of assertive behavior, Mary's comments about negotiation, Ada's clear boundary setting with her employer, and Joan's leaving her position focus on the employer-employee relationship within a particular situation, suggesting smaller scale and individual actions. As the class discussion illustrates, choices about the target, scope, and type of action will be greatly influenced by how we explain women's experiences.

 Now watch the videotape.

V. REVIEW QUESTIONS

1. What is the philosophy and method of oral history? Select one of the issues you identified in your reflection and think about who you could interview for this topic.

2. As you look over the list of issues compiled by you, the students, and the women on the video clip, note which issues are likely to be of concern to all women (e.g. access to education) and which issues might be of particular concern to a group of women (e.g. both Andrea Smith and Marlene Jackson identify land as a key issue for native American women). Also note issues which might concern all women, but which pose additional barriers for some groups of women (e.g. employment concerns all women, but African-American women also face the barriers of racism). How might the sociological imagination help you understand these similarities and differences?

3. What is empowerment and how does it relate to analysis, theory, and action?

4. Describe an experience you have had where you felt demeaned, invisible, limited, or stereotyped. If you have not had such an experience, talk with someone who has. What key ideas are suggested by this experience? What explanation do you have for this experience? What changes would be needed to minimize the possibility of this experience being repeated.

VI. INTERVIEW EXCERPT

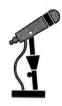

Transportation is an issue which affects many women. Judy Panko Reis, Health Center for Women with Disabilities, tells us why transportation is such an important issue for women with disabilities and gives us an overview of efforts to meet the transportation regulations of the Americans with Disabilities Act.

 Judy Panko Reis:

I cannot get on public transportation. Transportation's a really major problem for many disabled people because it's going to connect us with other people. It's the thing that's going to make interpersonal connection a reality. It's going to help us get jobs, it's going to help us get medical attention, medical services, it's going to help us get the resources we need to be viable people. However, in my situation, because my visual deficits prevent me from driving and I have a fairly severe mobility limitation, I have a tremendous problem getting around. I cannot get on main-line buses or trains and I can't walk far. I can walk comfortably a few yards. So what that means is I virtually have to either be driven around or I have to take taxis which are very, very expensive. Now if I was in a wheelchair I probably wouldn't even be able to take taxis because most taxis are not accessible. What the transportation situation right now for most disabled people means that we are left to resort to paratransit and the paratransit is a $1 ride service that fills up very, very quickly. We have to call 24-hours in advance and try to get through all the busy signals and possibly get a reservation for a ride the next day at the time that we made the doctor's appointment, for example. And that was how I got my child around. That was how I got my child to doctors' appointments, that's how I got myself to the University of Chicago where I took my first masters degree. A lot of people are losing jobs because they cannot get to work on time and they cannot get to work reliably. Paratransit is a very inefficient way to get disabled people around and yet that's it, at this point in time, until everything becomes, not only lift-equipped, but equipped with drivers and operators that are sensitive to our needs and know how to use the equipment and give us the transportation service that we require. We are left to the horrors and the limitations of having to get up at 5 in the morning, the day before we need a ride, to compete for the possibility of getting a ride just to go to the grocery store.

You can take your child sometimes on paratransit. It's all again very, very individual. It depends what kind of relationship the transit agency, whether it's the CTA, or the Suburban Transit Agency, has with that particular contractor. We have pretty much, I think, today successfully gotten to the point where disabled parents are able to take their nondisabled children with them. I mean there was a time and I still think there is still a practice in many parts of the country where if the disabled parent is trying to take a nondisabled child somewhere, they will be turned down for a ride. I should also say while we're talking about this that another important thing about getting children around is that schools have to be accessible. Even though your child is not disabled, you need an accessible school. I couldn't get Lewis into preschools that had a lot of stairs in them and I couldn't get Lewis into doctors' offices cause they were inaccessible as well. And so often the problems that confront a disabled parent really have a lot to do with what the child will be able to partake in - which after school programs, which school programs, which schools that they're going to attend, and the transportation practices are going to determine how or if you're even going to be able to get your child there.

I sit on a number of advisory boards. I sit on the Suburban Transit Advisory Board, I sit on the Regional Transportation Advisory Board, all are looking at providing accessible transit for the severely mobility impaired. And also for people that have developmental disabilities that might prevent them from independently accessing public transit. Our boards are made up of cross-disabilities; we have blind and visually impaired, and deaf and hearing impaired, as well as mobility impaired and developmentally disabled representatives on these boards. What we're trying to do is implement the regulations of the ADA that mandate that stations, commuter rail stations, whether they be transit stations or Metra stations, are accessible as well as the rail cars and the buses that are purchased. So all new buses and rail cars to be purchased from now on should be purchased with lifts. And we're still working on fine-tuning some of these regulations. For example, I was in a meeting a few weeks ago with some people from Washington, D.C. talking about how we needed to make sure the doors in between rail cars are accessible so we can go from car to car to get into our commuter rail train. We need to prioritize seating for people who are disabled that are not in wheelchairs but are ambulatory and have invisible dis-abilities. There's a whole range of our people that have disabilities that are not visible. So often ambulatory people are considered nondisabled even though they have very severe mobility impairments; they might have kidney dialysis problems, they might have heart problems. People with AIDS are also included in the Americans With Disabilities Act and are often considered to be transportation disabled because they just don't have the energy to walk up a flight of stairs to access transportation.

VII. SOURCES AND FURTHER READING

Allen, Paula Gunn. 1992. "Angry women are building: issues and struggles facing American Indian women today." Pp. 42-46 in *Race, Class, and Gender: An Anthology*, edited by Margaret L. Andersen and Patricia Hill Collins. Belmont, CA: Wadsworth Publishing.

Asch, Adrienne and Michele Fine. 1988. "Introduction: Beyond Pedestals." Pp. 1-37 in *Women with Disabilities: Essays in Psychology, Culture, and Politics.* Philadelphia, PA: Temple University Press.

Anzaldúa, Gloria (ed.). 1990. "Still Trembles Our Rage in the face of Racism, There is War: Some Losses Can't Be Counted," Section 1 in *Making Face, Making Soul: Haciendo Caras: Create and Critical Prespectives by Women of Color.* San Francisco: Aunt Lute Foundation Book.

Blood, Peter, Alan Tuttle, and George Lakey. 1992. "Understanding and fighting sexism: a call to men." Pp. 134-140 in *Race, Class, and Gender: An Anthology,* edited by Margaret L. Andersen and Patricia Hill Collins. Belmont, CA: Wadsworth Publishing.

Goode, William J. 1992. "Why men resist." Pp. 287-310 in *Rethinking the Family: Some Feminist Questions*, edited by Barrie Thorne with Marilyn Yalom. Boston: Northeastern University Press.

Hartsock, Nancy. 1979. "Feminist theory and the development of revolutionary strategy." Pp. 56 -74 in *Capitalist Patriarchy and the Case for Socialist Feminism*, edited by Zillah R. Eisenstein. NY: Monthly Review.

Morgen, Sandra and Ann Bookman. 1988. "Rethinking women and politics: an introductory essay." Pp. 3 - 29 in *Women and the Politics of Empowerment,* edited by Ann Bookman and Sandra Morgen. Philadelphia, PA: Temple University Press.

Rappaport, Julian. 1981. "In praise of paradox: a social policy of empowerment over prevention." *American Journal of Community Psychology,* 9 (1): 1 - 25.

Sarachild, Kathie. 1975. " Consciousness raising: a radical weapon." Pp. 131 - 137 in *Feminist Revolution,* edited by Redstockings. New Paltz, NY: Redstockings.

VIII. ORGANIZATIONS

Council for Disability Rights, 208 South LaSalle, Suite 1330, Chicago, IL 60604. (312) 444-9484. TDD (312) 444-1967.

Genesis House, 911 W. Addison, Chicago, IL 60613. (773) 281-3917.

Health Resource Center for Women with Disabilities, c/o Dr. Kristi Kirschner. Rehabilitation Institute of Chicago, 345 E. Superior, Chicago, IL 60610. (312) 908-4744.

The Hopi Tribe, P.O. Box 123, Kykotsmovi, Arizona 86039. (602) 734-2441.

IMPACT Self-Defense for Women, Self Empowerment Group, 6219 N. Sheridan, Chicago, IL 60660. (773) 338-4545.

Women of All Red Nations (WARN), 4511 N. Hermitage Ave., Chicago, IL 60640. (773) 493-2791.

Women's Program, Korean Self-Help Center, 4934 N. Pulaski Rd., Chicago, IL 60630. (773) 545-8348.

Women's Studies Program, Northeastern Illinois University, 5500 N. St. Louis Ave., Chicago, IL 60625. (773) 583-4050 x 3308.

WOMEN AND SOCIAL ACTION: CLASS 2
Perspectives on Women

 Before you read this Chapter of the Study Guide
Read Andersen, Chapter 1, "Studying Women: Feminist Perspectives"

 JOURNAL
ASSIGNMENT

> What has been your prior experience with feminism or feminists? What does feminism mean to you? As you view the tape, look for similarities and differences in views and experiences between yourself and others.

I. INTRODUCTION

Does the word "feminist" fill you with admiration for the power of women? Does it conjure up negative hostile images when you see it? Are you indifferent to the label? Do you think biology is destiny? Do you think society must undergo massive transformation to create a gender-free society? What would it take to create a woman-centered society? Do you think the way to create equality is by changing sexist laws? Do you think gender is the major framework for defining and limiting women? Do you think capitalism and patriarchy intersect to maintain women's oppression? Do you see racism as more of a problem for women of color than sexism? Do you struggle with understanding the connections between racism, sexism, and class structure?

I don't expect you to answer all these questions, but I raise them to give you an idea of the complex topic we are setting out to address in this session: perspectives on women. There are many points of view about whether or not gender is an important issue; whether or not differences in behaviors based on gender are the result of biology, society, or both; whether or not the way to end sexism requires changing laws, resocialization, restructuring all social institutions, ending capitalism, or creating a lesbian nation; whether or not women should fight for change with men or without them; whether or not women should organize in small collectives, large-scale hierarchial groups, or community-based organizations. If you would like to explore the specific lines of arguments developed by different groups of feminists, I encourage you to read the articles found below under "Sources and Further Reading."

As we discovered in the first class session, we each have a perspective or a point of view which reflects a set of assumptions about reality. Andersen introduces us to the notion of a paradigm which represents the idea that each discipline also has a perspective on what reality is, how to study it, and how to change it. In Class 2 we will see the range of perspectives on women within our classroom, explore ways in which people's life experiences influence the development of their perspectives, and touch upon ways that perspectives and paradigms can shift in response to social action and social change.

II. CLASS THEMES

Key themes introduced in this session include:

- Variations in perspectives on women
- Ways in which our life experiences influence the development of our perspectives
- How our perspectives influence our choices about social action
- How the concepts of feminism, the sociological imagination, and paradigm can enhance our understanding of perspectives on women

III. VIDEOTAPE SYNOPSIS

- Introduction of guest, Mary Ann Schwartz, Professor of Sociology and Women's Studies, Northeastern Illinois University
- Overview of class session
- Video composite of women talking about perspectives on women
- Class discussion of video
- Interview and discussion with Mary Ann Schwartz

IV. VIDEOTAPE COMMENTARY

I suggest you read this section before you watch the videotape. You will find that it will help you organize your thoughts in a more useful way than if you just watch the tape "cold." When you have finished viewing the tape you may want to read this section again.

A. Introduction of guest and overview of the class session

To enhance our appreciation for what a perspective is, how it develops, and how it influences our social actions, I asked Mary Ann Schwartz to talk with our class. Mary has a well-developed perspective on women and has been involved in social action for over twenty years. Examining her experience and ideas will give us an opportunity to explore the issue of perspective in more depth.

B. Video composite of women talking about perspectives on women

In this video clip several women talk about their views on feminism or their observations of how assumptions about gender affect people's lives. Their names and affiliations are listed below in the order they appear on the tape. As you watch the clip, note what they see as the central component of their views on women or what they suggest as ways gender influences social life.

Pauline Bart, Department of Psychiatry, University of Illinois-Chicago

Laura McAlpine, Director, Chicago Women's Health Center

Radhika Sharma, Legal Advocate and Community Educator, Apna Ghar, Chicago

Rachel Lucas-Thompson, 10 years old, my daughter

Rabbi Ellen Dreyfus, Congregation Beth Sholom, Park Forest, Illinois

Betty Achinstein, Social Studies, Thurgood Marshall Middle School, Chicago

C. Class discussion of video

Students identify commonalities, differences, and issues after watching the videotaped interviews. What commonalities and differences do class members mention? What would you add?

Some of the differences noted raise issues for class members. Debbie feels women varied in the negativity and hostility of their perspectives. Mary disagrees as did our guest, Mary Ann Schwartz. What do you see as the key arguments each one makes to support her position? What is your position on this issue?

My daughter Rachel's comments also stimulate discussion which shows differences in perceptions of gender expectations. Rachel was responding to a question I asked her about her thoughts on ways girls and boys are treated differently. I think Rachel's comments show a keen awareness of gender expectations, but some see her comments as superficial or outdated. What arguments do you see our guest and class members making to support their views on whether or not gender expectations exist? We see from the class discussion that class members respond differently to the video interviews. These varying reactions are related to different perspectives on women.

D. Interview and discussion with guest, Mary Ann Schwartz

Mary Ann Schwartz tells us about her background and her views on feminism. How do her early life experiences relate to her current views and social actions? Gail, Joe, Mary, Virginia, Trenace, Judy, and Helen raise questions and make points about feminism, learning, curriculum change, racism, and personal change. In response to Gail's question about the feminist movement, what issues does Mary identify as areas for continued work? What do Joe and Mary mean by unlearning and how do they see it working in women's studies classes?

Throughout our discussion, Mary Ann Schwartz as well as other members of the class make references to ways in which their own background or experiences have influenced their perspectives on women. Let's see how a sociological imagination can help us understand the idea of perspective. Mary, Gail, and Helen offer helpful definitions. Mary, Virginia, Trenace, and Judy give us examples from their own experience. What do we learn about perspectives on women from their comments?

Joe, Ada, and Trenace suggest a sociological imagination can help us challenge the traps of social expectations. Joe talks about making a distinction between what we ought to do and what we want to do. Trenace gives examples of ways she has challenged stereotypes of African-American women. Ada sees the utility of the concept in creating more choices and possibilities for women.

Class members also discuss their own and others' resistance to challenging socially restrictive patterns. For example, Trenace, Judy, Ada, and Gail give examples from their own experience. What is the challenge Trenace is facing with her daughter? What would you do? Why do you suppose it was so hard for Judy's mother and father to change their habits in sharing the newspaper? Given Ada's comments, what kinds of conflicts about views on women do you imagine mothers and sons might have? What is the struggle with language Gail describes? What would you do? Gunther raises his concern about what children's toys have to do with how people grow up. I respond to his question and summarize this discussion of the sociological imagination with the idea that it is no one thing that creates and reproduces sexism. It is, instead, an accumulation of activities, expectations, and opportunities. Because sexism is created through our everyday activities, we can all contribute to social change by developing an awareness of sexism and challenging it when we see it. Mary Ann Schwartz comments that an important part of our discussion was in recognizing that we are not alone in this struggle and that it is important for us to share our experiences with each other.

 Now watch the videotape.

V. REVIEW QUESTIONS

1. What is a sociological imagination? Compare your answer after this session with the answer you had after Class 1.

2. What is feminism? Compare your answer after this session with the answer you gave in your reflection prior to viewing this session.

3. What is "women's studies"? Why does this discipline exist? What is men's studies? How are they similar and different?

4. What are McIntosh's phases of curriculum change? In what phase is "Women and Social Action?" Think about some of the other courses you have taken. In what phase would you put them?

5. Describe ways in which our perspectives can influence our choices for social action. Give an example.

VI. INTERVIEW EXCERPTS

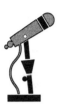

> Jean Lachowitz, Director, Genesis House; Irene Campos Carr,
> Coordinator of Women's Studies, Northeastern Illinois University; and
> Andrea Smith, Women of All Red Nations, offer different perspectives
> on feminism. Jean focuses on individuals, Irene on relationships,
> Andrea on the intersection of sexism with other forms of oppression.
> As you read these, think about the specific ways in which their perspec-
> tives differ and consider what types of social action might be most
> consistent with each.

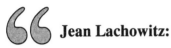 **Jean Lachowitz:**

Feminism means empowerment. It means being a full human person, it means having enough
self-esteem and enough self-worth to take your rightful place in society that's equal in every way
to any other gender or skin color or anything else. I feel very strongly that you can be a good
feminist and be a happily married person, like I am, which is really fun because I'm able in my
life to be a way that the women can see that there are some men of integrity. In their lives they
[prostitutes] haven't seen many. And so it's a way to mainstream because if you think that all
men are crummy, you'll never be able to mainstream, you'll never take your place in society.
And so that all rolls into feminism. I think that, I wish that it didn't have to be—I wish it could
just be humanism—but at this point in time it has to be feminism because we need men of
integrity and we need women who realize that they don't have to always evaluate themselves
based on how men see them. After a woman has been in prostitution for a long time and she's
been in competition with other women for her life's blood, you know, her dollar, her quotas,
what have you, it's very difficult and very personal to have the woman see that it doesn't matter
how men or anyone else perceives this person. It matters how she perceives herself. And so a
large part of what we do is just that. It doesn't have to do with externalities. It has to do with
internalities and so our feminist message is very, very strong and it surpasses some of the issues.
I know in feminist circles there is, as I alluded to, the issue of legalization. There are many
women who feel that that's a very strong component of the prostitution issue - having it legalized
so that women can make choices about their own bodies. Now granted that's true that a woman
is free to choose but we feel that very, very few women, if any, are truly, freely making the
choice to take on a life of prostitution. It somehow is put on them by society and by the breaks
they've had in life. That really isn't a decision that she made from her heart and soul. One of
the great things about my job, and I do believe I have the best job in the entire world, no question
about it, is I can be enraged 4 or 5 times a day and I can really be enraged and see the injustice
and feel that maybe I'm doing a little something. When a woman comes to me who's still
working out there and she tells me about something that happened to her on the streets and I say
that really makes me angry that that happened to you and you don't deserve that. And we will
just do anything in our power to help you not have that happen again. Well to me, that's the
highest call of feminism in my own heart and so the feminist issue is very much a part
of us and not all of us call it that but it certainly is the spirit of our whole staff. You

know, we're all there to help the women self-actualize and do what they want to do in their lives. "

Irene Campos Carr:

I usually ask my class, especially Europeans, what feminism means to them and they all get very puzzled because they start thinking of weird women parading down the street. I would say that for me feminism means a transformation of interrelations between men and women, women and women and men and men. I believe that feminism can ultimately change our relationships so that they are egalitarian relationships and not top/bottom ones. "

Andrea Smith:

I think most Indian women don't relate to the term feminism. But for me, I don't have a problem with the term. I think it is very important that we take sexism as seriously as we take racism and vice versa, but for any person experiencing oppression, there might be one thing that seems more pressing at the time. Anti-semitism, ableism, etc., are all equally important and what we're fighting is not one oppression, we're fighting a web-like thinking in which all of these things reinforce each other. Feminism to me means working for the liberation of all women, poor women, women of color, women with disabilities, Jewish women, old women, etc., and anything less than this to me is not feminism. And feminism just means taking sex as seriously as I take everything else. "

VII. SOURCES AND FURTHER READING

Ackelsberg, Martha A. 1988. "Communities, resistance, and women's activism: some implications for a democratic party." Pp. 297 - 313 in *Women and the Politics of Empowerment*, edited by Ann Bookman and Sandra Morgen. Philadelphia, PA: Temple University Press.

Baca Zinn, Maxine. 1982. "Mexican-American women in the social sciences." *Signs: Journal of Women in Culture and Society.* 8 (Winter): 259-72.

Bernard, Jessie. 1981. *The Female World.* NY: Free Press.

Bunch, Charlotte. 1978. "Lesbian-feminist theory." In *Our Right to Love, A Lesbian Resource Book*, edited by Ginny Vale. NY: Prentice Hall.

Brewer, Rose M. 1989. "Black women and feminist sociology: the emerging perspective." *American Sociologist 20 (spring)*: 57-70.

Chow, Esther Ngan-Ling. 1985. "Teaching sex and gender in sociology: incorporating the perspectives of women of color." *Teaching Sociology.* 12 (April): 299-311.

Collins, Patricia Hill. 1989. "The social construction of black feminist thought." *Signs: Journal of Women in Cluture and Society.* 14 (4): 745 - 773.

Cotera, Marta. 1980. "Feminism: the Chicana and Anglo versions: a historical analysis." Pp. 217-234 in *Twice a Minority: Mexican American Women,* edited by Margarita B. Melville. St. Louis: The C.V. Mosby Company.

Firestone, Shulamith. 1970. "The dialectic of sex." In *The Dialectic of Sex.* NY: Bantam.

Freeman, Jo. 1989. "The legal revolution." Pp. 371-394 in *Women: A Feminist Perspective,* fourth edition. Mountain View, CA: Mayfield.

Frye, Marilyn. 1992. "Oppression." Pp. 37-42 in *Race, Class, and Gender: An Anthology,* edited by Margaret L. Andersen and Patrica Hill Collins. Belmont, CA: Wadsworth Publishing.

Gilligan, Carol. 1982. *In a Different Voice.* Cambridge, MA: Harvard University Press.

Hartsock, Nancy. 1979. "Feminist theory and the development of revolutionary strategy." Pp. 56-77 in *Capitalist Patriarchy and the Case for Socialist Feminism,* edited by Zillah Eisenstein. NY: Monthly Review.

Mills, C. Wright. 1959. *The Sociological Imagination.* NY: Oxford University Press.

Morris, Jenny. 1991. *Pride Against Prejudice: Transforming Attitudes to Disability.* Philadelphia, PA: New Society Publishers.

Smith, Dorothy E. 1987. *The Everyday World As Problematic: A Feminist Sociology.* Boston: Northeastern University Press.

VIII. ORGANIZATIONS

Apna Ghar. 4753 N. Broadway Ave. Chicago, IL 60640. (773) 334-4663.

Chicago Women's Health Center. 3435 N. Sheffield Ave. Chicago, IL 60657. (773) 935-6126.

Genesis House. 911 W. Addison. Chicago, IL 60613. (773) 281-3917.

Women of All Red Nations (WARN). 4511 N. Hermitage Ave. Chicago, IL 60640. (773) 493-2791.

Women's Studies Program. Northeastern Illinois University. 5500 N. St. Louis Ave. Chicago, IL 60625. (773) 583-4050, Ext. 3308.

WOMEN AND SOCIAL ACTION: CLASS 3
Leadership and Social Action

Before you read this Chapter of the Study Guide

Read Cantarow, Chapter 2, "Ella Baker: Organizing for Civil Rights"

JOURNAL ASSIGNMENT

Identify an action or activity which has involved many people and took place in your neighborhood, school, place of worship, workplace, or other group. Describe who was in charge and how they led the group, how decisions got made, and how people were involved in the activity. As you view the tape for this class session, compare the approach to leadership and organizing you have described with the approach discussed in Class 3.

I. INTRODUCTION

Social justice work is going on around you right now—in your neighborhood, school, place of worship, and workplace. There are leaders who live near you, sit next to you in class, work beside you, and say hello at the grocery store. You will seldom see them or their work discussed in the newspaper or on network television. You, your family, friends, and co-workers are likely to have benefited from their leadership but may never know it unless you have a broad understanding of leadership and social action.

The dominant view of leadership focuses our attention on public, visible social actions and leaders. Within this view, important social actions are created and shaped by highly visible individuals who hold public office, head major organizations, have prestigious positions, or are in the spotlight for leading highly dramatic events. This view of leadership and social action emphasizes the large-scale, the far-reaching, the gripping, the dangerous, or the one-time event. This view of leadership can render invisible the social justice work women do in their families, neighborhoods, places of worship, workplaces, and the larger society. This work is invisible not because women hide their work, but because our assumptions about leadership and organizing allow us to ignore or devalue the leadership and organizing that is done right before us.

In Class 3, we present an alternative view of leadership. We focus our attention on the behind-the-scenes, small scale, ordinary, everyday struggles of women to discover the problems people face, to understand the roots of these problems, and to create and sustain social actions which will empower themselves and others. The concept of group-centered leadership is key to understanding this view of leadership. Group-centered leadership, in contrast to leader-centered groups, focuses on the needs of the group, not the leader, for identifying problems, seeking explanations, and formulating social actions (Payne, 1989). As you watch Class 3, you will have an opportunity to hear about concrete examples of group-centered leadership. Compare and contrast these examples with other forms of leadership with which you are familiar.

II. CLASS THEMES

We will focus on the following themes in this class session:

- Key principles of a model for social action and empowerment
- Distinguishing characteristics of group-centered leadership and how it differs from typical views of leadership.
- Significant influences and social actions in Ella Baker's life and how they relate to her perspective on leadership and social action
- Similarities between Ella Baker's and Regina Curry's perspectives on leadership and social action
- Ella Baker's historical significance and why her contributions have been less recognized than those of other civil rights leaders
- The relationship of leadership style and the type of social action in which groups engage

III. VIDEOTAPE SYNOPSIS

- Summary of Classes 1 and 2
- Overview of principles of leadership and social action
- Class discussion of Ella Baker
- Video visit with Regina Curry, Associate Director, WE CAN
- Interview and class discussion with Charles Payne, Associate Professor of African-American Studies, Sociology, and Urban Affairs, Northwestern University
- Summary of key ideas from Class Session 3

IV. VIDEOTAPE COMMENTARY

I suggest you read this section before you watch the videotape. You will find that it will help you organize your thoughts in a more useful way than if you just watch the tape "cold." When you have finished viewing the tape you may want to read this section again.

A. Recap of key ideas in Classes 1 and 2

As an introduction to Class 3, I highlight key ideas from Classes 1 and 2. Use these concepts to aid you in thinking about the alternative view of leadership and social action discussed in Class 3.

B. Overview of principles of leadership and social action

To introduce you to Class 3, I identify distinguishing characteristics of leadership that facilitate the empowerment of group members. How are these characteristics illustrated by quotes from Florence Luscomb, Ella Baker, and Jessie Lopez De La Cruz? What other characteristics are added by class discussion of Ella Baker and interviews with Regina Curry and Charles Payne?

PERSPECTIVES ON WOMEN

An individual's perspective on women is situated within a specific social and historical environment.

Perspectives on women vary in assumptions about

- What reality is
- How to study reality
- How to change reality

To understand women and social action we need to

- Hear stories of ordinary women's experience
- Develop an understanding of the theories used to explain these experiences
- Examine goals and methods of social change

"My theory is, strong people don't need strong leaders."

ELLA BAKER

"There is nothing in the world that is so transitory and fragile as a snowflake, and there is nothing so irresistible as an avalanche, which is simply millions of snowflakes.

So that if each one of us, little snowflakes, just does our part, we will be an irresistible force."

FLORENCE LUSCOMB

"It doesn't take courage. All it takes is standing up for what you believe in, talking about things that you know are true, things that should be happening, instead of what is happening."

JESSIE LOPEZ DE LA CRUZ

C. Class discussion of Ella Baker

I ask class members to identify significant influences and social actions in Ella Baker's life and to identify aspects of her perspective on leadership and organizing. Students identify several important things to know about Ella Baker. For example, Janet, Trenace, and Virginia talk about how Ms. Baker's family influenced her philosophy. Carlos and Claudia comment upon her leadership style. Helen tells us how reading about Ms. Baker brought back memories of her own participation in the civil rights movement. Using notes from your own reading as well as class members' comments, make a list of key influences in Ella Baker's life, her significant social actions, and the key components of her approach to leadership and organizing. How has reading about Ella Baker and the class discussion expanded your own knowledge of the civil rights movement?

D. Video interview with Regina Curry, Associate Director, Woodlawn East Community and Neighbors (WE CAN), Chicago.

Regina Curry is an outstanding contemporary example of someone who uses a group-centered leadership approach. She is deeply committed to her community and her beliefs about people finding answers for themselves. In addition to talking with us about her over twenty years of organizing experience and her philosophy of organizing, Ms. Curry and two of her co-workers took us for a tour of their neighborhood so we could see firsthand the challenges they face and the successes they have had. As you view this segment, identify the key ideas of her philosophy of organizing and identify the strategies she has used to put this philosophy into social action.

E. Interview and class discussion with Charles Payne, Associate Professor of African-American Studies, Sociology, and Urban Affairs, Northwestern University.

Charles Payne's respect for and knowledge of Ella Baker and the civil rights movement are quite compelling as is his enthusiasm for teaching and learning. Charles not only introduces us to a major behind-the-scenes figure in U.S. history, but he compares and contrasts approaches to leadership which have contemporary significance. Charles Payne provides us with an historical context for appreciating Ella Baker and her approach to leadership. His comments about Regina Curry's leadership style draw out the key ideas of a group-centered approach to leadership and how it contrasts with typical views of leadership.

 Now watch the videotape.

VI. REVIEW QUESTIONS

1. What is Ella Baker's perspective on leadership and organizing? How does this compare to Regina Curry's perspective?

2. What are similarities and differences in the social actions in which Ella Baker and Regina Curry have participated?

3. What are the characteristics of group-centered leadership? How do Ella Baker and Regina Curry reflect this approach to leadership in their philosophy and social actions?

4. What are three principles of social action and empowerment exemplified by the words of Ella Baker, Florence Luscomb, and Jessie Lopez De La Cruz?

5. What is the historical significance of Ella Baker? Why has she been recognized less than other civil rights leaders?

VI. INTERVIEW EXCERPT

Norma Seledon-Telez is the Coordinator of the Latina Leadership Program at Mujeres Latinas En Acción. Norma tells us how the program provides women with an opportunity to recognize and develop leadership skills. What similarities do you see between Norma's discussion of leadership development and that demonstrated by Regina Curry and Ella Baker?

 Norma Seledon-Telez:

A lot of the women will not even recognize themselves as leaders so you need to begin with education about what leadership means. Generally, Latinas are geared to be moms and wives and be very good at those roles. And these are very nurturing, giving roles which are okay, which I think are an essential part of leadership development. But in the process they exclude themselves. So one of the things that the leadership program does is focus on self-development of the woman. Give her some time, give her a couple of months to talk about who she is, where she's coming from, what experience she's had, what role history, religion, and culture have to do with her development as a person. We do a lot of self-esteem, self-assertiveness, and confidence building in the first portion of the leadership development program.

Martha: Could you describe or explain to me what leadership is? How do you define it in this program?

Norma: Actually we explore the issue of power and how there are different ways that power is manifested, different types, different styles of leadership, and actually the leadership that we focus on is shared leadership, understanding issues and understanding that individuals have different views on different issues and that there's a way to work with different people and share the leadership. And there are different abilities that everybody has and it contributes to organizing or to addressing some of those issues.

Martha: How does shared leadership work?

Norma: Well, one of the things that you really need to be aware of is that you're working in a group and that there are different personalities and as I mentioned before different vision, different ways of addressing issues. And you need to understand how a group functions. You need to understand that as a group, as an entity, there is an identity. You need to respect different personalities and you need to learn how to work with them and there are strengths in different personalities in a group.

Martha: What are examples of success stories?

Norma: We place the women in internships through the leadership program and we have some of them who are employed. We have a woman who was an accountant in her country of origin and was here doing housekeeping, cleaning. When she was enrolled through the program we placed her in an agency to do some accounting work, she was hired on as the accountant for the agency. A lot of the women—most of the women, it's not all— have gone back to being enrolled in English classes, GED classes, we have a couple of women who have enrolled in college courses. I could go on and on.

Martha: Can you think of anything else you would like people to know about the leadership program?

Norma: There are different ways that Latinas develop leadership and I think to expect them to start organizing right away is difficult because they're going through a major development or a major change within themselves and so it takes a while. Leadership development is not a one year program, it's an ongoing program and we need to be sensitive to that and we need to be able to keep in touch with those who graduate from the program and let them know that when they're ready we're here and that we're going to help them and support them to address the major issues in the communities: gangs and housing and education. And that we're here to support them.

VII. SOURCES AND FURTHER READING

Thanks to Maha Jarad for a list of references for further reading.

Baker, Andrea. 1982. "The problem of authority in radical movement groups: a case study of lesbian-feminist organizations." *Journal of Applied Behavioral Science* 18:323-341.

Baker, Ella. 1973. "Developing community leadership." Pp. 345-352 in *Black Women in White America: a Documentary History,* edited by Gerda Lerner. NY: Vintage Books.

Blumberg, Rhoda Lois. 1990. "White mothers as civil rights activists: the interweave of family and movement roles." Pp. 166-179 in *Women and Social Protest,* edited by Guida West and Rhoda Lois Blumberg. NY: Oxford University Press.

Diao, Nancy. 1992. "From homemaker to housing advocate: an interview with Mrs. Chang Jok Lee." Pp. 477-485 in *Race, Class, and Gender,* edited by Margaret L. Andersen and Patricia Hill Collins. Belmont, CA: Wadsworth Publishing.

22

Evans, Sara. 1980. *Personal Politics. The Roots of Women's Liberation in the Civil Rights Movement and the New Left.* NY: Vintage.

Fundi: the story of Ella Baker. 1980. 63 min. Color. 16mm. Fiorello La Guardia Community College Library.

Giddings, Paula. 1984. "Dress rehearsal for the sixties." Pp. 261-275 in *When and Where I Enter: the Impact of Black Women on Race and Sex in America.* Toronto: Bantam.

Gilkes, Cheryl Townsend. 1988. "Building in many places: multiple commitments and ideologies in black women's community work." Pp. 53-76 in *Women and the Politics of Empowerment*, edited by Ann Bookman and Sandra Morgen. Philadelphia, PA: Temple University Press.

Kautzer, Kathleen. 1992. "Growing numbers, growing force: older women organize." Pp. 456-462 in McAdam, Doug. 1988. *Freedom Summer.* NY: Oxford.

McAdam, Doug. 1988. *Freedom Summer.* NY: Oxford.

McCormack, Thelma. 1975. "Toward a nonsexist perspective on social and political change." Pp. 1 - 33 in *Another Voice: Feminist Perspectives on Social Life and Social Science,* edited by Marcia Millman and Rosabeth Moss Kanter. Garden City, NY: Anchor Books.

Millman, Marcia and Rosabeth Moss Kanter. 1975. "Editorial Introduction." Pp. vii - xvii in *Another Voice: Feminist Perspectives on Social Life and Social Science,* edited by Marcia Millman and Rosabeth Moss Kanter. Garden City, NY: Anchor Books.

Payne, Charles. 1989. "Ella Baker and models of social change." *Signs: Journal of Women in Culture and Society,* 14 (4): 885-899.

Payne, Charles. 1990. "'Men led, but women organized': Movement participation of women in the Mississippi delta." Pp. 156 -165 in *Women and Social Protest*, edited by Guida West and Rhoda Lois Blumberg. NY: Oxford University Press.

The Women Organizers' Collective: "Women organizers: a beginning collection of references and resources." NY: The Women Organizers Collective.

VIII. ORGANIZATIONS

Mujeres Latinas En Acción (Latin Women in Action). 1823 West 17th St., Chicago Il 60608. (312) 226-1544.

Women Organizers' Collective. c/o ECCO, Hunter College School of Social Work. 129 East 79th St., New York, NY 10021. Greater Chicagoland: (800) 400-4010.

Woodlawn East Community and Neighbors (WE CAN). 1541 E. 65th Street, Chicago, IL 60649. (773) 288-3000.

WOMEN AND SOCIAL ACTION: CLASS 4
Commonalities and Differences

 Before you read this Chapter of the Study Guide

Read Cantarow, chp. 3, "Jessie Lopez De La Cruz"

JOURNAL ASSIGNMENT

Describe an experience you have had in working (e.g. in employment, community work, religious work, political work) with people who differ from you. This difference could be by age, class, disability, ethnicity, gender, political orientation, race, religion, or sexual orientation. Reflect on what contributed to your working together effectively and inhibited you from working together effectively.

I. INTRODUCTION

Below is a journal entry I made while teaching a women's studies class a few years ago.

"'What does that poor black dyke's experience have to do with me?!' As the woman's words exploded into the middle of the group, I felt intense hostilities sweep through the room. As group members shouted at her and then at each other, the veneer of common purpose was chipped away. If only this were a nightmare, but it was happening right before my eyes. I dripped with sweat, wishing for someone to stop what was happening, accepting that that someone would have to be me."

The example I just described forcefully brought to my attention the need to deal with differences among group members before they explode into hostility. Since this experience, I have worked to develop strategies for dealing constructively with diversity in groups (Thompson, 1993; 1987a; 1987b; 1983). As long as I can remember, I have had some awareness of the hatred that differences deemed socially significant can bring out. My mother grew up in Mississippi, but moved to the north when she married. I occasionally sensed animosity bubbling beneath the surface when strangers heard her accent just as I sensed it when some southerners heard mine. I felt similar vibrations in my small town when Protestants and Catholics talked about each other or when people who lived on one side of town talked about people on the other side. I later felt those same undertones when I began to explore issues of racism. When I became part of the women's liberation movement at Kent State, I realized through discussion and reading that our common struggle as women was not enough to override ageism, class bias, homophobia, or racism. In recent years, I have become aware of the anger and fear directed toward women with disabilities.

It took the experience I describe above for me to recognize awareness was not enough, that leaders need to deal with the diversity among group members as well as work to develop common goals. In Class 4, we will have an opportunity to explore some of the principles and strategies leaders use to facilitate united social action where there are socially significant differences among group members.

II. CLASS THEMES

- Principles and strategies for building on commonalities and differences
- Distinguishing characteristics of a centerwoman
- Jessie Lopez De La Cruz' approach to organizing

III. VIDEOTAPE SYNOPSIS

- Overview of the topic
- Class discussion of Jessie Lopez De La Cruz
- Video interview with Norma Seledon-Tellez, Coordinator, Latina Leadership Program and Alicia Amador, Youth Outreach worker, Mujeres Latinas En Acción, Chicago
- Interview and class discussion with Yvonne Murry-Ramos, Executive Director, American Indian Economic Development Association, Chicago

IV. VIDEOTAPE COMMENTARY

A. Overview of the topic

As an introduction to the topic of building on commonalities and differences, I briefly outline some of the differences in groups and introduce the concept of centerwoman to make the point that building cohesive groups consisting of people with diverse backgrounds requires skill and commitment. What are some of the key skills needed?

B. Class discussion of Jessie Lopez De La Cruz

Several class members contribute to the discussion of Jessie Lopez De La Cruz and identification of centerwoman skills. What are some of the skills Ada, Judy, Mary, and Sharon identify? Joe and Virginia point out aspects of her vision and leadership. What are the key ideas here? Claudia raises the issue of guilt. Have you ever experienced guilt around a political issue? What do you think Jessie Lopez De La Cruz might have said to you?

C. Video interview with Norma Seledon-Tellez, Coordinator, Latina Leadership Program and Alicia Amador, Youth Outreach worker, Mujeres Latinas En Acción, Chicago

What does a group do when its target membership is highly diverse? What does a group do when the community in which it is situated considers the group as different from the community? To get a sense of the challenges such a group faces, I met with Norma Seledon-Tellez and Alicia Amador from Mujeres Latinas En Acción. Mujeres Latinas En Acción brings together Latinas who vary in age, class, cultural origins (e.g. Puerto Rican, Mexican, Colombian), environmental origin (e.g. urban or rural), and generation in the United States.

In the videotape, Norma and Alicia give us an overview of some of the work Mujeres Latinas En Acción does. Norma highlights aspects of the leadership project for women developed by Mujeres Latinas En Acción. What skills does she mention they work on and how would these skills help leaders deal with diversity in groups? Alicia gives examples which highlight the importance of relationship building. What roles do relationships play in individual and group development?

D. Interview and class discussion with Yvonne Murry-Ramos, Executive Director, American Indian Economic Development Association (AIEDA), Chicago

Yvonne Murry-Ramos is an urban Native American who has in-depth experience with groups working toward a common goal, but which have a diverse membership. The Native American community consists, of course, of many different nations. She also has a background in building coalitions and doing community organizing with groups which vary in age, class, cultural origins, environmental origins, and political clout and expertise. In introducing Yvonne, I mention that she prefers to say she is centered in the community rather than saying she is a centerwoman. What do you see as the difference in these two concepts?

In her brief description of her background, Yvonne tells us she is quite comfortable with diversity. How does she see being an urban Indian contributing to that comfort? Yvonne also gives us an overview of some of her organizing experiences. How does she define organizing? Joan asks her to explain more about the American Indian Economic Development Association (AIEDA). What does Yvonne say the mission of the organization is? In response to Phyllis' question about networking, Yvonne gives us an overview of how she was guided along in her development through networks. What are some of the ways that other people assisted her? What advice does she give Trenace about economic development work?

Ada, Trenace, Gail, and Peg pursue some additional lines of questioning. Ada wonders about similarities and differences between issues facing urban and reservation Indian women. How do you think gangs and alcoholism affect women and men differently? In response to Gail's question about alcoholism, what does Yvonne mean by the trickle-down effect? Trenace asks how Yvonne takes care of herself and deals with issues of femininity. Peg raises a question about the acceptance of Native American men toward women's leadership. How does Yvonne take care of herself and view her relationships with Native American men? How do perceptions of women leaders differ among different tribes or nations?

In conclusion Yvonne sums up two key ideas for organizing in diverse communities. What are those two key ideas?

 Now watch the videotape.

V. REVIEW QUESTIONS

1. What is Jessie Lopez De La Cruz's perspective on organizing?

2. What are examples of Jessie Lopez De La Cruz's work that demonstrate her willingness to work with people from diverse backgrounds?

3. What were important experiences and influences in Jessie Lopez De La Cruz's ability to work with people from a variety of backgrounds, experiences, and beliefs?

4. What is a centerwoman and how does this concept relate to the notion of group-centered leadership?

5. What is the importance of mentoring and leadership development in organizing in diverse communities?

6. What is meant by "relationship building?"

7. What are principles and strategies for organizing in diverse communities?

VI. INTERVIEW EXCERPT

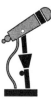

Theo Pintzuk has been involved in feminist, leftist, lesbian, and gay politics for over twenty years. Her prior affiliations include: the Madison Women's Center, Madison Welfare Rights Alliance, Madison Defense League, Madison Lesbians, the Detroit Committee to End the War Against Vietnam, the Mother Jones Brigade, the Chicago Women's Liberation Union, Gay Socialists, and Chicago Women's Uprising. She is currently working in the Women's Program, Howard Brown Health Center. Theo consistently brings issues of power and diversity to her political work. When I realized I had not adequately covered lesbian politics in the videotape, I asked Theo to talk about the complexity of organizing lesbians who vary in race, ethnicity, social class, age, and political perspective and of doing coalition building with gay men and heterosexual feminists.

Theo talked about what she wants from an ally, what has to happen for coalition building to occur, the reasons she does coalition building, and essential elements of building bridges among groups.

Martha: What do you want from an ally?
Theo: As someone with a stigmatized identity, I was thinking about what I want from an ally. The bottom line for me is that I don't always want to be the one to manage the stigmatized identity. Someone feels like an ally to me if they do some of that work and the more of it they do the more they feel like an ally. For instance, when I feel I have an ally is when someone will stop things going on and then approach me about it to discuss it. There is a willingness to open up discussion and to take risks around the subject matter. These may be risks in what someone is saying or behavioral risks or giving up privileges. The tricky thing is that it works both ways when we talk about the diverse groups you were listing. It does not simply mean someone being an ally to a politically active lesbian. It also means understanding how a politically active lesbian can be an ally to others who have stigmatized identities. It means understanding the specifics of that "outsideness" or oppression and being willing to take risks. What gets real tricky is when you've got two people with limited internal and external resources for them both to be able to extend toward the other in taking these sorts of risks and survive the distrust from the other and have timing on the process. It's no wonder it so seldom works.

I am thinking about some situations that came up in Gay Socialists. We did a series of discussions on pornography. We had a common subject and the women and the men were all trying to openly understand what this stuff called pornography is. The role that pornography has in the lives of gay men is real different than the role for women. To suppress pornography would be to suppress gay male identity in ways that women have never even understood. To embrace pornography is to hurt many women that the men never really got.

I was talking with one of the men a few years later who was praising how many lesbians have been involved in A.I.D.S. work. He was sort of musing if there was anything in women's lives that would be the equivalent that men could do. I just looked at him. He said, "Oh, rape, right." There are some men who do rape victim advocacy, but it is nothing like what women have done around A.I.D.S.

Martha: What has to happen for commonalities and differences to be dealt with effectively?
Theo: I think what really has to happen is that it is not enough to talk about this stuff. Talking is important. Talking has to take place before action, but we must do concrete things that create bridges between women of color and white women, women who are poor and women who are not, women with disabilities and those without. If we don't do that, then our talking doesn't mean all that much. The real work comes in doing that piece of it. In doing action to bring different groups together, a lot of notions about women, about assertiveness, free time, availability, language, all that stuff is up for grabs. I have to decide what I am keeping and not keeping; what is racist and classist to keep; what I have the right to claim that has race and class underpinnings. Can I deal with not being trusted and having to prove my intentions? Is it OK for me to make mistakes? What happens when I hear back from these women is not only ways that I am fucking up, but their homophobia and anti-Semitism? How do I take that on? We're dealing in 19 or 20 dimensions simultaneously.

Martha: Why take on the challenge of building bridges between diverse groups?
Theo: I do like being politically correct (laughter!). I really don't think that things are going to be changed by middle-class, primarily white, college educated women even though that group of women has done some remarkable things. I like having a belief that how I see the world is exactly how the world is, but I also like having that challenged, knowing that what I actually see of the world is a particular take and a limited view. It's a much richer life. Also, I don't see how there can be true social justice in one area without it being across the board.

Martha: What are other things that somebody who wants to build bridges should know about?
Theo: It's important for the person who is going to be an ally to take responsibility for learning about who they are being an ally to, not simply by relying on that other person to be their source of information. Seek other sources of information. In order to cleanly be an ally, you have to in some fundamental, firm way take pride in who you are. If you are doing it out of shame for who you are, it comes out really messy and fucked up. Not for guilt reasons, not for shame. This is one of the benefits of doing this work, because if you really get into doing it, it's a way of grounding yourself in who your group is in really positive terms. To be an ally it is also important to understand power, not just understand difference. You have to understand the unequal distribution of power in society and how that plays its way through difference.

VII. SOURCES AND FURTHER READING

Adamson, Nancy, Linda Briskin, and Margaret McPhail. 1988. *Feminists Organizing for Change: the Contemporary Women's Movement in Canada.* Toronto: Oxford University Press.

Aragon de Valdez, T. 1980. "Organizing as a political tool for the Chicana." *Frontiers*, 5: 7 - 13.

Cross, Tia, Freada Klein, Barbara Smith, and Beverly Smith. 1982. "Face-to-face, day-to-day—racism CR." Pp. 52 - 56 in *But Some of Us Are Brave: Black Women's Studies,* edited by Gloria T. Hull, Patricia Bell Scott, and Barbara Smith. Old Westbury, NY: The Feminist Press.

Davis, Barbara Hillyer. 1984. "Women, disability, and feminism: notes toward a new theory." *Frontiers.* VIII, 1: 1 - 5.

Garland, Anne Witte. 1988. *Women Activists: Challenging the Abuse of Power.* NY: The Feminist Press.

Joseph, Gloria I. and Jill Lewis. 1981. *Common Differences: Conflicts in Black and White Feminist Perspectives.* Garden City, NY: Anchor.

Sacks, Karen Brodkin. 1988. "Gender and grassroots leadership." Pp. 77 - 94 in *Women and the Politics of Empowerment*, edited by Ann Bookman and Sandra Morgen. Philadelphia, PA: Temple University Press.

Thompson, Martha E. 1993. "Building groups on students' knowledge and experience." *Teaching Sociology,* 21 (1): 95-99.

Thompson, Martha E. 1987. "Diversity in the classroom: creating opportunities for learning feminist theory." *Women's Studies Quarterly,* Fall/Winter: 81 - 89.

Thompson, Martha E. 1983. "Racism and sexism: a strategy for understanding." *American Sociological Association Teaching Newsletter*, 8 (4): 4 - 5.

Thompson, Martha E. 1987. "Teaching new ways to think about race, class, and gender." In *An Inclusive Curriculum: Race, Class, and Gender in Sociology Instruction,* edited by Margaret Andersen and Patricia Hill Collins. Washington, D.C.: American Sociological Association.

VIII. ORGANIZATIONS

American Indian Economic Development Association (AIEDA). 4753 N. Broadway Ave. Chicago, IL 60640. (773) 784-0808.

Mujeres Latinas En Acción (Latin Women in Action). 1823 West 17th St. Chicago, IL 60608. (312) 226-1544.

Native American Educational Service (NAES). 2838 West Peterson Ave. Chicago, IL 60659. (773) 761-5000.

Organization of the North East (O.N.E.). 5121 N. Clark St. Chicago, IL 60640. (773) 769-3232.

Urban League. 4510 S. Michigan Ave. Chicago, IL 60653. (773) 285-5800.

Women's Program, Howard Brown Health Center. 945 W. George, Chicago, IL 60657. (773) 871-5777.

WOMEN AND SOCIAL ACTION : CLASS 5
Gender Socialization

Before you read this Chapter of the Study Guide

Read Andersen, Chapter 2, "The Social Construction of Gender"

JOURNAL
ASSIGNMENT

Find a picture of yourself when you were between the ages of six and 18. What are you wearing in the picture? How similar are these clothes to what you wore everyday? What were your favorite activities at that time? What did you dislike doing? Think about ways gender expectations influenced what you were wearing, what you liked to do, and what you disliked doing.

I. INTRODUCTION

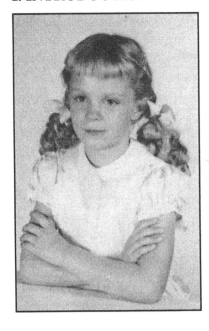

This is a picture of me when I was six years old. I'm wearing a dress and have my hair in curly ponytails tied with ribbons. Though I can't see them in the picture, I am probably wearing anklets and dress shoes. I typically wore blouses and skirts to school and wore my hair in pigtails. I loved to read, climb trees, swim, explore the woods behind our house, and play with the other kids in the neighborhood. I was unhappy that my parents wouldn't let me have a bike. They thought a bike was too dangerous.

My gender socialization was, no doubt like yours, complicated. For some activities, there was a clear distinction between girls and boys, for other things there was not. For instance, I wore dresses or blouses and skirts for special photographs, school, church, and any formal function. When I played outside after school, on vacations, or during the summer, my clothes were indistinguishable from the clothes of the boys with whom I played. Girls were excluded from organized sports activities and almost no girls played marbles at recess, but girls and boys played ball together during recess. I never had a bicycle, but almost all other girls I played with did. Though I never learned to play marbles, as an adult I did join a softball league when the opportunity arose and purchased a bike.

Andersen gives us an overview of biological sex differences, socialization and gender identity, theoretical perspectives on gender formation, and the limitations of a socialization perspective for explaining gender inequality. Think about how her overview can help you understand the girl or boy in the picture you chose for your reflection. Think about how you have changed since this picture was taken. Given these changes, which theoretical perspective on gender makes the most sense to you?

II. CLASS THEMES

- Gender socialization is a multi-dimensional, socially constructed process in which we actively participate.
- Gender socialization changes over time and in different circumstances.
- Gender socialization affects our self-esteem, feelings, behavior, and perspectives.
- Gender socialization has to be considered within the context of race and class.
- Gender socialization cannot fully explain gender inequality.
- Gender socialization can be altered through social action.

III. VIDEOTAPE SYNOPSIS

- Overview of gender socialization
- Class discussion of sex, gender, and socialization
- Video interview with B.J. Richards, preschool teacher, B.J.'s KIDS
- Interview and class discussion with Barbara Scott, Assistant Professor of Sociology and Women's Studies, Northeastern Illinois University
- Summary of key ideas

IV. VIDEOTAPE COMMENTARY

A. Overview of gender socialization

As an introduction to the topic of gender socialization, I open the class with the key questions we will be addressing during this class session and tell a story about my daughter being mistaken for a boy. As you listen to this story, think about your own experience with gender identity. Have you ever been mistaken for a male if you are a female or a female if you are a male? Or has your child ever been misidentified? How did it make you feel? Have you ever been confused about whether or not someone is female or male? Think about what made it difficult for you to determine another person's sex. Think about how it affected your treatment of the person. Think about what information you typically rely upon to determine if someone is female or male.

B. Class discussion of sex, gender, and socialization

Listen carefully to the discussion concerning sex, gender, and socialization. Joe and Debbie offer definitions of these terms. Christine, Joe, Peg, Janet, and Judy share stories and raise questions that offer insight into the complex process of gender socialization. Their stories and questions point us to issues concerning gender identity, the intense feelings surrounding gender identity, and ways that gender affects our experiences. For example, Christine shares a story about her own experience of being mistaken for a boy and how angry it made her. Peg tells us the grieving she has done concerning a male friend who is in a sex change process. Joe tells us about how a man in one of his classes was almost arrested when he undertook a class project to explore gender expectations.

In response to issues raised about gender identity, I introduced the concept of homophobia. Audre Lorde (1992) defines homophobia as "[t]he fear of feelings of love for members of one's own sex and therefore the hatred of those feelings in others." A related term, used less often, is lesbophobia. Cherie Lyn (1992) describes lesbophobia as "[m]isogyny directed specifically at lesbians." Often people who challenge gender expectations, regardless of sexual orientation, are vilified as "dykes" or "fairies." Can you think of examples where homophobic language has been used to describe someone who does not fit within conventional gender expectations?

After listening to this discussion and reading Andersen, how would you define sex, gender, and gender socialization? How do you see homophobia related to gender socialization? How are people discouraged from stepping outside gender lines? What benefits are there for people who are not limited by gender expectations?

C. Video interview with B.J. Richards, preschool teacher, B.J.'s KIDS, Chicago

B.J. Richards is featured in William Ayers book, *The Good Preschool Teacher* (she's identified as JoAnne). She was also highlighted in *Ms.* "B.J.'s KIDS: A Day-Care Dream Come True" (Wohl, 1986). B.J. is a preschool teacher for whom quality care includes a commitment to nonracist and nonsexist education. During her years as a preschool teacher, she has worked with students, teachers, and parents on the challenges of growing up in a society where racism and sexism are part of the air we breathe and where children's need to develop self-confidence and skills are often neglected. We have the opportunity in this video interview to hear B.J. talk about her views on early childhood socialization and ways to challenge sexism and racism in a way that empowers children.

B.J. Richards offers us a glimpse of her complex philosophy on socialization. What specific things does she do to create a nonsexist, multicultural environment at her preschool? Think of children you know and consider the books they read, the toys they have, their playmates, the games they play, their favorite television shows, the posters or pictures they see routinely. What messages are they getting about gender and race?

D. Interview and class discussion with Barbara Scott , Assistant Professor of Sociology and Women's Studies, Northeastern Ilinois University

In the more than 10 years I have known Barbara, she has actively served the Sociology department and Women's Studies Program, the university, the faculty union, sociology and women's studies professional societies, and her neighborhood. In addition to her active involvement in improving the lives of people around her, Barbara has also done research and writing on numerous issues, including the socialization of upwardly mobile African-American women and her development as a feminist sociologist. Her personal, professional, and political experiences offer rich sources of insight into gender socialization and how it interacts with other social dynamics, such as race and class.

As we begin the interview with Barbara, Christine and Gunther raise a concern about B.J. Richards' reaction to a poster one of the children brought to school one day. Barbara Scott works with us to gain a better understanding of the ways in which the repetition of images reproduces racism and sexism. What is your reaction to the way B.J. Richards handled the situation? How does the class discussion of her reaction influence your thinking about the issue?

Barbara gives us an overview of her background and some of the social actions in which she has been engaged. Barbara has not typically thought of herself as an activist. "Activists" are people who publically and collectively challenge social injustice (Kramarae and Treichler, 1992). Based on what you have heard Barbara say about her own work do you see why I thought of her as an activist? Barbara also gives us some of her thoughts about ways in which her background influenced her development of a feminist perspective. What do you see as important experiences in her life? What are the key components of her perspective on feminism?

Gail, Peg, and Joe raise questions about developing a consciousness, challenging racism in research, and a vision for younger generations. Barbara's answers demonstrate a complex understanding of the intersection of sexism and racism. Barbara's discussion shows that we cannot look at gender socialization in isolation from other forms of oppression.

E. Summary of key ideas

To wrap-up Class 5, I review the key ideas we covered in the session concerning gender socialization. We didn't get an opportunity to explore the limits of a gender socialization approach. Reread the section in Andersen on "Limitations of the socialization perspective." In future class sessions we will address institutionalized patterns of inequality so that you will see the limits of gender socialization for explaining gender inequality.

 Now watch the videotape.

V. REVIEW QUESTIONS

1. What are the arguments concerning nature versus nurture in understanding differences between females and males?

2. Distinguish between sex and gender. Give an example.

3. Define gender socialization and give an example.

4. What is gender identity? How does gender identity vary by race and class? Across the life cycle?

5. What are benefits for individuals in challenging gender stereotypes? What are ways people are punished for not meeting gender expectations?

6. What are different theories about socialization?

7. Identify specific actions people can take for encouraging nonsexist, multi-cultural socialization.

8. In what ways does socialization influence our participation in social action? Give an example from Barbara Scott's or Ella Baker's experience.

9. How is gender socialization related to other forms of oppression (e.g. homophobia, racism)? Give examples.

10. What are the limits of a socialization perspective for understanding gender inequality?

VI. INTERVIEW EXCERPTS

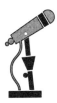

I interviewed Della Mitchell, Coordinator for the Chicago Coalition for the Homeless Empowerment Project for Homeless Women and Children, about her work with the Project. During the interview, I asked her to talk about what influenced her to become an organizer. She talked about her early experiences with racism. Think about your first awareness of racism or sexism and what feelings you had about it.

" Della Mitchell:

If I talk about how I became an organizer I probably would go back to when I was about 4 or 5 years old. It had to do with a lot of the racial prejudice in the South. I was out shopping with my Mom one day at what was called at that time a dime store. They had water fountains, two water fountains, one had "colored: on it and the other one had "white" on it. I went up to the water fountain, you know a kid, I bounced over to get a drink of water and started to drink from the one that was marked "white." And my Mom screamed so, kind of a muffle cause she didn't want to raise any excitement from the other people, and that frightened me and I couldn't understand why can't I drink from this fountain? What is it? So she explained to me that I had to drink from the one marked "colored." And from that day on I knew that something was wrong with this and I would have to do something about it. I have to change it. It was 20 years before I was really able to do something about it but as I grew up I looked at all of the injustices - going in the backdoor of a restaurant, not being able to sit down in a front seat at a restaurant, all of those things are the things that motivated me to become an organizer. I guess when I was about 20 I started doing something about it. This was in North Carolina where I organized a group of students to deal with the issues of not being able to go into a restaurant or blacks just not being able to register and vote. It was a lot more dangerous then than it is now. It was easier in the South than it is in Chicago because you knew exactly what you're dealing with. This particular weekend we had been doing a lot of picketing at a theater in High Point. It was in a building that was owned by the city where blacks couldn't go. So this particular weekend "To Kill a Mockingbird" was playing at the theater where blacks couldn't go. We planned to form a human chain and block the entrance. If we can't go in, then nobody else is going to go in. We knew we were going to get arrested if we did that. But we planned it anyway and we were indeed arrested. We spent that whole weekend in jail and I fasted and prayed during that whole time and we refused bail and they got so concerned about us not eating, they were afraid somebody was going to get sick. But that Sunday we heard this mumbling outside, nobody but one of the groups that went in with us could see out the window. They were looking out the window so the word got to us that all of the churches in the city had come down to support us. They had their services out in the parking lot and that was kind of the beginning of opening up the city of High Point, North Carolina. I was instrumental in doing that. There were big rallies and there were a few times where my life was even threatened but that was motivated within itself too because I had this drive that had been in me since I was a child that this just has to change. It has been my life since then. "

VII. SOURCES AND FURTHER READING

Anzaldua, Gloria (ed.). 1990. *Making Face, Making Soul/Haciendo Caras: Creative and Critical Perspectives by Women of Color.* San Francisco: Aunt Lute Books.

Ayers, William. 1989. "JoAnne: to make a difference" [B.J. Richards] *The Good Preschool Teacher: Six Teachers Reflect on Their Lives.* NY: Teachers College Press.

Beck, Evelyn Torton (ed.). 1982. *Nice Jewish Girls: A Lesbian Anthology.* Watertown MA: Persephone Press.

Bem, Sandra. 1981. "Gender schema theory and its implications for child development: raising gender-aschematic children in a gender-schematic society." *Signs: Journal of Women in Culture and Society*, 8: 598-616.

Chodorow, Nancy. 1978. *The Reproduction of Mothering: Psychoanalysis and the Sociology of Gender.* Berkeley: University of California Press.

Garber, Marjorie. 1993. "Spare parts: the surgical construction of gender." Pp. 321-336 in *The Lesbian and Gay Studies Reader*, edited by Henry Abelove, Michele Aina Barale, and David M. Halperin. NY: Routledge.

Glickman, Rose L. 1993. *Daughters of Feminists.* NY: St. Martin's Press.

Goffman, Erving. 1976. *Gender Advertisements.* NY: Harper Colophon.

Hancock, Emily. 1989. *The Girl I Left Behind.* NY: Fawcett Columbine.

Harris, Adrienne and Dana Wideman. 1988. "The construction of gender and disability in early attachment." Pp. 115-138 in *Women with Disabilities: Essays in Psychology, Culture, and Politics,* edited by Michele Fine and Adrienne Asch. Philadelphia, PA: Temple University Press.

Kimmel, Michael S. and Michael A. Messner (eds.). 1989. *Men's Lives.* NY: Macmillan.

Kramarae, Cheris and Paula A. Treichler (eds.). 1992. *Amazons, Bluestockings, and Crones: A Feminist Dictionary.* London: Pandora Press.

Lips, Hilary M. 1989. "Gender-role socialization: lessons in femininity." Pp. 197 - 216 in *Women: a Feminist Perspective,* edited by Jo Freeman. 4th ed. Mountain View, CA: Mayfield Publishing.

Lorde, Audre. 1992. "Homophobia." P. 195 in *Amazons, Bluestockings, and Crones: A Feminist Dictionary.*, edited by Cheris Kramarae and Paula A. Treichler. London: Pandora Press.

Lyn, Cherie. 1992. "Lesbophobia." P. 230 in *Amazons, Bluestockings, and Crones: A Feminist Dictionary* edited by Cheris Kramarae and Paula A. Treichler. London: Pandora Press.

Rossi, Alice. 1977. "Toward a biosocial perspective on parenting." *Daedulus*, 106 (Spring): 1-31.

Seifer, Nancy (1976). *Nobody Speaks for Me: Self-Portraits of American Working Class Women.* NY: Touchstone.

Thorne, Barrie. 1993. *Gender Play: Girls and Boys in School.* New Brunswick, NJ: Rutgers University Press.

Wittig, Monique. 1993. "One is not born a woman." Pp. 103-109 in *The Lesbian and Gay Studies Reader*, edited by Henry Abelove, Michèle Aina Barale, and David M. Halperin. NY: Routledge.

Wohl, Lisa Cronin. 1986. "B.J.'s Kids: A Day-Care Dream Come True." *Ms.*, February: 73-75.

VIII. ORGANIZATIONS

B.J.'s KIDS Day Care Home. 2473 N. Albany, Chicago, IL 60647. (773) 342-3054.

Chicago Coalition for the Homeless Empowerment Project for Homeless Women with Children. 1325 S. Wabash, Suite 205, Chicago, Il 60605-2504. (312) 435-4548.

WOMEN AND SOCIAL ACTION: CLASS 6
Transforming Knowledge

Before you read this Chapter of the Study Guide

Read Andersen, Chapter 3, "Images of Gender: Women and the Social Construction of Knowledge"

I. INTRODUCTION

JOURNAL ASSIGNMENT

List the main characters of your three favorite movies or television shows. List three of your favorite books. List three books you remember reading in high school literature. List three scientists, discoveries, events, or inventions you remember learning about in high school science. Look over the list you have made. To what extent are gender and multicultural concerns represented on the list? How diversified are the authors by gender and race?

What do we learn about women and girls on television and in film? What do we learn about women and girls in school? To what extent are women and girls visible in the programs we watch or the books we read? When women and girls are visible how are they presented? These same questions can be asked about people of color, poor people, gay people, people with disabilities, people over 65 (groups which include females).

What does it matter for us as individuals and for our society if the media and educational institutions ignore or stereotype portions of the population? The media and educational institutions are powerful systems for shaping what we believe reality is. If our base of knowledge is rooted in sexist and racist assumptions then we will have a distorted view of reality which, in turn, will hinder us in dealing effectively with issues we face in our personal lives, in society, and in the world.

Andersen gives us an overview of the ways in which the media and educational institutions perpetuate sexist and racist assumptions. She also offers us a description of the major theories which attempt to explain these narrow images. Andersen provides us with a broad framework for thinking about ways our view of the world is developed. In Class 6, we will look at ways people are challenging sexism and racism in education.

Andersen does not discuss the issue of "political correctness," but I want to address it before you view the videotape (for more on this topic, check out Berman, 1992). The purpose of this session is for you to hear about the ways in which dedicated teachers are working to create a quality learning environment for all their students. This effort has sometimes been misrepresented as sacrificing quality for the sake of a rigid adherence to gender and racial politics. This videotape will give you an opportunity to determine for yourself why and how teachers are trying to create gender fair and multiculturally inclusive content and pedagogy. Weigh all these comments in light of your educational experience and your vision of the kind of education you would like for yourself and children important to you.

II. CLASS THEMES

- The impact of gender and culturally biased curricula on girls and boys
- The current state of schools concerning gender fair and multiculturally inclusive curricula
- Curriculum change includes both content and pedagogy
- Ways teachers are working within educational systems for change

III. VIDEOTAPE SYNOPSIS

- Welcome and introduction of Wendy Stack, Director, Professional Development Program, University-Schools Collaborative Project, Chicago Teachers' Center, Northeastern Illinois University
- Overview of transforming knowledge
- Interview and class discussion with Wendy Stack about her background
- Video visit with Betty Achinstein, Social Studies, Thurgood Marshall Middle School
- Interview and class discussion with Wendy Stack about curriculum change
- Video visit with Pat Beardon, Metcalf Elementary School, and Yolanda Simmons, King High School
- Interview and class discussion with Wendy Stack about changing teaching styles

IV. VIDEOTAPE COMMENTARY

A. Welcome and introduction of Wendy Stack, Director, Professional Development Program, University-Schools Collaborative Project, Chicago Teachers' Center, Northeastern Illinois University

I invited Wendy Stack to visit with us because of her past and current experience in education. Wendy has a particular interest in gender fair and multicultural curricula and is the director of a unique project in which university professors and kindergarten through twelfth grade teachers work together to improve teacher education. This is not a "top-down" approach, but a collaboration in which teachers are learning with each other.

B. Overview of transforming knowledge

Prior to talking with Wendy, I give a brief overview of what issues are important when we discuss transforming knowledge.

C. Interview and class discussion with Wendy Stack about her background

Wendy begins by telling us about her educational background and teaching experiences. What do you think about her observations that girls' self-esteem goes down as they go through school? Later on in the videotape, we will hear about her discovery that this applies only to white girls, not African-American girls. What hunches do you have about why there might be this variation in girls' self-esteem in schools? What other variations among girls would you expect to find?

Wendy wanted to hear about class members' experiences in school. Christine, Judy, Joe, and Gail tell us about some of their experiences and observations. What does Christine's example tell us about sex segregation in classrooms? What does Joe's story illustrate about the challenges women and men face when highly skilled women enter into male-dominated activities? What does Judy's example show us about the effect a lack of role models has on the development of girls' potential? What does Gail's experience suggest about the range of changes that have to occur in male-dominated fields for a gender-fair curriculum to be developed?

The experiences Christine, Judy, Joe, and Gail talk about happened a while ago. How different are things now? Wendy gives us an overview of a current study done by the American Association of University Women (AAUW) about gender issues in schools. What does she tell us about the importance of gender as an issue in schools, ways in which girls' and boys' skills with language are equalized, changes in self-esteem, and the challenges of creating a gender-fair curriculum?

D. Video visit with Betty Achinstein, Social Studies, Thurgood Marshall Middle School

Betty Achinstein is an outstanding example of a teacher committed to transforming knowledge. Betty gives us an overview of the ways in which both content and pedagogy are transformed in a gender fair curriculum. How does her discussion of curriculum change compare to Peggy McIntosh's (Andersen: pp.10 -13)? Betty also identifies her sources of inspiration and support for engaging in curriculum transformation. If you plan to be a teacher (or already are), what would be your sources of inspiration and support for creating a gender-fair curriculum? What sources of support would you need from students, other teachers, school administrators, and parents?

E. Interview and class discussion with Wendy Stack about curriculum change

Wendy discusses her approach to supporting teachers who are making efforts to transform the curriculum. She poses a decision that people working for change must make: do I work from the outside or the inside? What do you see as the advantages and disadvantages for working for change inside educational institutions or outside them? What choice would you be likely to make?

Gail, Mary, and Sharon's comments raise important questions about curriculum change. For example, Gail's question stimulates us to think about ways we can expose children we know to works by women when they are not getting this exposure in school. What does Wendy offer as a suggestion? Mary's comments point to challenges teachers face in changing the curriculum. What do you see as the key issues she raises? In response to Sharon's question about ways preschool children might be stifled, Wendy discusses several issues for teachers to consider, including how children play and how teachers talk to students. What strategies for change do you hear suggested by Wendy's comments?

F. Video visit with Pat Beardon, Metcalf Elementary School, and Yolanda Simmons, King High School

Pat Beardon and Yolanda Simmons are both excellent examples of dedicated and inspiring teachers who are engaged in developing a multicultural curriculum. Pat and Yolanda talk about how their teaching project "It's a Cultural Thang" evolved and the challenges they have faced along the way. With humor and respect for each other and their students, they provide us with a rich source of information about ways teachers can build on the resources available in the classroom, in the school, and in the community to build a multicultural curriculum. Identify those resources and think about ways you or teachers you know could use these ideas in their classrooms.

G. Interview and class discussion with Wendy Stack about changing teaching styles

Wendy draws out for us more explicitly how transforming knowledge involves changing teaching style not just changing content. Helen brings up the issue of objectivity. How do you see this related to transforming knowledge? Judy raises a question about boys' reactions to a gender-fair curriculum. How does Wendy see a gender-fair curriculum benefiting both girls and boys?

 Now watch the videotape.

V. REVIEW QUESTIONS

1. What does Andersen mean by the social construction of knowledge?

2. What are images of women in the media? How do these images contribute to the social construction of knowledge about gender?

3. What are the dominant explanations for images of women in the media?

3. What is the position of women in education? How does gender stratification in education affect the development of knowledge?

4. How does Andersen define sexism? How does she define racism? How does she define ideology? How does she link these concepts?

5. What is the impact of gender and culturally biased curricula on girls and boys?

6. What is the current state of schools concerning gender fair and multiculturally inclusive curricula?

7. What are ways in which content and pedagogy must change to create a gender fair and multiculturally inclusive curricula?

8. How are teachers working within educational systems for change?

VI. SOURCES AND FURTHER READING

Thanks to Mary Grady and Wendy Stack for recommendations for further reading on sex equity in education.

American Association of University Women. 1992. *Shortchanging Girls, Shortchanging America.* Report available for $16.95 from American Association of University Women. 1011 Sixteenth Street NW, Washington D.C. 20036-4873. To order, call: 1-800-225-9998, ext. 252.

Belenky, Mary Field, Blythe McVicker Clinchy, Nancy Rule Goldberger, and Jill Mattuck Tarule. 1986. *Women's Ways of Knowing: The Development of Self, Voice, and Mind.* NY: Basic Books.

Berman, Paul (ed.). 1992. *Debating P.C.: the Controversy over Political Correctness on College Campuses.* NY: Dell.

Bunch, Charlotte and Sandra Pollack. 1983. *Learning Our Way: Essays in Feminist Education.* Trumansburg, NY: The Crossing Press.

Collins, Patricia Hill. 1990. *Black Feminist Thought: Knowledge, Consciousness, and the Politics of Empowerment.* Boston: Unwin Hyman.

Feminist Teacher. $12/year for three copies. Order from Ballatine 442, Indiana University, Bloomington, IN. 47405.

Freire, Paulo. 1970. *Pedagogy of the Oppressed.* NY: Seabury Press.

Freire, Paulo. 1985. *The Politics of Education: Culture, Power, and Liberation.* South Hadley, MA: Bergin and Garvey Publishers.

García, Alma M. 1990. "Studying Chicanas: bringing women into the frame of Chicano Studies." Pp. 19-29 in *Chicana Voices: Intersections of Class, Race, and Gender*, edited by Teresa Córdova et al. Albuquerque, NM: University of New Mexico Press.

Hull, Gloria T., Patricia Bell Scott, and Barbara Smith (eds.). 1982. *But Some of Us Are Brave: Black Women's Studies.* Old Westbury, NY: The Feminist Press.

Hurston, Zora Neale. 1978. *Their Eyes Were Watching God.* Urbana, Il: University of Illinois Press.

Gilligan, Carol. 1982. *In a Different Voice: Psychological Theory and Women's Development.* Cambridge, MA: Harvard University Press.

McIntosh, Peggy. 1983. "Interactive phases of curricular revision: a feminist perspective." In *Working Papers Series.* Wellesley, MA: Center for Research on Women.

McIntosh, Peggy. 1990. "Interactive phases of curricular and personal re-vision with regard to race." In *Working Papers Series*. Wellesley, MA: Center for Research on Women.

McKenna, Teresa and Flora Ida Ortiz (eds.). 1988. *The Broken Web: The Educational Experience of Hispanic American Women*. Tomas Rivera Center and Floricanto Press.

Rich, Adrienne. 1979. "Toward a woman-centered university." *On Lies, Secrets, and Silence*. NY: W.W. Norton.

Rothenberg, Paula. 1983. "Teaching 'racism and sexism in a changing America.'" Pp. 35 - 45 in *Learning our Way: Essays in Feminist Education*, edited by Charlotte Bunch and Sandra Pollack. Trumanburg, NY: The Crossing Press.

Sadker, Myra and David Sadker. 1982. *Sex Equity Handbook for Schools, 2nd ed.* NY: Longman. (914)993-5000.

Schniedewind, Nancy. 1990. "Feminist values: guidelines for teaching methodology in women's studies." Pp. 11 - 21 in *Politics of Education,* edited by Susan Gushee O'Malley, Robert C. Rosen, and Leonard Vogt. Albany, NY: State University of New York Press.

Sierra, Christine Marie. 1993. "The university setting reinforces inequality." Pp. 5 - 7 in *Chicana Voices: Intersections of Class, Race, and Gender*, edited by Teresa Cordova et al. Albuquerque, NM: University of New Mexico Press.

Spier, Peter. 1980. *People.* NY: Doubleday.

Stummer, T. Christina F. 1992. "The ABCs of disability." Pp. 165 - 173 in *Imprinting Our Image: An International Anthology by Women with Disabilities,* edited by Diane Driedger and Susan Gray. Canada: Gynergy Books.

Torres, Sasha. 1993. "HeartBeat and prime time lesbianism." Pp. 176 - 185 in *The Lesbian and Gay Studies Reader*, edited by Henry Abelove, Michèle Aina Barale, and David M. Halperin. NY: Routledge.

Women's Action Coalition (WAC). 1993. "Media." Pp. 35 - 37 in *WAC Stats: The Facts About Women.* NY: The New Press.

VII. ORGANIZATIONS

American Association of University Women. 1111 Sixteenth Street NW, Washington, D.C. 20036-4873. (202) 785-7700.

Professional Development Program, University-Schools Collaborative Project, Chicago Teachers' Center. 770 N. Halsted, Suite 420, Chicago, Il 60622. (312) 733-7330.

The Research Clearinghouse and Curriculum Integration Project on Women of Color and Southern Women. Center for Research on Women. Memphis State University. Memphis, TN 38152.

Seeking Educational Equity and Diversity (S.E.E.D.). National S.E.E.D. Project on Inclusive Curriculum. Wellesley College for the Center for Research on Women. Wellesley, MA 02181. (617) 283-2522.

Telling Women's Lives Historical Encyclopedia of Chicago Women Project. Contact: Rima Schultz, 320 N. Ridgeland, Oak Park, IL 60302. (708) 383-7026.

Wellesley College. Center for Research on Women. 106 Central Street, Wellesley, MA 02181-8259.

WOMEN AND SOCIAL ACTION: CLASS 7
Families

 Before you read this Chapter of the Study Guide

Read Andersen, Chapter 6, "Women and Families"

I. INTRODUCTION

JOURNAL
ASSIGNMENT

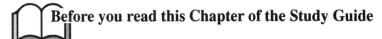

> Find a picture of a family or household to which you have belonged or now belong. Briefly describe the family or household in the picture, including one or more of the following in your description: what were their ages in the picture, what was or is their relationship to each other, what was the source (s) of income for the family or household, how are or were chores done and who did or does them?

To how many different family situations or households have you belonged? Was it difficult deciding which family or household on which to focus? At what point in time? I have belonged to many different family and household situations during my life and at times have belonged to several at the same time. For instance, now I live with my spouse, Jim Lucas, and my daughter, Rachel Lucas-Thompson. My family also includes my mother and three sisters (my father died in 1983). My extended families include brothers-in-law, aunts, uncles, nieces, nephews, and cousins on my father's side of the family and on my mother's side. My extended families also include Jim's mother, his three brothers, sisters-in-laws, nieces, nephews, aunts, uncles, and cousins on both sides of his family (Jim's father also died in 1983). I also have family relationships with neighbors and friends, not established by marriage or birth, but by the quality of the relationship. These family networks include a variety of family and household relationships which create a richly diverse picture of families.

Until the late 1960s, most of my experience with families, my own and others, was that of a husband, wife, and children where females and males had different family responsibilities. Like other families in our community, my mother had responsibility for the children and household; my father was responsible for earning a income. I don't remember anyone questioning this division of labor at the time. Not only was there a division of labor, but my family adapted its daily life to the structure of my father's job. For instance, when my father was in town, my mother set mealtimes according to his work schedule. When he was traveling, our evening mealtimes varied. When my father's new job required considerable travel, my mother's day-to-day responsibilities increased. She took on financial decision-making responsibilities that had previously been my father's.

By the time Jim and I got married in 1971, we both had been exposed to many alternative families and households. Jim and I lived together for a brief time before deciding that it was best for our standing in our small community if we got married. Influenced heavily by the ideas of the women's liberation movement, we set out to create an egalitarian family situation. We faced challenges in every aspect of family life, including housework, parenting, and sexuality. These challenges came not only from our individual gender socialization, but also from our families, friends, political allies, neighbors, co-workers, employers, and every imaginable social organization. We devised what we think are creative responses to these challenges (see sources and further reading for articles I have written on these topics).

Our gender socialization was the smallest barrier we faced. The most painful barriers were put forward by people who loved and cared about us. The most inspiring barriers were provided by backward social organizations. For instance, in 1971 it was uncommon for spouses to have different last names. The bank where we had both had separate checking accounts prior to marrying asked us to leave once we married and kept our own names and own bank accounts. The bank manager's reason: "We are not in the business of underwriting unstable marriages." The new bank which had recently opened in our community was delighted to have our business. Our level of income, academic degrees, and work environments have often given us resources to draw upon to create equality in our relationship.

In Class 7, we will explore a framework for thinking about families that assumes families are an integral part of society and are interwined with other social institutions, social values, and norms. By reflecting on your particular family or household experience, you can ground our discussion in your own experience. With this concrete backdrop in mind, you can check out whether or not the perspective we discuss broadens your understanding of your own family and offers insight into ways social policies and social practices have an impact on families and households.

II. CLASS THEMES

- Issues facing families today
- The centrality of families in society
- Gender and families
- Need for changes in social policies and social practices

III. VIDEOTAPE SYNOPSIS

- Introduction to thinking about families
- Class discussion of issues facing families
- Videotape composite of visit with women from The Hopi Tribe, Keams Canyon, Arizona
- Interview and class discussion with Harriet Gross, Professor, Humanities and Social Sciences, Governors State University

IV. VIDEOTAPE COMMENTARY

A. Introduction to thinking about families

We are bombarded in the media with contemporary problems facing the family, but often do not have a framework for thinking about these problems. Through class discussion and with the help of our guest, Harriet Gross, we will work in Class Session 7 on developing a perspective on families and considering the implications of this perspective for social policies and social practices. As you look over the headlines which appear on the screen, think about the issues each suggests. Think about other headlines related to families you have seen recently. What additional issues can you identify?

"If the '90s man is doing half of chores, it's news to women"
"Families to keep changing, but slower"
"Men Seek Changes In Custody Process"
"Studies Find No Disadvantages in Growing Up in a Gay Home"
"Demographic changes put new face on U.S. family"

B. Class discussion of issues facing families

Through storytelling and examples, Judy, Claudia, Virginia, Gail, Joan, Peg, Laura, Debbie, and Joe help us develop a list of issues facing families. For example, Judy, Claudia, and Peg introduce examples that point to conflicts between family and work or educational worlds. Can you think of other types of conflicts you or others have experienced? What issue does Virginia bring to our attention? How is gender involved in her example? Gail, Joan, Laura, Joe, and Debbie bring up issues around family relationships. In thinking about some of their examples, how do you see conditions in the economy or government influencing some of their experiences? Make a list of the issues class members identify. Add any that haven't been mentioned. What broad themes do you see in this list?

C. Videotape composite of visit with women from the Hopi Tribe, Keams Canyon, Arizona

As class members pointed out, family and work responsibilities are often in conflict. Resolving these conflicts typically falls upon women. What stresses and dilemmas do these conflicts create for women? What are strategies women use to deal with these conflicts? What are social policies and practices that can alleviate individual stresses?

To get a sense of the complexity of these conflicts, we talked with people who daily must struggle for survival and the maintenance of traditions. The Hopi have rich and beautiful traditions which depend heavily upon the work of women (see **Hopi: Song of the Fourth World**; Waters, 1977). Because of the economic and political circumstances of the Hopi, women must often go off reservation for education and employment (see Qoyawayma, 1964). Without women's education and employment, families and the Hopi nation could not survive. How, then, do women balance their responsibilities to Hopi traditions, the survival of their families, and to themselves?

With the support of LuAnn Leonard, Acting Secondary Education Specialist of the Hopi Tribe, the Hopi Tribal Council, and Lynn Ables, physician, Keams Canyon Public Health Service, we were able to meet and interview several members of the Hopi Tribe as well as two Anglo women working as medical doctors on the reservation. The people we interviewed while visiting the Hopi tribe (not all appear here), included: Lynn Ables, Marla Dacawyma, Marlene Jackson, Carol James, Lynn Kalectaca, LuAnn Leonard, Nicole Marietta Leonard, Farron Lomakema, Grace Nejman, Beatrice Norton, Thelma Tewahaftewa, Ethelene Tootsie, Ellen Wadsworth.

The Hopi we interviewed were willing to talk about the importance of Hopi traditions in their lives and the challenges they face in meeting their responsiblities to their families, their clan, the Hopi tribe, their work, and their education.

As you watch the videotape composite, note the amount of time and effort Hopi traditions require, particularly the wedding ceremony. Think about what would be lost if women stopped giving their time and effort. You will hear about the hardships of reservation life, but also the benefits. What are all the ways you hear gender playing a role in Hopi traditions and Hopi life?

D. Interview and class discussion with Harriet Gross, Professor, Humanities and Social Sciences, Governors State University

Sociologist Harriet Gross has done extensive thinking, research, and writing about families. Her work on families and work with co-author Naomi Gerstel includes two books: *Commuter Marriage* (1984) and *Families and Work* (1987). Harriet has also been involved in numerous educational efforts to enhance the general public and policymakers' understanding of the complex dynamics of family life and the implications for public policy and social change.

Harriet discusses how her views and her scholarship on families has changed since she wrote *Commuter Marriage*. What was her view originally? What is it now? What difference does this change make for family policies and practices?

Phyllis, Gail, Judy, and Peg make comments and raise important questions which give Harriet an opportunity to elaborate on her perspective. For example, Phyllis and Gail address the notion of an ideal family. What does Harriet see as some of the consequences for the idea that there is an ideal family type? What does she see real, not ideal, families needing to make them work effectively? What important points do Judy and Peg make? What implications does Harriet draw out for social policies and social practices? What does Harriet mean by a band-aid approach? What kinds of social action work does she see we can begin right now?

 Now watch the videotape.

V. REVIEW QUESTIONS

1. Because there is so much contained in each segment of Andersen's chapter, read thematically, according to your interests.

   a. Select one of the following to guide your reading: How have changes in the state influenced family life? How have changes in the economy influenced the family? How has gender, race, or class affected family life? Select one period in history discussed here and think about ways political institutions, economic institutions, and gender, race, and class influenced the family in this period.

   b. Andersen identified five revisions in the family suggested by feminist scholarship. Select any one to think about. What changes in political institutions, economic institutions, or gender, race, and class would have to happen for this revision to occur?

   c. In the section on contemporary households, read for ways political institutions, economic institutions, gender, race, or class have affected changes in the family.

2. What does Harriet Gross mean by production and reproduction?

3. What are gender issues in balancing family and work?

4. Distinguish matriarchal, matrilineal, patrilineal, and patriarchal.

5. Describe how the experiences of Hopi women illustrate the conflicts between family and work discussed in our reading and in class.

VI. SOURCES AND FURTHER READING

Baca Zinn, Maxine. 1989. "Family, race, and poverty in the eighties." *Signs: Journal of Women in Culture and Society* 14 (4): 856-874.

Baca Zinn, Maxine and Stanley Eitzen. 1990. *Diversity in American Families.* NY: Harper-Collins.

Browne, Susan E., Debra Connors, and Nanci Stern. 1985. "Growing Up in Our Families," Chapter 3. *With the Power of Each Breath: A Disabled Women's Anthology.* Pittsburgh, PA: Cleis Press.

Collins, Patricia Hill. 1989. "A comparison of two works on black family life." *Signs: Journal of Women in Culture and Society* 14 (4): 875-884.

Di Leonardo, Micaela. 1992. "The female world of cards and holidays: women, families, and the work of kinship." Pp. 246 - 261 in *Rethinking the Family: Some Feminist Questions*, edited by Barrie Thorne with Marilyn Yalom. Boston: Northeastern University Press.

Elsasser, Nan, Kyle MacKenzie, and Yvonne Tixier Y. Vigil. 1980. "The Soul of the Home," Chapter two. *Las Mujeres: Conversations from a Hispanic Community.* Old Westbury, NY: The Feminist Press.

Gerson, Kathleen. 1985. *Hard Choices: How Women Decide About Work, Career, and Motherhood.* Berkeley: University of California Press.

Gerstel, Naomi and Harriet Gross. 1984. *Commuter Marriage.* NY: Guilford.

Gerstel, Naomi and Harriet Engle Gross (eds.). 1987. *Families and Work.* Philadelphia: Temple University Press.

Gerstel, Naomi and Harriet Engel Gross. 1989. "Women and the American family: continuity and change." Pp. 89 - 120. In Jo Freeman (ed.) *Women: A Feminist Perspective,* 4th edition. Mountain View, CA: Mayfield Publishing.

Hochschild, Arlie. 1989. *The Second Shift: Working Parents and the Revolution at Home.* NY: Viking-Penguin.

Hopi: Song of the Fourth World. Video. The Hopi Tribe. P.O. Box 123. Kykotsmovi, Arizona, 86039. (602) 734-2441.

Malos, Ellen (ed.).1980. *The Politics of Housework.* London: Allison & Busby.

Oakley, Ann. 1976. *Women's Work: The Housewife, Past and Present.* NY: Random House, Vintage.

Qoyawayma, Polingaysi (Elizabeth Q. White) as told to Vada F. Carolson. 1964. *No Turning Back: A Hopi Indian Woman's Struggle to Live in Two Worlds.* Alburquerque, NM: The University of New Mexico Press.

Rich, Adrienne. 1980. "Compulsory heterosexuality and lesbian existence." *Signs: Journal of Women in Culture and Society* 5(4): 631 - 660.

Rosenbaum, Jill L. 1993. "The female delinquent: another look at the role of the family." Pp. 399 - 414 in *It's A Crime:Women and Justice,* edited by Roslyn Muraskin and Ted Alleman. Englewood Cliffs, NJ: Regents/Prentice Hall.

Rubin, Lillian Breslow. 1976. *Worlds of Pain: Life in the Working-Class Family.* NY: Basic Books.

Schwartz, Mary Ann and BarBara M. Scott. 1994. *Marriages and Families: Diversity and Change.* Englewood Cliffs, NJ: Prentice Hall.

Stack, Carol B. 1974. *All Our Kin: Strategies for Survival in a Black Community.* NY: Harper and Row.

Thompson, Martha E. 1984. "Gender and parenthood: a feminist experience." Pp. 1 - 5 in *Midwest Feminist Papers,* edited by Carla Howery. Midwest Sociologists for Women in Society.

Thompson, Martha E. 1984. "Housework: putting theory into practice." *Feminism Lives* 10: 16 -31. Edited by Brooke Williams and published by the Radical Feminist Organizing Committee. 109 Ellerbee Street, Durham, NC 27704.

Thompson, Martha E. 1979. "On confusing heterosexism with having a male partner." *Off Our Backs* IX (11): 30.

Thompson, Martha E. 1981. "Comment on Rich's 'Compulsory heterosexuality and lesbian existence. " *Signs: Journal of Women in Culture and Society* 6 (4): 790-794.

Thorne, Barrie. 1992. "Feminism and the family: two decades of thought." Pp. 3 -30 in *Re-thinking the Family: Some Feminist Questions,* revised edition, edited by Barrie Thorne with Marilyn Yalom. Boston: Northeastern University Press.

Waters, Frank. 1977. *Book of the Hopi.* NY: Penguin.

Weston, Kath. 1992. "The politics of gay families." Pp. 119 - 139 in *Rethinking the Family: Some Feminist Questions,* 2nd edition, edited by Barrie Thorne with Marilyn Yalom. Boston: Northeastern University Press.

VII. ORGANIZATIONS

The Hopi Tribe. P.O. Box 123. Kykotsmovi, Arizona 86039. (602) 734-2441.

Radical Feminist Organizing Committee (RFOC). 109 Ellerbee Street, Durham, NC 27704.

WOMEN AND SOCIAL ACTION: CLASS 8
Child Care

 Before you read this Chapter of the Study Guide
Read Andersen, "Teenage Pregnancy," pp. 179-181 "Child Care," pp. 181-184

I. INTRODUCTION

 JOURNAL ASSIGNMENT

Describe an experience you or someone you know has had with child care. Give a brief overview of the available options at the time, the choices made, and the feelings you or the person you talked with had about their choices. Think about how societal views of motherhood and/or fatherhood affected this child care experience.

The care of children is simultaneously exalted and devalued. Children are hailed as the future of our country while public schools are in crisis, increasing numbers of children live in poverty, and there is resistance to a comprehensive national child care program.

To make sense of these contradictions, we need to consider societal assumptions about gender, motherhood, and families. Norgren (1989) argues that the development of a national child care policy has been hampered by the belief that motherhood is women's central role, that mothers belong in the home, and that families must be independent of outside intervention.

Historically, women of color have been expected to sacrifice their role as mother for their role as laborer for white people, therefore, the above ideas are mostly directed to white women. The idea that women's place is in the home also appears to apply only to women with economic resources. Consider how mothers receiving public assistance are characterized as free-loading and lazy. The little attention to child care for children with disabilities or the child care needs of disabled parents suggests that child care is typically assumed to be an issue only for nondisabled people (Morris, 1991). Our policies and practices concerning child care must, therefore, consider assumptions about race, class, and disabilities.

Finally, if we look at the history of child care in the United States, we see that when it has been in the interests of society to put adult women to work, then subsized child care has materialized; for example, during the Depression and World War II (Norgren, 1982). What is in the best interests of children is seldom considered. We, then, must also consider beliefs about children, their needs, and their role in society.

Our societal orientation to child care, then, reflects a mix of assumptions about gender, children, families, race, class, and disabilities. To develop national child care policies and practices which work for people will require us to examine and change these assumptions, where necessary.

In Class 8, we explore child care within the current social climate; a climate whereby children are still seen as the responsibility of their mothers or families, not the society; a climate where parents must make do with limited options while often shouldering alone their fears about the barriers and challenges their children may face; a climate where child care is often narrowly limited to the care of young children during daytime hours; a climate where the needs of disabled parents, disabled children, older children, and teenagers are often neglected. Through class discussion, our video visit, and studio visit, we will explore ways parents can get support, ways people without children can advocate for children, and ways we can work together to develop empowering child care policies and practices.

II. CLASS THEMES

- What child care is
- Gender and child care
- Issues, concerns, and fears concerning child care
- Child care as societal, not individual, responsibility

III. VIDEOTAPE SYNOPSIS

- What child care is
- Class discussion of experiences with child care, concerns, and fears
- Video composite of visit with teachers, students, and children at Orr Community Academy Infant and Family Development Center
- Interview and class discussion with Brenda Chock Arksey, Director, Child Education and Development Services, Chinese American Service League

IV. VIDEOTAPE COMMENTARY

A. What child care is

I open Class 8 with stories about my own recognition of the importance of child care and the different ways people think about taking care of children. What do you see as my motivation for working to start a child care center over twenty years ago, even though I had no children of my own? How would you persuade others without children to make a commitment to quality child care? What does it mean to you if a father talks about taking care of his own children as babysitting? If you were collecting statistics about child care, what questions would you ask?

B. Class discussion of experiences with child care, concerns, and fears

Laura, Joan, Janet, Mary, Judy, and Gail share examples, ask questions, and raise concerns. For example, Laura tells us about the range of options she has used. How do these options fit within the categories shown on the graphic? Janet tells us about her experience as a child care provider. What conflict did she experience in this role?

Mary and Judy share examples which point to variations in attitudes about child care. What are some of the variations you hear them identify? Joan and Gail address fears about child care. How might these concerns and fears affect child care policies and practices?

C. Video composite, Orr Community Academy Infant and Family Development Center

The availability of child care is critical to the survival of many women and their families. We visited Orr Community Academy to see firsthand what access to child care means for teen mothers and their children. At Orr we visit with teachers, students, and children. The Orr Infant and Family Development Center is operated by Jane Addams Center. The purpose of the program is to prevent teen parents from dropping out of high school, to give teen parents an opportunity to learn parenting skills, and to provide quality early childhood education for the children of teen parents. Catherine Moore, Director of the Center, gives us an overview of the typical day at the center, some of the controversy surrounding the opening of the center, and the rewards of the work. Some of the teen parents tell us about the challenges of being a parent. Betty Sandifer, teacher of the teen parenting class, addresses the purposes of the center.

Based on this video visit, what advantages and disadvantages do you see in providing on-site child care at a high school? What are ways in which you see the teen parents, the children, and the staff benefitting from this experience?

D. Interview and class discussion with Brenda Chock Arksey, Director, Child Education and Development Services, Chinese American Service League

Brenda Chock Arksey has been involved in various aspects of child care and early childhood education for over a decade, including administration of a community-based child care center, day care advocacy and referral services with Headstart and the Day Care Action Council, and involvement with educators and other professionals through her connection with the National and Chicago Associations for the Education of Young Children.

Brenda Chock Arksey was quite moved by the opening comments of class members and wanted the opportunity to address ways that parents could enhance their ability to select child care services for their children. Brenda urges parents to take an active responsibility for selecting child care services. In response to a question from Joan, she identifies ways parents can make choices that are best for their families. What are benefits and drawbacks you see to parents having this responsibility? Brenda makes reference to brochures on choosing child care. For copies of these brochures, more information, or referrals, you may contact Cook County Child Care Resource and Referral, (312) 769-8000.

Laura addressed the benefits of child care for children. Make a list of the benefits she identifies. Can you add others to this list?

A range of issues is brought to light in class discussion with Brenda. She alerts parents to their rights as consumers and tells us about resource and referral services (see a list at the end of this chapter). Jan's comments remind us of the low salaries associated with child care work. Why do you suppose the salaries are so low? Helen and Brenda put the child care dilemma in an historical perspective. Whose interests stimulated the massive supports for child care in the 1940s? How did these interests change in the late 40s and early 50s? Brenda's overview of her center's services and comments about quality child care show how broad a high quality program should be. If you were designing a high quality child care program, are there additional elements you would include? Phyllis and Carlos share their experiences in working on behalf of children. What are ways they identify that people with and without children can work for quality child care?

Brenda concludes her visit with us by summarizing social actions concerning child care. What are the three major things she identifies that we can do?

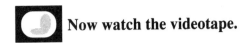 **Now watch the videotape.**

V. REVIEW QUESTIONS

1. What is meant by the privatized and exclusive character of child care? Give an example.

2. What are the differences in meaning between the notions of taking care of your own child, babysitting, and child care?

3. What are consequences for families when child care is a private responsibility? What are the consequences for society?

4. How do approaches to child care relate to assumptions about women and motherhood? men and fatherhood? disabled and nondisabled people as parents?

5. What has been the history of child care in the U.S.?

6. What are alternative models for child care?

7. What are ways we can support the development of effective child care policies and practices?

VI. INTERVIEW EXCERPT

B.J. Richards of B.J.'s KIDS has been involved with family day care programs since 1979. She started doing child care for neighbors to earn extra money. She found she really enjoyed interaction with the children. With the encouragement and support of parents, she started B.J.'s KIDS in New York City. She later moved to Chicago. She has integrated an anti-bias curriculum into her family day care program. Her work has been featured in Ayers, 1989 and Wohl, 1986 (see "Sources and Further Reading" below). In this excerpt from her interview, she talks about the rewards of child care work and the value to parents and in society.

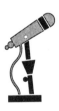 **B.J. Richards:**

Well I don't think family care is very valued in this society. Most people consider us just to be babysitters. That's the one big hurdle that every family day care provider has to get over. I've been very lucky where the parents are almost constantly telling us or writing how much they appreciate us, not always and not every parent and not every day. One parent typed a 2-page letter to us telling us how she will never look at children's books again in the same way. One of her daughters brought home a book from here. She said she was raised on Golden Books and never really thought about how important a good library was for her own daughter and that's changed her. Her daughter also asked her aunt in Ohio for a brown-skinned Barbie for Christmas and the aunt said why, why would she want one? So the mother challenged the aunt on that and tried to educate her and she said: "See, it's even reaching out to aunts in Ohio." And so that was great to hear because that's the way you want it. So things like that keep you going. Even kids themselves, when you hear them use the word "snowperson" or "firefighter." In New York we were right across the street from the fire station and we saw them every day, and the truth was they were all firemen so we could use "firefighter" until we were blue in the face. Reality was across the street where they were all white men, until one day we saw this woman walking down the street with her raincoat on, doing the grocery shopping. They had sent her out to the grocery store and we knew there was a graduating class of women joining the fire department and sure enough she was assigned to the station across the street and we were so thrilled that finally we had a role model to show them. But before she was there we took the children to the fire station. One of the little children went up to a firefighter and said, "Can you tell us when are the women going to be here? are they going to be here?" And this guy's name was Jimmy, I'll never forget him, and he looked down at this little girl and said, "God, we hope not. You know, we certainly don't want any women here." Well, she was just appalled and spoke up. We wrote a whole children's book about it with photographs of the trip and she actually went with me on a national speak-out in New York on equity. She stood right up to the microphone and told that story. And she is one of the success stories, she is now 15 years old and has been outspoken about what's fair and what's not fair her entire life. But it all went back to that firefighter, she was so outraged. We actually showed the children's book to the firefighter they got and she found it interesting.

But see, you use every teachable moment like that and seek it out. It's a lot of letter writing that I see as an activist approach that we do with them. When I see something that I object to or find offensive I'll immediately write a letter and then we'll see the response and the response says "Thank you very much, we'll pass it on to the person in charge of that." I think it's important that they see that as a way to help challenge people. And it might not work but then it might work. So I'm lucky, but I know it's undervalued. I know people who work in centers, who are terribly underpaid and have no health insurance. Even though I feel the children actually learn the first five years the most they're going to learn their entire lives. So why caregivers are not as well respected as college professors I don't understand, I just don't get it. Why are they so underpaid, because these are the years that children are just absorbing everything. And I feel like we'd all be in such a better place if the teachers weren't burnt out or were trying to serve too many kids because they really need the money. I think that happens a lot in family day care, especially unlicensed family day care. If the caregivers were supported for what they're doing, they'd do a better job and in the end the results would be better.

VII. SOURCES AND FURTHER READING

Thanks to Diane Haslett for her list of recommendations for further reading.

Ayers, William. 1989. "JoAnne: to make a difference" [B.J. Richards] *The Good Preschool Teacher: Six Teachers Reflect on Their Lives*. Pp. 57 -78. NY: Teachers College Press.

"Child care and child development." 1990. Pp. 41 - 55 in *S.O.S. America! a Children's Defense Budget*. Washington, D.C.: Children's Defense Fund.

Glenn, Evelyn Nakano. 1985. "Racial ethnic women's labor: the intersection of race, gender, and class oppression." *Review of Radical Political Economics*, 17: 102.

Joffe, Carole. "Why the United States has no child-care policy." Pp. 168 -182 in Irene Diamond (ed.). *Families, Politics, and Public Policy*. NY: Longman.

Norgren. Jill. 1989. "Child Care." Pp. 176 - 194 in *Women: A Feminist Perspective,* edited by Jo Freeman. 4th edition. Mountain View, CA: Mayfield.

Norgren, Jill. 1982. "In search of a national child-care policy: background and prospects." Pp. 124 -143 in *Women, Power, and Policy,* edited by Ellen Boneparth. NY: Pergamon Press.

Morris, Jenny. 1991. "Feminist Research and Community Care." Pp. 146 -168 in *Pride Against Prejudice: Transforming Attitudes to Disability*. Philadelphia, PA: New Society Publishers.

Wohl, Lisa Cronin. 1986. "B.J.'s Kids: A Day-Care Dream Come True." *Ms.* February: 73 - 75.

VIII. ORGANIZATIONS

B.J.'s KIDS Day Care Home. 2473 N. Albany, Chicago, IL 60647. (773) 342-3054.

Chicago Association for the Education of Young Children. 410 S. Michigan, Suite 525, Chicago, IL 60605. (312) 427-5399.

Child Care Initiatives. 1300 W. Belmont Avenue. Suite L100. Chicago, IL 60657.

Child Development Center, Chinese American Service League. 310 W. 24th Place, Chicago, IL 60616. (312) 791-0454 or (312) 791-0418.

Cook County Child Care Resource and Referral. (773) 769-8000.

Day Care Action Council of Illinois. 4653 N. Broadway, Suite 726. Chicago, IL 60640.

Jane Addams Hull House Association. 118 N. Clinton St. Chicago, IL 60661. (312) 726-1526.

National Association for the Education of Young Children. 1509 16th St. NW, Washington, DC 20036-1426. (800) 424-2460 or (202) 232-8777.

Orr Community Academy Infant and Family Development Center. 730 N. Pulaski Ave. Chicago, IL 60624. (773) 826-1090.

WOMEN AND SOCIAL ACTION: CLASS 9
Women and Health

 Before you read this Chapter of the Study Guide

Read Andersen, Chapter 7, "Women, Health, and Reproduction"
Andersen, pp. 86 - 89 "Sexual Development over the Life Cycle"

I. INTRODUCTION

JOURNAL
ASSIGNMENT

> Describe an experience you have had with the health care system. Reflect on ways in which gender, race, or economics influenced your experience.

Below I describe an experience I had the first time I went to a new doctor other than my family doctor.

> I was nervous about going to this new doctor. Dr. Smith had taken care of my family and me for my whole life, so it felt odd going to someone else. I felt very uncomfortable about there being no nurse in the room and that he asked me to take off all my clothes and didn't even provide me with a paper gown. I was uncomfortable, but not knowledgeable about common practices. I didn't raise any questions or express my feelings of discomfort. However, when he stroked my breasts, I decided that I was getting out of there. I talked with a dentist I knew about what to do. After listening to my story, he advised me to get another doctor and forget about it. He said that it would be the doctor's word against mine and that the chances I would be believed over a doctor of his prominence were highly unlikely.

This was an experience I had almost 25 years ago. I mostly took the dentist's advice. I did find another doctor and I forgot the doctor's name. I haven't, however, forgotten the experience.

My story illustrates some of the challenges women face with the medical system; for example, lack of knowledge about accepted practices, lack of knowledge of patient's rights, lack of a doctor review process by patients, the power of male doctors in the health care system. My story also highlights the strong feelings that can be evoked by health care practices.

As we address women and health in Class 9, think about your own experiences with the health care system. Consider the knowledge and support you have had and what difference more or less knowledge or support would have made in your experience. Consider the cost of the health care you have had and consider who has paid for it. Consider the access you have had to health care and how your access may have been influenced by gender, race, class, or disability. Think about your own vision for an empowering system of health care.

II. CLASS THEMES

- Issues in health care
- Gender and health care
- Social action and health care
- Women's health movement and Native American health movement

III. VIDEOTAPE SYNOPSIS

- Overview of women's health
- Class discussion of women's health issues
- Video composite of visit with women from the Lesbian Community Cancer Project, Mary McCauley II, Director; Sandra Steingraber, Robin Stein, and Carol Zimmerman
- Class discussion of video
- Video visit with Laura McAlpine, Director, and Sharon Powell, Outreach Coordinator, Chicago Women's Health Center
- Interview and class discussion with guest Geri Shangreaux, Dean of Chicago Campus, Native American Educational Services (NAES)

IV. VIDEOTAPE COMMENTARY

A. Overview of women's health

Using *The New Our Bodies, Ourselves* as a symbol, I point to the gains of the women's health movement over the last twenty years. Think about the graphics which appear on the screen. What does the phrase "Killing Us Quietly" as applied to breast cancer mean to you? Have you ever done self-examination with a speculum or know someone who has? What do you see as the potential power in women being able to do self-examination?

B. Class discussion of women's health issues

Through stories of their own experience, class members identify a range of issues in health care and give examples of the benefits of having access to information. For example, Virginia, Jan, Gail, and Judy share examples concerning menstruation and menopause. What insights do we gain about the need for access to information and a supportive network? Peg mentions the strides in treatment of breast cancer. What specific changes does she mention? Laura and Judy also address changes in practitioners and health care centers. What are the key changes they identify?

C. Video composite of visit with women from the Lesbian Community Cancer Project

Mary McCauley II, Director, Sandra Steingraber, Robin Stein, and Carol Zimmerman offer us insightful and moving analyses and stories of women's experiences with cancer. Sandra discusses the invisibility of cancer and the courage of women who make it visible. What do you think about breast reconstruction? What have you done or what would you do if you or someone close to you was faced with this decision? What are the benefits? What are the disadvantages?

Sandra also draws our attention to the need to address prevention and environmental sources of cancer rather than focusing almost solely on treatment. Find out for yourself where dollars for cancer are going. When you hear or read news stories about cancer, check out whether the emphasis is on prevention or treatment. If the emphasis is on prevention, what is the relative emphasis on the environment, personal lifestyle, or inherited factors?

Robin discusses the value of support groups, particularly the benefits of support groups for lesbians with cancer. What does she tell us about the value of such groups for dealing with cancer?

Mary and Carol give us an overview of the tremendous impact dealing with cancer has on women, their friends, and families. Carol tells us of the deep feelings she has experienced in dealing with cancer. We see the tremendous power unleashed when she expresses these feelings.

All these women are breaking silence about cancer. What are things we all can do to contribute to heightened public awareness of the causes and consequences of cancer?

D. Class discussion of video

Class members reinforce and draw out issues raised in the interviews with women from the Lesbian Community Cancer Project. For example, Claudia, Judy, and Joan's comments enhance our understanding of women's experience of breast cancer. What are the feelings expressed? How has the experience changed for women in the last three decades?

Carlos, Judy, Sharon, and Felicia identify important things we can do in the fight against cancer. What do they offer as important elements in this fight?

E. Video visit with Laura McAlpine, Director, and Sharon Powell, Outreach Coordinator, Chicago Women's Health Center

Sharon Powell and Laura McAlpine give us an overview of the Chicago Women's Health Center, the services it provides and how it operates. What do they see as the advantages of a collective organization which is constantly evolving? What benefits do you see in this approach to women's health care? They mention menstrual extraction and Norplant. Laura describes menstrual extraction, but not Norplant. For more on Norplant, see *The New Our Bodies, Ourselves*.

F. Interview and class discussion with Geri Shangreaux, Dean of Chicago Campus, Native American Educational Services (NAES)

Geri Shangreaux describes her background and the current focus on Native American health issues. She contrasts the approach to Native American health issues and women's health issues. What do you see as the differences? What do you see as the similarities? In her overview, Geri talked about genograms. Jan asks Geri to elaborate on what a genogram is. What do you understand a genogram is?

In response to Gail's question about the differences between urban and reservation Native American health care issues, Geri discusses the politics of health care. What are the key issues? What is her vision of health care and how does it contrast with an individualistic approach?

Helen and Peg ask questions concerning traditional Native American healing practices. What role do these play in the work Geri does? What influences how they are used?

 Now watch the videotape.

V. REVIEW QUESTIONS

1. How is gender related to health care? Give an example.

2. How is race and ethnicity related to health care? Give an example.

3. What are major issues in work environments and health?

4. How is sexism involved in protective legislation?

5. According to Andersen, in what ways is women's health interwoven with men's power in medicine and the profit structure of modern medicine?

6. What are the goals of the women's health movement? What are accomplishments of the women's health movement?

7. How has feminist scholarship challenged conventional ideas about menstruation and menopause?

8. What are ways to make the cancer epidemic visible?

9. What are the benefits of a collective decision-making process in women's health? Give an example of how it works in the Chicago Women's Health Project.

10. What are health issues among Native Americans? What are the politics of health care for Native Americans?

VI. INTERVIEW EXCERPTS

Judy Panko Reis, Health Resource Center for Women with Disabilities, gives us an overview of the reasons why the Center for Women with Disabilities was founded.

" Judy Panko Reis:

The Center for Women With Disabilities is at the Rehabilitation Institute of Chicago. It was founded by two doctors who are physiologists and attending physicians at the rehab and what they wanted to do is start placing more of a medical focus on providing accessible health care to women with disabilities. What they realized was that many women with disabilities were not given standard OB and gynecological care and that was the first of a number of reasons. Another is that medical professionals themselves were often not recognizing that women with disabilities were sexually active and capable of producing children and fertile. So issues like birth control, menopause, osteoporosis, parenting concerns, mammograms, and venereal disease were basically overlooked. Not to mention that a lot of technology and equipment were not accessible. Women in wheelchairs were not getting mammograms because mammogram machines were not accessible. And this was some of the impetus for the founding of the center. The doctors came out into the community and said that we really need to get the community involved in the formation of this group. They started an advisory board and wanted to have a newsletter, a publication that was coming out on a regular basis. So I was recruited as one of the members of the advisory board and was shortly thereafter made chair of the advisory board and also hired as editor of our publication. I should also say that one of the reasons I was recruited was because prior to the establishment of this center at the Rehabilitation Institute I had just finished guest-editing a publication on women with disabilities [for *The Creative Woman*]. And the reason I did that was because there were virtually no resources about women with disabilities and I thought that if nothing else I wanted to have a parenting article in there and that was actually the lead story in that magazine. So a lot of the doctors had heard about the magazine and a lot of my peers and colleagues were aware of that so it was pretty much what brought me into it.

Sandra Steingraber of the Lesbian Community Cancer Project offers a framework for understanding cancer as a human rights issue.

Martha: Give us an overview of cancer and women

Sandra Steingraber: Cancer, unfortunately, right now is really at an epidemic proportion in every literal and biological sense of that word. More and more people are being diagnosed with cancer all the time. For women in particular the kind of cancers that are particular to women, like ovarian cancer and breast cancer, are on the rise; particularly breast cancer. About when I was born, in 1959, about one in every 20 women would be diagnosed with breast cancer and about half of those would survive and half of those would die. Now it's one in every nine and perhaps one in every eight. So in the course of my lifetime just the incident rate has gone way up, so it effects more and more of us all the time and the survival rate hasn't changed at all. About half of us survive and half of us die.

Martha: Tell us about the relationship of cancer to the environment

Sandra: Strangely enough the increase in cancer is really well understood biologically, although it seems to me that the word isn't really getting out to people about what's going on. It's really not disputed at all in the scientific literature that about 80% of all cancers, and it's the same for breast or uterine or ovarian, are caused by repeated, long-term exposure to contaminants in the environment. They're called environmental insults. What that means to you and me is things that should not be in our air, food and water that we're being exposed to that can cause a cascade of physiological effects inside our body, eventually leading to the formation of a tumor. This can be triggered by the breaking up of DNA, it can change the way our immune system responds, can change the way cells recognize each other. About 80% of cancers are caused by these environmental exposures. They can be in your home, in your workplace, just in the general environment in the air and water that we all need to live. What this means is that the entire scientific community all agree on this. What's amazing to me is that when people are diagnosed with cancer they often ask the "why me" questions, they often ask it in a very nonmaterial way. They see this as fate or destiny, and if they think about the biology of the situation, very often they come to the conclusion that there's something wrong with their genes. It's very easy to blame our mothers, for example, if there's a history of breast cancer in the family, we're more susceptible to it. It's true that some of us are more sensitive than others to these contaminants but our genes don't suddenly, spontaneously cause a tumor. It takes that environmental trigger to do that. So what I wonder about is if everyone in the scientific community agrees, why is it that people with cancer aren't talking about the environment? There's a breakdown in the analysis somewhere and it seems to me the breakdown comes from a kind of deep-rooted summation of the issue by the very institutions that are supposed to be advocating for cancer victims. By that I mean the American Cancer Society and the National Cancer Institute, which are two big cancer establishments, and which have really downplayed the environmental connection with cancer when that's the most important thing we should be talking about.

Martha: Tell us more about the politics of cancer

Sandra: Politics and cancer are both elaborate and very simple. I think one can understand it on one level as a simple conflict of interest. Let me make that comparison with the AIDS epidemic for a moment. When AIDS came on to the scene, there really were no established bodies in the government or large nonprofit organizations clinging to represent AIDS, claiming to be finding a cure. It's because it initially attacked a group of people who already were considered invisible by society and suffered a lot of discrimination. It was really up to those people to force the medical and scientific communities to deal with this disease. And I saw this as a human rights issue. So the organizations that have sprung up to raise money and to fight for the rights of these people to get treatment and to fight the disease itself came from these groups and they've made incredible progress. In contrast, with women with cancer these powerful organizations are already in place. Let me explain how this interlocking system works. The National Cancer Institute is a branch of our government that's a part of the National Institute of Health. It has a direct line of communication to the White House. So it's supposed to be doing research, it's responsible for the war on cancer, as it was declared by President Nixon quite a long time ago. So that's the Institute. Along with the Institute is a nonprofit organization, that's the big cancer charity, the American Cancer Society. So that has a board of directors and most of those directors are heads of large chemical corporations, pharmaceutical corporations, etc. They have a very high stake, I believe, in promoting cancer as a lifestyle issue. They want to promote the idea that cancer runs in families. And that you can change your risk of getting cancer by changing your behaviors. So if you stay out of the sun, you eat a high fiber diet, you don't smoke, all the things that we really are propagandized to believe are primary causes of cancer, the way they get their message out is to publish brochures and literature that go to doctor's offices so that public education around cancer comes from the American Cancer Society. And again, I want to say a few more things about the National Cancer Institute. Pretty much 95% of the money that they get from the federal budget goes for treatments of cancer. And right now, as they have been for the last four years, treatment of cancer falls into three categories. Some of us who have researched this have a gallows kind of humor, they're often referred to as slash, burn, and poison; mainly surgery, chemotherapy and radiation therapy. Those three sectors haven't changed very much at all in the decades that I've been alive. So the money goes to perfecting new techniques of one of those three. That's where the lion's share of the money is going.

A real cancer prevention campaign would mean, as far as I'm concerned as a biologist, is not more mammograms, which detect, not prevent anything, but would mean cleaning up our whole environment. It would mean radically changing the way we deliver goods and services in this country. It would mean letting people in South Chicago know, for example, that South Chicago has the most concentrated amount of hazardous waste anywhere in the United States, and it's raising their cancer risk in that area. It would mean that all the well-documented cancer clusters around petro chemical refineries, pesticides and farm fields, nuclear reactors, where all these things would be documented, people would know that they're at risk and people would begin to make the connections. It's very simple, the health of the earth and our health are interconnected because we take in energy and matter from our environment and whatever is in that goes into our bodies. That's what I think the National Cancer Institute and the American Cancer Society should be doing. That would explain 80% of the cancers that we're seeing. It's not what they do. So they've really created an invisibility around these issues.

Martha: I know you're doing something different. You talked about this is why you became an activist and became involved in this project. Talk about how you made this shift from being a biologist studying the problem to including or expanding your role as an activist as well?

Sandra: Well, cancer has touched me personally for a long time. I'm 33 years old now. My mother was diagnosed with breast cancer when I was about 13 and it metastasized to her bones so she was ill for most of my adolescence. She is in remission, actually, against all odds and is still alive and doing fine now, but I as a young girl watched her go through all the different treatments, all the surgeries, and the chemotherapy and the radiation. Then I myself was diagnosed at the age of 20 with bladder cancer which is actually called an unusual kind of cancer for someone both of my gender and of my age.

I guess in a way I became a biologist because of my experiences both with my mother and with myself. And this is a footnote—I'm going to interject that I'm an adoptee—so a lot of people in my community think, oh, her mother's got it, she's got it, you know, there it is, it's in the genes, which is what a lot of families think. Of course families who have a history of cancer also tend to drink the same water supply or they live next to the same toxic waste dump. They tend to be compounded variables in those families. And from a biologist's point of view, my family is a kind of controlled experiment because none of us is genetically related and yet we see cancer in the area where I grew up which is in downstate Illinois. And my attempt to understand the question, "why me?" "why my mother?" is one I've asked every day of my life since I've been 13. I think about cancer as an issue, it's an ongoing part of my relationship with my family. I wanted to know the answers and I began to read the medical literature, I began to study biology, and the more I found out and the more anyone would read, the more you realize that it's what's in our environment that affects us. So in a way I ended up choosing a career goal that reflected my needs, to come to terms with this. So I asked the "why me" questions in a very material and very ecological way and it helps me demystify the disease. It was no longer a monster that was going to overwhelm, it was no longer just a random shake of the dice, you know, there were very specific reasons for it. I could understand that we lived down the river from a coal burning power plant in my home town, that we drank ground water there, we were surrounded by pesticide intensive agribusiness, you know, I could start to sort it all out. At some part of my life, when I was helping my mother get healthy again, I didn't use biology directly to understand cancer, I worked on a lot of other things.

And now I see how it's all connected, at the time I didn't. I was doing work in the rain forest in Central America, I was in Ethiopia and Sudan in the 80s and looking at the famine there and ecological reasons for that and the whole political situation and what I realize now is that all of this was an ongoing attempt to understand how ecology and human rights are related. And I now understand cancer as a human rights issue. When you cut down the rain forests and the people there cannot live anymore, that's an environmental rights violation. When there's war as there is now going on in Somalia and people can't grow food to feed themselves, that's a human rights violation. So I feel that 10 years really engaged in third world issues and it's been a very interesting metamorphosis for me to come back around and to look at myself and my family and the women in the Lesbian Community Cancer Project as victims of a larger environmental policy that I think is killing people. Just as if our government picked people out and shot them to death, we'd go to the UN and say you can't just assassinate people, you can't torture them, you can't imprison them without due process. Well, I also say you can't poison people and contaminate their air, food and water in such a way that they're going to get sick and die. I know that most people don't look at cancer that way and when people die a death from cancer, even if they live in the inner city, that's not considered a political death.

VII. SOURCES AND FURTHER READING

Blume, Judy. 1970. *Are you there God? It's Me, Margaret.* Englewood Cliffs, NJ: Bradbury Press.

Boston Women's Health Book Collective. 1992. *The New Our Bodies, Ourselves: Updated and Expanded for the 90s.* NY: Simon and Schuster.

Brown, Susan E. 1985. "Infusing blues." Pp. 15 -22 in *With the Power of Each Breath: A Disabled Women's Anthology,* edited by Susan E. Browne, Debra Connors, and Nanci Stern. Pittsburgh: Cleis.

Corea, Gena. 1985. *The Hidden Malpractice: How American Medicine Mistreats Women,* rev. ed. NY: Harper.

Dreifus, Claudia (ed.) 1978. *Seizing Our Bodies.* NY: Vintage.

Ehrenreich, Barbara and Deidre English. 1978. *For Her Own Good.* Garden Center, NY: Anchor-Doubleday.

Franchild, Edwina Trish. 1985. "Untangling the web of denial." Pp. 36 - 51 in *With the Power of Each Breath: A Disabled Women's Anthology,* edited by Susan E. Browne, Debra Connors, and Nanci Stern. Pittsburgh: Cleis.

Laws, Sophie. 1993. "Who needs PMT?" Pp. 385 - 388 in *Women's Studies: Essential Readings,* edited by Stevi Jackson. Washington Square, NY: New York University Press.

Levy, Emily. 1985. "How the rhino got its flaky skin." Pp. 26 - 35 in *With the Power of Each Breath: A Disabled Women's Anthology,* edited by Susan E. Browne, Debra Connors, and Nanci Stern. Pittsburgh: Cleis.

Lorber, Judith. 1984. *Women Physicians: Career, Status, and Power.* NY: Tavistock.

Lorde, Audre. 1980. *The Cancer Journals.* Argyle, NY: Spinsters Ink.

Luxenburg, Joan and Thomas E. Guild. 1993. "Women, AIDS, and the criminal justice system."
   Pp. 77 - 92 in *It's a Crime: Women and Justice*, edited by Roslyn Muraskin and Ted
   Alleman. Englewood Cliffs, NJ: Regents/Prentice Hall.

Millman, Marcia. 1977. *The Unkindest Cut: Life in the Backrooms of Medicine.* NY: William
   Morrow.

Reis, Judy Panko. 1991. "Swimming Upstream: Managing Disabilities," Special issue. *The
   Creative Woman* 11 (2, Summer).

Women's Action Coalition. 1993. "AIDS," "Breast Cancer," "Health," "Hysterectomy," and
   "Menopause; Osteoporosis." NY: New Press Edition.

White, Evelyn. 1990. *The Black Women's Health Book: Speaking for Ourselves.* Seattle, WA:
   Seal Press.

VIII. ORGANIZATIONS

Boston Women's Health Book Collective. Women's Health Information Center,
P.O. Box 192. West Somerville, MA 02144.

Chicago Women's Health Center. 3435 N. Sheffield Ave. Chicago, IL 60657.
(773) 935-6126.

Health Resource Center for Women with Disabilities. c/o Dr. Kristi Kirschner, Rehabilitation
Institute of Chicago, 345 E. Superior, Chicago, IL 60610. (312)908-4744.

Lesbian Community Cancer Project. 1902 W. Montrose Ave., Chicago, IL 60613.
(773) 561-4662.

National Latina Health Organization/Organizacíon Nacional de la Salud de la Mujer Latina,
P.O. Box 7567, Oakland, CA 94601. (415) 534-1362.

Native American Educational Service (NAES). 2838 West Peterson Ave., Chicago, IL 60659.
(773) 761-5000.

Native American Women's Health Education Resource Center. P.O. Box 572. Lake Andes, SD
57356. (605) 487-7072.

Planned Parenthood Information and Referral Hotline. 14 E. Jackson Blvd. Chicago, IL 60604.
(312) 427-2275.

Women's Program, Korean Self-Help Center. 4934 N. Pulaski Rd. Chicago, IL 60630. (773) 545-8348.

Y-Me National Organization for Breast Cancer Information and Support. 18220 Harwood Ave. Homewood, IL 60430. 24 hour Emergency Breast Cancer Hotline (708) 799-8228. Monday - Friday, 9 am - 5 pm CST, call 1-800-221-2141.

WOMEN AND SOCIAL ACTION: CLASS 10
Women, Weight, and Food

 Before you read this Chapter of the Study Guide

Read Andersen, pp. 197-203, "Gender, Health, and Social Problems"
Andersen, Chp. 4, "Sexuality and Intimate Relationships"

I. INTRODUCTION

JOURNAL
ASSIGNMENT

> Describe your experience with dieting or body image. Reflect on ways cultural messages about thinness may have affected you.

Look through a fashion, body building, or exercise magazine. Look carefully at each photo or drawing in the magazine. How would you characterize the body weight and height of each person represented? Notice the range of skin color. Notice the age range. Notice how many people represented are in a wheelchair, using a cane, or have a hearing aid. Now look at yourself in a full-length mirror; really look. How similar are you to the people in the magazine? How do you feel about your body? Are there parts of your body you avoid looking at? Are there parts you enjoy looking at? What about when you look at other people. What do you notice first? Do you notice different things about women and men? Go back and think about the reflection assignment again; note any additions or changes.

One year my Aunt Ruth arranged to have t-shirts printed for the Thompson family. They contained an apt motto "Till we eat again." Food is at the center of Thompson family gatherings. Food represents so much more than eating in my family; it represents gifts we share with each other; it represents our uniqueness and creativity; it represents our family solidarity. However, I also see the conflicts about eating that different family members have experienced at family gatherings; the dilemmas about staying on a diet; the desire to have a second helping of a favorite dish, but also the desire to fit into a smaller size bathing suit; the chagrin at weighing more at this gathering than at the last one.

When we talk about women, weight, and food, we have to examine the topic from all the angles I've mentioned above: what are the messages we get through the media and other social institutions; what is our family's approach to weight, food, and sexuality; and how do we feel about our own bodies and our own sexuality. We need to think about the size of airplane seats, clothing sizing, the food industry, the diet industry. We need to think about how much food and weight are topics of conversations with our family and friends. We need to think about how our self-esteem and our sexual feelings are tied into what we eat, how much we eat, and how much we weigh. We need to think very carefully about the myriad ways women's lives are affected by social values concerning women's bodies and food.

Imagine a world where our body size and type were honored and celebrated and not at the expense of others. Imagine a world where sexual expression and sexual feelings were not linked to the size and shape of our bodies. Imagine a world where we all eat and exercise for our health, not for our appearance. Think about what changes have to occur for such a world to exist.

II. CLASS THEMES

- The diversity in our bodies
- The effects of the cultural obsession with thinness on our lives
- How weight and food issues are related to gender, sexuality, and power
- Ways to take our bodies back

III. VIDEOTAPE SYNOPSIS

- Overview of class session and introduction of Demetria Iazzetto, contributor to *The New Our Bodies, Ourselves: Updated and Expanded for the '90s.*
- Overview of Demetria Iazzetto's background
- Interview and class discussion with Demetria Iazzetto

IV. VIDEOTAPE COMMENTARY

A. Overview of class session and introduction of Demetria Iazzetto, contributor to *The New Our Bodies, Ourselves: Updated and Expanded for the '90s.*

I have known Demetria for over 15 years and have had the opportunity to see her explore issues of weight and food from personal, political, and professional angles. With humor, compassion, and insightful analysis in her writing and presentations on body image, Demetria has raised the consciousness of countless people about the impact social messages about food, weight, and body image have on women.

After introducing Demetria, I give an overview of the themes for Class Session 10 on "Women, Weight, and Food."

B. Overview of Demetria Iazzetto's background

Demetria gives us an overview of her own experience in dealing with weight and food, her research on the topic, and her work with the Boston Women's Health Book Collective. Later in the videotape Demetria will talk about her own body size and how it affects people's responses to her. As you listen to her introduction, notice your reactions to her body size and shape.

C. Interview and class discussion with Demetria Iazzetto

With a combination of graphics and discussion, we explore diet mania, height and weight tables, fat myths and facts, and actions for social change.

Demetria gives us an overview of what she calls diet mania. What do you think she means by that term? What examples does she give to support her viewpoint? Demetria briefly addresses the issues of heterosexism and homophobia. How do you see these issues relating to our knowledge of eating problems?

Mary, Gail, and Ada share moving examples from their own lives about weight and food issues. Demetria responds to Mary's example by distinguishing between eating being the problem and becoming a problem. What do you see as the difference?

Gail talks about her experience with eating. How does she describe the problem? In response to Gails's story, Demetria talks about distorted body image and internationalization. What do these concepts mean to you? Ada's example reminds us that having the "ideal" figure can also pose problems for women. What issues does her story reveal about sexuality and body image?

Ada's example leads into talking about height and weight tables which presumably are to represent ideals to which we should strive. Demetria gives us a brief overview of the history of these tables and formulae and then compares the different models. What are similarities and differences in the tables? What changes do you see over time in the tables? What differences do you see for females and males? What does Demetria mean by the social construction of these tables? How does Demetria's example of an historical replica of a goddess illustrate this point?

In response to Gunther's question about health and diet and a question from me, Demetria talks about better ways to measure health. What are these measures? Joe provides a concrete example for discussion about the flaws in the height and weight tables. What is the key flaw in these tables his example reveals? Debbie shares her own experience with these charts. What does her experience tell us about these ideals? In response to a question from Gunther about eating, Demetria talks about the cultural messages females and males receive. What are these messages? Trenace describes her own experience with negative messages and asks Demetria to elaborate on who gives us negative messages. What does Demetria tell us about who sends these negative messages and how they are sent?

Demetria briefly addresses levels of change. What are these three levels? How does Gail's example illustrate Demetria's point about the individual level?

In response to our review of fat myths and facts, Trenace provides an example concerning her and her sister. Demetria talks about the role of heredity, metabolism, and yo-yo dieting. What roles do heredity and metabolism play in our body weight? How does Trenace's example illustrate this? What health problems does Demetria identify with yo-yo dieting?

In conclusion, Demetria summarizes what the cultural obsession with weight and food means for social action. What are her key points?

 Now watch the videotape.

V. REVIEW QUESTIONS

1. What is meant by a cultural obsession with weight and thinness? What effects does it have on our lives?

2. What are ways that gender, sexuality, and power are related to issues of weight and food? How do they relate to substance abuse rates?

3. What is diet mania? What is yo-yo dieting? What health risks do they present?

4. What is meant by anorexia nervosa? bulimia? compulsive eating?

5. What role do heredity and metabolism play in body size?

6. What is the difference between an eating disorder and an eating problem?

7. What are three patterns in the history of sexuality? How do these patterns affect women's bodies?

8. What is meant by compulsory heterosexuality? heterosexism? homophobia? How do these concepts relate to issues of weight and food?

9. What is meant by sexual politics? patriarchy? power? How do they relate to issues of weight and food?

10. Briefly describe the ideal weight tables, their history, and their flaws. What are better indicators of health?

11. What are three levels of change associated with women, weight, and food? Give an example of one thing that could be changed at each level.

12. What does the cultural obsession with weight and food mean for social action?

VI. INTERVIEW EXCERPT

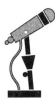

Sharon Powell, Outreach Coordinator, Chicago Women's Health Center, talks about the importance of grounding policies about women's health and women's bodies in women's experience and the importance of women advocating for themselves.

❝❝ Sharon Powell:

I would like to see, in terms of other organizations, women really working toward doing something that's direct service in nature. I don't know—sometimes I call it a field trip, to come and deal with what is actually going on in organizations that face direct services. Because I think that once you've been involved—if you're giving health education, if you're providing services— you have a better understanding of what would work on a higher level in terms of policy. Sometimes we sit around having meetings, and we get so far away from the real issues of providing services that we're not able to really make those clear decisions. I would suggest that groups try to find a way where they can have that kind of link between what's really happening in health care agencies and then what kind of advocacy work that they're doing. Also, to provide forums for health education because a lot of this is going to be about prevention and information— women knowing about their bodies, being able to act on that information, and then being able to be in a health care situation and actually advocate for themselves there. A lot of times we think about picketing and having marches and that kind of thing, when a real, very serious advocacy thing happens when a woman is able to advocate for herself. **❞❞**

VII. SOURCES AND FURTHER READING

Thanks to Demetria Iazzetto for her list of recommendations for further reading.

Browne, Susan E., Debra Connors, and Nanci Stern, (eds.). 1985. "This Body I Love-Finding Ourselves," Chp. 5 in *With the Power of Each Breath: A Disabled Women's Anthology*. Pittsburgh, PA: Cleis Press.

Chernin, Kim. 1981. *The Obsession: Reflections on the Tyranny of Slenderness*. NY: Harper and Row.

Espin, Oliva M. 1992. "Cultural and historical influences on sexuality in Hispanic/Latin women." Pp. 141 - 146 in *Race, Class, and Gender: An Anthology*, edited by Margaret L. Andersen and Patricia Hill Collins. Belmont, CA: Wadsworth Publishing.

Frank, Gelya. 1988. "On embodiment: a case study of congenital limb deficiency in American culture." Pp. 41 - 71 in *Women with Disabilities: Essays in Psychology, Culture, and Politics*, edited by Michele Fine and Adrienne Asch. Philadelphia, PA: Temple University Press.

Freedman, Rita. 1988. *Bodylove: Learning to Like Our Looks—and Ourselves*. NY: Harper and Row.

Hall, Lesley. 1992. "Beauty quests - a double disservice: beguiled, beseeched and bombarded— challenging the concept of beauty." Pp. 134 - 139 in *Imprinting Our Image: An International Anthology by Women with Disabilities,* edited by Diane Driedger and Susan Gray. Canada: Gynergy Books.

Hutchinson, Marcia Germaine. 1985. *Transforming Body Image*. NY: Crossing Press.

Lyons, Pat and Debby Burgard. 1990. *Great Shape: the Fitness Guide for Large Women*. Palo Alto, CA: Bull.

Orbach, Susie. 1978. *Fat Is A Feminist Issue*. NY:Berkeley Publishing.

Polivy, Janet and C. Peter Herman. 1983. *Breaking the Diet Habit*. NY: Basic

Schoenfielder, Lisa and Barbara Wieser (eds.). 1983. *Shadow on a Tightrope*. San Francisco: Spinsters/Aunt Lute.

Radiance: the Magazine for Large Women. P.O. Box 31703, Oakland, CA 94604. (415) 482-0680.

Rome, Esther. 1992. "Food." Pp. 30 -54 in the Boston Women's Health Book Collective (eds.). *The New Our Bodies, Ourselves*. NY: Simon and Schuster.

Sanford, Wendy with update by Demetria Iazzetto. 1992. "Body Image." Pp. 23 -29 in the Boston Women's Health Book Collective (eds.). *The New Our Bodies, Ourselves.* NY: Simon and Schuster.

Women's Action Coalition. 1993. "Cosmetics/cosmetic surgery" and "Eating disorders/dieting" Pp. 18 - 21 in *WAC Stats: the Facts About Women.* NY: The New Press.

"Women's Bodies." 1990. *Woman of Power*, 18 (Fall). Available from Women of Power, Inc. P.O. Box 2785, Orleans, MA 02653.

VIII. ORGANIZATIONS

Boston Women's Health Book Collective. Women's Health Information Center. P.O.Box 192, West Somerville, MA 02144.

Chicago Women's Health Center. 3435 N. Sheffield Ave. Chicago, IL 60657. (773) 935-6126.

WOMEN AND SOCIAL ACTION: CLASS 11
Pregnancy and Childbirth

 Before you read this Chapter of the Study Guide

Read Andersen, pp. 209-216 "The Politics of Birth" and "Reproductive Technology"

I. INTRODUCTION

JOURNAL
ASSIGNMENT

> Describe your own experience with pregnancy, childbirth, or breastfeeding/bottlefeeding or that of someone you know. Reflect on ways the politics of birth influenced this experience.

In *The Dialectic of Sex,* Shulamith Firestone (1970) argued that women's capacity for childbearing is **the** root of the class/caste system as well as the basis for women's oppression. Further she argued that for women to gain control over their bodies and lives, women need to replace biological reproduction with the option of artificial reproduction. Even while advocating artificial reproduction, Firestone emphasized that unless women control the means of reproduction, potentially liberating technology will be another means of oppression.

In "Women and Social Action," we will explore several ways that women are working to gain control of reproduction. In Class 11, we will explore ways women are working to make pregnancy and childbirth a woman-centered experience in which pregnancy, labor, birth, and lactation are seen as interconnected parts of a natural process. We will contrast these efforts with the dominant medical model which separates these experiences, intervenes in each stage of the process, and places control in the hands of medical personnel. In upcoming class sessions, we will examine alternative (artificial) insemination, abortion, and other reproductive issues.

Firestone's provocative argument challenges us to consider whether or not women must give birth for the species to survive. She does not permit us to excuse current treatment of pregnancy and childbirth with a nod to biological imperatives. In Class 11 we will, like Firestone, challenge the dominant approach to childbearing in the United States. We will, in contrast to Firestone, challenge the dominant approach by focusing on the ways that pregnancy and childbirth can be empowering experiences for women. We will explore the conditions under which women can experience the power of their bodies. We will touch upon the largely unexplored subject of female sexuality and reproduction. A model of sexuality based solely on male experience sees the linkage of sexuality and childbearing as perverted. With little vocabulary yet available to us, our studio guest, Marge Altergott will ask us to consider the possibility that female sexuality is much more encompassing than we have ever imagined.

II. CLASS THEMES

- The social construction of pregnancy and childbirth
- Medical and midwifery models of pregnancy and childbirth
- Empowerment in pregnancy and childbirth

III. VIDEOTAPE SYNOPSIS

- Introduction to the topic of pregnancy and childbirth
- Class discussion of pregnancy and childbirth experiences
- Video visit with Judy Panko Reis, Health Resource Center for Women with Disabilities
- Interview and class discussion with Marge Altergott, health educator. Adjunct Faculty, Department of Sociology, Northeastern Illinois University.

IV. VIDEOTAPE COMMENTARY

A. Introduction to the topic of pregnancy and childbirth

I introduce the idea of the social construction of pregnancy and childbirth by comparing my mother's and my experience. What do you see as the similarities and differences in our experiences?

B. Class discussion of pregnancy and childbirth experiences

Class members share a range of experiences with breastfeeding and bottlefeeding .
Notice the differences in social support for choices about how to feed babies.
For example, Joan, Janet, Laura, Virginia, Debbic, and Trenace give examples of ways that their or another woman's choice to feed their child was not supported. What are ways that people indicated their disapproval or undermined their choice? What were the consequences in each of the examples? Debbie expresses feelings shared by many women who have had their pregnancy or childbirth experience defined and confined by the medical model.

Judy, Ada, and Trenace give examples of ways they received support. What ideas do you have about the differences in these experiences? Gunther raises questions about what to do when someone else is breastfeeding? What has been your experience? What ideas do you have about ways people could show their support while not invading someone's personal space?

C. Video visit with Judy Panko Reis, Health Resource Center for Women with Disabilities

Judy turned her experience with the lack of resources for pregnant women with disabilities into social action. Judy was instrumental in developing the Health Resource Center for Women with Disabilities. In recognition of the work she has done to bring health services to women with disabilities, Judy received a $100, 000 grant from the Robert Wood Johnson Foundation. $95,000 will go to the Health Resource Center. Judy also has a Master of Science in Communication from Northwestern and uses her communication skills in many ways. She founded the *Resourceful Woman*, a newsletter for women with disabilities and was a guest editor for a special issue of *The Creative Woman* on "Swimming Upstream: Managing Disabilities." For this special issue, she worked with Helen Hughes, the editor of *The Creative Woman* and "Women and Social Action" class member.

On the videotape, Judy describes her background, the brutal act of violence which resulted in her disability and the death of her fiance, and ways this violence has changed her life. She also describes her experience with pregnancy and childbirth, offering insights into the need for a model for pregnancy and childbirth which adapts to the needs of a pregnant woman and new mother. No woman's pregnancy and childbirth is exactly like any other woman's. Judy's experience shows the limitations of a system which assumes all women are the same. What particular resources would have been helpful to Judy? How would a flexible system help other women?

D. Interview and class discussion with Marge Altergott, Adjunct Faculty, Department of Sociology, Northeastern Illinois University and a health educator.

Marge is a highly effective health educator. As part of her work, she has examined pregnancy and childbirth through feminist literature, history, and sociology. She is currently working on her doctorate in public health. She has worked actively on many community health projects, including the Health Policy Project of Women United for a Better Chicago. In the midst of all of this work, she has given birth to five children.

On the videotape, Marge gives us an overview of her background, particularly her commitment to home births. She also identifies two major concerns about pregnancy and childbirth: the narrow focus of the medical model and the lack of recognition of the social nature of health. She compares and contrasts the medical and midwifery models. What do you see as the key differences? She also introduces us to the concept of home birth. Gunther raises a question about the safety of home births and Trenace asks Marge to describe what would be done in a specific situation like she experienced with the birth of her first child (i.e. meconium aspiration). What safeguards does Marge tell us about? What point does Ada make about infant mortality rates?

In response to Jan's questions about midwifery schools and insurance, Marge took the opportunity to tell us about variations in support for midwives by state. She asked me to let you know not only are there certificate programs in Oregon, Texas, and Arizona, but there are degree programs in midwifery in Seattle, Washington and Taos, New Mexico. The names and addresses of the schools are under "Sources and Further Reading." Christine had a question about the role of midwives in hospitals. What did we learn from Marge about why midwives work in hospitals?

When you saw the graphic Marge brought with her, what did you think it was? Marge and I were both surprised when Jan guessed correctly right away. Marge uses this graphic to talk about how a male model of sexuality has affected women's experience with pregnancy and childbirth. Claudia, Laura, and Judy give examples of different reactions to women's bodies and women's sexuality during pregnancy and childbirth. What does Marge mean by a male model of sexuality and how does she see it affecting women's experience of pregnancy and childbirth? What does Marge mean when she says we have no vocabulary to describe women's sexuality during reproduction?

In conclusion Marge tells us about ways to make pregnancy and childbirth an empowering and positive experience for women. What are the levels that she says we have to deal with?

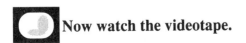 **Now watch the videotape.**

V. REVIEW QUESTIONS

1. What is a social history of childbirth?

2. What is meant by the medicalization of pregnancy and childbirth?

3. What is meant by a midwifery model of pregnancy and childbirth?

4. Compare and contrast the medical model and midwifery model.

5. What is a midwife and how does support for midwifery vary by state?

6. What is a home birth? What safeguards do midwives take when doing home births?

7. What are the benefits and limitations of reproductive technologies?

8. What is a male model of sexuality and how does it affect women's experience of pregnancy and childbirth?

9. How are midwifery, the health system, and social stratification interrelated?

10. What are ways pregnancy and childbirth can be empowering for women?

VI. INTERVIEW EXCERPT

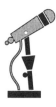

> Melissa Josephs, Policy Associate at Women Employed, says one of the most common questions about pregnancy Women Employed hears is "what are my rights as a worker when I'm pregnant?" Melissa tells us how to find out what your rights are and addresses some of the major policy changes required for employers to deal realistically and compassionately with pregnancy and childbirth.

" Melissa Josephs:

If a company has a three week policy or a one week policy, whether it's paid or unpaid, it's all up to the company. Whether they keep your job open for you when you come back is all dependent on the company and it is dependent upon how they treat other people. So the answer to all these questions we get about what are my rights when I'm pregnant, the answer is always check and see if the company has a short-term disability policy and how they treat other employees who have used it. If they held the job open for the man who came back after the broken leg, they have to do the same for you. If they allowed this person six weeks off with pay, then they have to do the same thing for you. They can't treat you any worse, they can't discriminate against you, that's where it comes in. Like I said, there's no affirmative duty. There are few employers who are blatantly discriminating when you announce you're pregnant and they fire you. Even then if that's the case, the pregnancy discrimination act protects you as well, so it's not always a strict disability comparison, but that's usually the same way it's interpreted. So it's not great. There are so many people who call the office, who work somewhere where there is no short-term disability, where they may have already used up their vacation and sick days and so they don't have that to use. If the boss is not real sympathetic or understanding, then lots of times the job is not there for them when they get back. One large issue that Women Employed is working on which is slow in coming is getting employers to change the work place. So often in the past the situation for families and work has been one person works, and it's usually the husband or the father who works, and one person, usually the Mom, would stay home and take care of the child. Well, that's no longer the case. People don't have that luxury anymore of separating that out. That's what employers, the majority of whom are male, have to realize is that the situation that they may have had, which is that they may have been able to combine work and family because they never spent any time, or very little time on the family, is no longer the case. Now they have employees who have to handle both, they have to struggle and juggle. And so that's something that's slow in coming but we're working on it. And that leads to the importance of having a family medical leave act. Some states already have this and what this would provide is unpaid job protection leave. All industrial nations in this world have some kind of leave policy and many of them are better than ours, many of them include paid leave for six months or a year and it's truly an investment. What employers have to see is that it's important obviously for people to continue having children and that employers have to be more sensitive to the issues that people are struggling with.

VII. SOURCES AND FURTHER READING

Thanks to Marge Altergott for her list of recommendations for further reading.

Al-Hibri, Azizah. 1984. "Reproduction, mothering, and the origins of patriarchy."
Pp. 81-93 in *Mothering: Essays in Feminst Theory,* edited by Joyce Trebilcot. Totawa, NJ: Rowman and Allanheld.

Atwood, Margaret. 1986. *The Handmaid's Tale.* Boston: Houghton Mifflin.

Boston Women's Health Book Collective. 1992. "Childbearing," Chapter IV in *The New Our Bodies, Ourselves.* NY: Simon and Schuster.

Corea, Gena. 1985. *The Mother Machine: Reproductive Technologies from Artificial Insemination to Artificial Wombs.* NY: Harper and Row.

Dryfoos, Joy D. 1990. *Adolescents at Risk: Prevalence and Prevention.* NY: Oxford University Press.

Enrenreich, Barbara and Deidre English. 1973. *Witches, Midwives, and Nurses.* NY: The Feminist Press.

Firestone, Shulamith. 1970. *The Dialectic of Sex: the Case for Feminist Revolution.* NY: Bantam.

Haire, Doris. 1973. "The cultural warping of childbirth." *Environmental Child Health*. June: 172 - 191.

Hayes, Cheryl D. (ed.). 1987. *Risking the Future: Adolescent Sexuality, Pregnancy, and Childbearing*. Washington, D.C. : National Academy Press.

Kay, Margarita A. 1980. "Mexican, Mexican American, and Chicana childbirth." Pp. 52 - 65 in *Twice a Minority: Mexican American Women*, edited by Margarita B. Melville. St. Louis, MO: The C.V. Mosby Company.

Kittay, Eva Feder. 1983. "Womb envy: an explanatory concept." Pp. 94-128 in *Mothering: Essays in Feminist Theory,* edited by Joyce Trebilcot. Totawa, NJ: Rowman and Allanheld.

McFarlane, Judith. 1991. "Violence during teen pregnancy: health consequences for mother and child." Pp. 136 - 141 in *Dating Violence: Young Women in Danger*, edited by Barrie Levy. Seattle, WA: Seal Press.

Merlow, Alida V. 1993. "Pregnant substance abusers: the new female offender." Pp. 146 - 158 in *It's A Crime: Women and Justice,* edited by Roslyn Muraskin and Ted Alleman. Englewood Cliffs, NJ: Regents/Prentice Hall.

O'Brien, Mary. 1981. *The Politics of Reproduction*. Boston: Routledge and Kegan Paul.

Palmer, Gabrielle. 1988. *The Politics of Breastfeeding*. London: Pandora Press.

Reed, Susan O. 1993. "The Criminalization of pregnancy: drugs, alcohol, and AIDS." Pp. 93 - 117 in *It's A Crime: Women and Justice,* edited by Roslyn Muraskin and Ted Alleman. Englewood Cliffs, NJ: Regents/Prentice Hall.

Resourceful Woman, a newsletter for disabled women. (312) 908-4744.

Rich, Adrienne. 1976. *Of Woman Born: Motherhood as Experience and Institution*. NY: Norton, Bantam.

Robinson, Bryan. 1988. *Teenage Fathers*. Livingston, MA: DC Heath and Company.

Sakala, Carol. 1990. *Childbearing Policy within A National Health Program: An Evolving Consensus for New Directions*. Brighton, MA: Boston Women's Health Book Collective, the National Black Women's Health Project, the National Women's Health Network, and the Women's Institute for Childbearing Policy.

Well-Woman Journal. Women's Health Policy Project, Women United for a Better Chicago. 1325 S. Wabash, Chicago, IL 60605. (312) 939-3636.

Women's Institute for Childbearing Policy for the Public/Consumer Delegation of the Interorganizational Workgroup on Midwifery Education. 1991. *Bibliography on the Practice of Midwifery in the U.S.* $5.00 from Judith Dickson Luce. 30 Park St., Barre, VT 05641.

Women's Health Policy Project, Women United for a Better Chicago. 1325 S. Wabash, Chicago, IL 60605. (312) 939-3636.

VIII. ORGANIZATIONS

Thanks to Marge Altergott for a list of midwifery organizations.

American College of Nurse-Midwives (ACNM). 1522 K Street NW Suite 1120, Washington, D.C. 20005. (202) 345-5445.

Boston Women's Health Book Collective. Women's Health Information Center. P.O.Box 192, West Somerville, MA 02144.

Chicago Community Midwives. 4340 N. Central Park, Chicago, IL 60632. (773) 478-2458.

Health Resource Center for Women with Disabilities. c/o Dr. Kristi Kirschner, Rehabilitation Institute of Chicago. 345 E. Superior, Chicago, IL 60610. (312)908-4744.

Illinois Birth Center Task Force. Health and Medicine Policy Research Group. Women's Health Task Force. 332 S. Michigan Ave., Chicago, IL 60604. (312) 922-8057.

La Leche League International. P.O. Box 1209, Minneapolis Ave., Franklin Park, IL 60131. (708) 455-7730.

Midwives Alliance of North America (MANA). P.O. Box 1121, Bristol, VA 24202. (615) 764-5561.

National Black Women's Health Project. 1237 Ralph Abernathy Blvd., SW, Atlanta GA 30310. (404) 758-9590.

National College of Midwifery. Drawer SSS. Taos, NM 87571. (505) 758-1216.

National Women's Health Network, 1325 G Street NW, Washington DC 20005. (202) 347-1140.

Seattle School of Midwifery. 2524 16th Ave, Seattle, WA 98144. (206) 322-8834.

Traditional Childbearing Group. P.O. Box 638. Boston, MA 02118. (617) 541-0086.

Women Employed, 22 W. Monroe Ave., Suite 1400, Chicago, IL 60603. (312) 782-3902.

WOMEN AND SOCIAL ACTION: CLASS 12
Motherhood

Before you read this Chapter of the Study Guide

Read Andersen, pp. 162-174 "Gay and Lesbian Households," "Motherhood," "Fatherhood," and "Race, Gender, and Families"
Blumenthal, "Scrambled Eggs and Seed Daddies: Conversations with my Son," Appendix A, Study Guide

I. INTRODUCTION

JOURNAL ASSIGNMENT

In "Scrambled eggs and seed daddies," Amy Blumenthal shares journal entries about conversations she has had with her son Jonathon about his beginnings, her decision to be a mother, and his family. Take the stand-point of yourself as a child or now as an adult and write about **one** of the following:

a. Briefly describe what your parent(s) told you about your beginnings, their decisions about becoming a parent, and your family. Reflect on the messages this information or lack of information gave you about reproduction, motherhood or fatherhood, and families.

b. Briefly describe what you have told your child(ren) about their beginnings, your decision to be a parent, and your family. Reflect on the messages this information or lack of information gives them about reproduction, motherhood or fatherhood, and families.

I cannot remember thinking much about motherhood until one day when I overhead my mother and a neighbor discussing another woman in the neighborhood who had recently had a baby. I knew I had gotten some important piece of information—the meaning of which was not clear at the time—when I heard one of them say in hushed tones that she would not give the baby a present because the woman was "unwed." I knew enough to know that the lack of a present indicated disapproval, but I wasn't sure what was wrong. I didn't know what unwed meant or how to spell it so I couldn't look it up in the dictionary.

This was the first of many hushed conversations I heard over the years about reproduction, motherhood, and families that was at odds with religious teachings about the sanctity of motherhood and the family. I heard the religious teachings in church; the stories about the shadow side of motherhood I typically heard when I was playing in the same room while my mother and other adults talked. It was in this overheard context I also learned about teenagers giving their babies up for adoption to adult women who were not able to have children. I also heard jokes about "surprise" or "change of life" babies. I also overheard a conversation about a mother and father leaving their five children at the local orphanage because they weren't suited to raise children.

Not all conversations were hushed. Once I heard an adult comment loudly about a boy and girl, both of whom were retarded, who were holding hands, "Let's hope she's been fixed or she'll have a string of babies."

Though I was an adult before I really understood all the implications of what I heard as a child, I knew at a young age that motherhood and families were more complicated than formal teachings indicated. In Class 12, we explore social expectations about motherhood and families, the impact these expectations have on our lives, and strategies for challenging these socially restrictive conceptions of motherhood and families.

II. CLASS THEMES

- How motherhood is socially defined
- Differences between motherhood as a social institution and motherhood as a personal experience
- The consequences of the gap between the social institution and women's experience of motherhood
- Strategies for challenging restrictive conceptions of motherhood

III. VIDEOTAPE SYNOPSIS

- Introduction to the topic of motherhood
- Class discussion of motherhood
- Video visit with Jonathon and Amy Blumenthal
- Interview and class discussion with Amy Blumenthal, author of "Scrambled eggs and seed daddies: conversations with my son," *Empathy, Gay and Lesbian Advocacy Research Project*

IV. VIDEOTAPE COMMENTARY

A. Introduction to the topic of motherhood

In this introduction, I identify several experiences people have had which indicate there is a social definition of motherhood. Can you think of additional examples?

B. Class discussion of motherhood

Class members' comments vividly illustrate motherhood as a social institution, motherhood as a personal experience, and the consequences of the gaps between the social institution and women's experience. For example, Debbie, Mary, Gail, and Jan highlight some of the expectations associated with motherhood. Make a list of these expectations and add additional ones. Phyllis, Gunther, Ada, Peg, Judy, and Janet give examples of ways motherhood has been expressed in their own lives and how this differs from conventional conceptions. Make a list of these examples and add your own.

Ada, Mary, Gail, Christine, and Sharon talk about the gap between the motherhood ideal and people's actual experience. Christine's example shows the effect on a child when a mother doesn't live up to the ideal. Mary's and Sharon's discussion of baking cookies is a good example of how unrealistic expectations negatively affect women. Ada and Gail identify ways in which mothers not living up to the ideal can be beneficial for women and children. Identify other consequences of the gap between the ideal of motherhood and women's experience. How does this gap affect men, women, and children?

C. Video visit with Jonathon and Amy Blumenthal

I first met Amy when she was beginning the process of deciding whether or not to have a child. The process of motherhood for Amy has involved deep reflection about the social institution of motherhood and choices about how to live her life. As a lesbian feminist mother, she has taken the opportunity to sort through what aspects of motherhood and child development are rooted in assumptions about heterosexuality, what are rooted in assumptions about gender, and what are rooted in assumptions about childhood. What does Amy tell us about her parenting philosophy? What do we learn from Jonathon about ways to create babies?

D. Interview and class discussion with Amy Blumenthal, author of "Scrambled eggs and seed daddies: conversations with my son," *Empathy, Gay and Lesbian Advocacy Research Project*

Because of the thoughtful reflection Amy has brought to her mothering experience, she is an excellent person for us to talk with about strategies for challenging restrictive conceptions of motherhood while simultaneously being a responsible, loving, and honest parent.

Amy tells us about the variety of options she considered for having a baby. What are these options? What are the advantages and the disadvantages? If you were in Amy's position, which would you choose?

In response to a question from Gunther, Amy elaborates on the difference between Jonathon knowing there is a specific man who is his father and knowing that there is a man who donated sperm. What do you see as the main difference she is talking about?

Peg and Virginia ask Amy to elaborate on the societal aspects of being a lesbian mother. Amy gives a brief overview of her experience with social barriers as a lesbian, as a lesbian mother, and of Jonathon's experience at different ages. What are the social barriers lesbians face and how do they affect Amy as a mother and Jonathon as a child? In response to Helen's question about male role models, Amy talks briefly about role models and their importance. What is the key idea here?

Carlos asks Amy to expand on her idea of age appropriateness. What do you learn from this? Jan and Amy have a brief exchange about adoption. What do you learn about the adoption process from this exchange?

The issue of reproduction and how to talk with children about it is the focus of questions, comments, and examples from Christine, Ada, Mary, Judy, and Joe. What do we learn about ways to talk with children about reproduction from Amy, Ada, and Mary's examples? What do we learn about changes in medical screening of sperm donors in the last decade? Why do you think these changes might have occurred? What do we learn about Amy's openness to new problems in the future with her response to Joe's question?

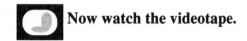 **Now watch the videotape.**

V. REVIEW QUESTIONS

1. What is meant by motherhood as a social institution? How does it differ from women's experience? Give examples.

2. How does the social institution of motherhood affect women's experience of motherhood? Give examples.

3. What are key ideas about what motherhood is? How do these ideas compare and contrast to key ideas about fatherhood?

4. What are key findings about gay and lesbian households? What are similarities and differences between gay and lesbian parents? Between gay fathers and heterosexual fathers? Between lesbian mothers and heterosexual mothers?

5. What is donor insemination? What are the advantages and disadvantages of anonymous and known donor insemination?

6. What are strategies for talking with children about reproduction? about parenting? about different types of families?

VI. SOURCES AND FURTHER READING

Anderson, Lois. 1985. "The Lois Anderson Story." Pp. 275 - 279 in *With the Power of Each Breath: A Disabled Women's Anthology,* edited by Susan E. Browne, Debra Connors, and Nanci Stern. Pittsburgh, PA: Cleis Press.

Arcana, Judith. 1983. *Every Mother's Son: the Role of Mothers in the Making of Men.* Garden City, NY: Anchor Books/Doubleday.

Arcana, Judith. 1979. *Our Mothers' Daughters.* Berkeley: Shameless Hussy Press.

Berryman, Julia. 1993. "Perspectives on later motherhood." Pp. 214 - 216 in in *Women's Studies: Essential Readings*, edited by Stevi Jackson. Washington Square, NY: New York University Press.

Brentan, Anne Glaser. 1991. "Acts of creativity, acts of love: mothering with disabilities." *The Creative Woman*, 11 (2): 5 - 10.

Chernin, Kim. 1983. *In My Mother's House: A Daughter's Story.* NY: Harper and Row.

Chodorow, Nancy. 1978. *The Reproduction of Mothering: Psychoanalysis and the Sociology of Gender.* Berkeley: University of California Press.

Collins, Patricia Hill. 1992. "Black women and motherhood." Pp. 215 - 245 in *Rethinking the Family: Some Feminist Questions*, edited by Barrie Thorne with Marilyn Yalom. Boston: Northeastern University Press.

Debold, Elizabeth, Marie Wilson, and Idelisse Malave. 1993. *Mother Daughter Revolution.* Reading, MA: Addison-Wesley Publishing Company.

de la Madrid, Maria Gil. 1991. *Lesbians Choosing Motherhood: Legal Implications for Donor Insemination and Co-Parenting*, 2nd edition. San Francisco: National Center for Lesbian Rights.

Hanscombe, Gillian E. and Jackie Forster. 1981. *Rocking the Cradle, Lesbian Mothers: A Challenge in Family Living.* Boston: Alyson Publications.

Harne, Lynne. 1993. "Lesbian custody and the new myth of the father." Pp. 217 - 220 in in *Women's Studies: Essential Readings*, edited by Stevi Jackson. Washington Square, NY: New York University Press.

Hubbard, Ruth with Wendy Sandford. 1992. "New reproductive technologies." Pp. 386 - 393 in *The New Our Bodies, Ourselves.* NY: Simon and Schuster.

Hyler, Donna. 1985. "To Choose a Child." Pp. 280 - 283 in *With the Power of Each Breath: A Disabled Women's Anthology*, edited by Susan E. Browne, Debra Connors, and Nanci Stern. Pittsburg PA: Cleis Press.

Kendrick, Deborah. 1990. "Just being mom: I just do what all mothers do." *Chicago Parent,* West/South, December: 19.

Laqueur, Thomas W. 1992. "The facts of fatherhood." Pp. 155 - 175 in *Rethinking the Family: Some Feminist Questions*, edited by Barrie Thorne with Marilyn Yalom. Boston: Northeastern University Press.

LeMaistre, JoAnn. 1985. "Parenting." Pp. 284 - 291 in *With the Power of Each Breath: A Disabled Women's Anthology*, edited by Susan E. Browne, Debra Connors, and Nanci Stern. Pittsburgh, PA: Cleis Press.

Lorde, Audre. 1992. "Man child: a black lesbian feminist's response." Pp. 253 - 259 in *Race, Class, and Gender: An Anthology*, edited by Margaret L. Andersen and Patricia Hill Collins. Belmont, CA: Wadsworth Publishing.

Mikotowicz, Joyce Malo. 1991. "Three mothers of spina bifida children." *The Creative Woman,* 11 (2) : 14 -15.

Phoenix, Ann. 1993. "Narrow definitions of culture: the case of early motherhood." Pp. 211 - 216 in *Women's Studies: Essential Readings*, edited by Stevi Jackson. Washington Square, NY: New York University Press.

Rich, Adrienne. 1976. *Of Woman Born: Motherhood as Experience and Institution.*
NY: Norton, Bantam.

Rothman, Barbara. 1989. *Recreating Motherhood: Ideology and Technology in a Patriarchal Society.* NY: Northon.

Ruddick, Sara. 1992. "Thinking about fathers." Pp. 176 - 190 in *Rethinking the Family: Some Feminist Questions*, edited by Barrie Thorne with Marilyn Yalom. Boston: Northeastern University Press.

Stack, Carol B. 1974. *All Our Kin: Strategies for Survival in a Black Community.* NY: Harper and Row.

Tan, Amy. 1991. *The Kitchen God's Wife.* NY: Ivy Books.

Trebilcot, Joyce (ed.). 1983. *Mothering: Essays in Feminist Theory.* Totowa, NJ: Rowman and Allanheld.

Woollet, Anne and Ann Phoenix. 1993. "Issues related to motherhood." Pp. 216 - 217 in in *Women's Studies: Essential Readings,* edited by Stevi Jackson. Washington Square, NY: New York University Press.

Women's Action Coalition. 1993. "Mothers." Pp 40 - 43 in *WAC STATS: The facts about women.* NY:The New Press.

VIII. ORGANIZATIONS

Chicago Women's Health Center. 3435 N. Sheffield Ave., Chicago, IL 60657. (773) 935-6126.

EMPATHY: Gay and Lesbian Advocacy Research Project. P.O. Box 5085, Columbia, S.C. 29250.

WOMEN AND SOCIAL ACTION: CLASS 13
Abortion and Reproductive Issues

Before you read this Chapter of the Study Guide

Read Andersen, pp. 203-209, "The Politics of Reproduction: Birth Control, Abortion, and Childbirth."

Andersen, pp. 242-244, "The Abortion Debate: the Conflict of Religious World Views."

I. INTRODUCTION

JOURNAL
ASSIGNMENT

> Describe an experience you or someone you know has had with birth control, abortion, or sterilization and how you felt about it. Reflect on ways in which societal views of women and /or mothers affected your experience.

Playground whispers about how babies are made.
Hallway whispers about girls who put on weight and then disappear for
    a few months.
Neighborhood whispers about shotgun weddings and marrying too young.
Hearing a friend tell me about her abortion. Not knowing what to say.
Hearing a group of women talk frankly about sexuality, abortion, and birth
    control, not realizing how much I would have to say, too.
Worrying if my period was a day late.
Pretending I was married so I could get birth control pills.
Attending a clandestine meeting to plan abortion referral when it was illegal.
Listening to women talk at a public hearing about their decision to have an
    abortion. Seeing them endure cat calls and spit.
Holding a woman's hand while she has an abortion.
Seeing La Operacion, a film about sterilization abuse in Puerto Rico.
Hearing an abortion rights activist tell about her friend who died from an
    illegal abortion.
Attending a session where members of JANE, an illegal abortion collective,
    talk about their history.
Investigating bogus abortion clinics and the impact on women who then delay
    their decision past the first trimester of pregnancy.

As I look at this laundry list of some of my experiences with abortion and other reproductive issues, I am on a roller-coaster of feeling: sadness, anger, fury, anxiety, joy, pride, curiosity, relief, embarrassment, fear, love. I am reminded why control of our fertility is essential to women's empowerment.

I am reminded of the limited choices and many traps that await women and girls when they do not have the power to determine with whom, when, and how they will experience sexuality and reproduction.

I am reminded why all of us — whether or not we are sexually active, whether or not we are heterosexual, bisexual, gay, or lesbian, whether or not we have ever been involved in a decision to terminate a pregnancy, whether or not we have ever been sterilized against our will, whether or not we have been denied access to birth control—must fight for women's right to control their fertility.

II. CLASS THEMES

- Views on abortion are related to social background and to attitudes about gender, sexuality, and reproduction.
- The controversy about abortion can only be understood in a socio-historical context.
- The controversy about abortion is played out in many ways and affects women differently depending upon their age, race, and social class.
- The struggle for women's control of reproduction is related to other struggles for social justice.

III. VIDEOTAPE SYNOPSIS

- Introduction to the topic of abortion and reproductive issues
- Class discussion of perspectives on abortion
- Video composite of demonstrations outside Cook County Hospital and visit with Rev. Cheryl Pero, Crossings Ministry (Lutheran), Harold Washington College Campus Ministry
- Interview and class discussion with Aida Giachello, Assistant Professor, Jane Addams College of Social Work, University of Illinois at Chicago and National Latina Health Organization

IV. VIDEOTAPE COMMENTARY

A. Introduction to the topic of abortion and reproductive issues

In my introduction to the topic I review Kristin Luker's findings about the relationship between views on abortion and social background and attitudes. I also give an overview of my own perspective and the influences on the development of my perspective. I also briefly described the forums in which the abortion controversy is being played out and the impact it has on different groups of people.

B. Class discussion of perspectives on abortion

Class members share a range of passionate viewpoints on abortion and birth control and point to their relationship to broader social issues. For example, Joan, Christine, Mary, and Gail share their own viewpoints on abortion. Helen offers a framework for consensus about the topic. Joe describes the evolution of his viewpoint. Judith raises the larger issues of power and control and Gail discusses denial of women's sexuality and different ideas about when life begins. Jan shares her experience of working in a pharmacy. Listen carefully to the range of perspectives presented. Do they all fit within Helen's suggested agreements? Joan, Christine, and Jan link the need for abortion with lack of access to birth control. How do you see abortion and birth control linked? Based on what you have heard in prior sessions, what relationship between abortion and other social attitudes do you see?

C. Video composite of demonstrations outside Cook County Hospital and visit with Rev. Cheryl Pero, Crossings Ministry (Lutheran), Harold Washington College Campus Ministry

In September 1992, Cook County reinstituted publically funded abortions after a 12 year hiatus. Within the first ten days of taking appointments, Cook County received over 4,000 calls from women wanting to schedule appointments. Almost immediately protests against the reinstitution of abortions at Cook County began. Simultaneously pro-choice advocates demonstrated in support of publically funded abortions. We set off to Cook County Hospital to find out what this change in county policy meant for people. The same day I interviewed Rev. Cheryl Pero about women and religion. As I finished the interview, I decided to ask her for her views on abortion because of her deep religious and social justice commitments. I wondered how these commitments were reflected in her position on abortion.

As you watch the videotape, note the differences in the the language people use. Consider the differences in choice of language to describe people's perspectives on abortion. Think about how language is related to the perspective of the person talking. Note also the feelings people express verbally and nonverbally. What strikes you about the demonstrations and the interview with Rev. Pero? What does Rev. Pero mean by the importance of considering the quality of life after birth?

D. Interview and class discussion with Aida Giachello, Assistant Professor, Jane Addams College of Social Work, University of Illinois at Chicago and National Latina Health Organization

Aida Giachello is committed to breaking silence about abortion and sexuality (Brotman, 1992), particularly in the Latino community. She is a founding member of the National Latina Health Organization, a member of Catholics for a Free Choice, served as the chairperson of the Chicago Commission on Women, and serves on the Mujeres Latinas En Acción Board of Directors.

On the videotape, Aida tells us about her own perspective on reproductive issues and how it evolved. What did she learn about the need for women to control their fertility?

She also gives us an overview of her approach to advocate for a pro-choice agenda. She elaborates this agenda as she responds to questions and comments from Gail, Christine, and Judith. What issues does she see as related to reproductive choice?

In response to a comment from Jan about sexual responsibility, Aida addresses ways in which cultural ideas about sexuality inhibit taking sexual responsibility. What do you see as her major point here?

Gail talks about her own experience with a supportive women's clinic. What does she identify as concrete examples of support? In what ways does Aida characterize this as model health care?

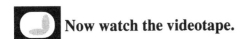 **Now watch the videotape.**

V. REVIEW QUESTIONS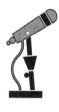

1. What is a feminist perspective on reproduction?

2. How does language reveal a person's perspective on abortion?

3. How does the availability of birth control relate to women's status in society?

4. What are issues for adolescents in reproductive rights?

5. How do cultural attitudes about women's sexuality inhibit the development of responsibility for being sexually active?

6. What are current legal and popular views of abortion?

7. In what ways are reproductive issues of abortion, birth control, and sterilization particularly significant for women of color?

8. What other issues are reproductive issues related to?

VI. INTERVIEW EXCERPT

Andrea Smith, Women of All Red Nations, addresses problems with limiting discussions of reproductive rights to abortion and an individual's right to choose. She makes a compelling argument for including sterilization, birth control, and birth defects. She also encourages us to focus on ways in which challenging racism requires us to consider community concerns as well as an individual's right to choose.

" Andrea Smith:

Women of All Red Nations deals with all the reproductive rights issues, including abortion rights. We happen to be working on this because the way it currently is framed it is not very inclusive of the needs of Indian women. People often frame abortion rights as an issue of women losing their rights to abortion when most Indian women have already lost that right. With restrictions on federal funding for abortions, Indian health services do not do abortions, although they give free sterilizations. We have to reframe those reproductive rights for Indian women. The other issue is that it is looked at as an individual right or women's individual right to choose. For Indian women the issue is more of selecting their own health care because when you have situations where Indian women are being given experimental forms of birth control and not being told what's going on, tribes don't have the right. Women are being sterilized without their consent; 25% of Indian women are sterilized without their consent. And then on some reservations there's a 60% birth defect rate - and that's primarily South Dakota and Arizona, where they have a birth defect rate 200 times higher than the national average and the infant mortality rate is 3 times higher. A lot of Indians see abortion rights differently in that they're very concerned about the future of their children. Although they won't necessarily make it illegal, their main concern is promoting good health for communities and tribes. "

VII. SOURCES AND FURTHER READING

Asch, Adrienne and Michelle Fine. 1988. "Shared dreams: a left perspective on disability rights and reproductive rights." Pp. 297 - 305 in *Women with Disabilities: Essays in Psychology, Culture, and Politics*, edited by Michelle Fine and Adrienne Asch. Philadelphia, PA: Temple University Press.

Banwell, Suzanna S. and John M. Paxman. 1992. "The search for meaning: RU 486 and the law of abortion. *American Journal of Public Health*, 82(10):1399 - 1405.

Bart, Pauline. 1981. "Seizing the means of reproduction: an illegal feminist abortion collective—how and why it worked." Pp. 109 -128 in Helen Roberts (ed.). *Women, Health, and Reproduction.* London: Routledge and Kegan Paul.

Bonavoglia, Angela. 1991. *The Choices We Made: Twenty-five women and men speak out about abortion.* NY: Random House.

Brotman, Barbara. 1992. "A silent minority: whites dominate the debate, but not the passion, over the abortion issue." Tempo, Section 5, *Chicago Tribune*, July 10: 1 -2.

Callum, Janet (Feminist Women's Health Center, Atlanta, GA) and Renate Klein, Lynette Dumble and Janice Raymond (FINNRAGE). 1992. "RU-486: A dialogue." *The Network News*, National Women's Health Network, September/October: 1 -8.

Chrisler, Joan C. 1993. "Whose body is it anyway? Psychological effects of fetal-protection policies." Pp. 285 - 290 in *It's A Crime: Women and Justice*, edited by Roslyn Muraskin and Ted Alleman. Englewood Cliffs, NJ: Regents/Prentice Hall.

Degener, Theresia. 1992. "Sterile without consent." Pp. 119 -123 in *Imprinting Our Image: An International Anthology by Women with Disabilities*, edited by Diane Driedger and Susan Gray. Canada: Gynergy.

Finger, Anne. 1985. "Claiming all of our bodies: reproductive rights and disability." Pp. 292 - 307 in *With the Power of Each Breath: A Disabled Women's Anthology*, edited by Susan E. Browne, Debra Connors, and Nanci Stern. Pittsburgh, PA: Cleis.

Gordon, Linda. 1990. *Woman's Body, Woman's Right: Birth Control in America*, rev. ed. NY:Penguin.

Luker, Kristin. 1984. *Abortion and the Politics of Motherhood.* Berkeley, CA: University of California Press.

Mertus, Julie A. 1990. "Fake abortion clinics: the threat to reproductive self-determination." *Women and Health*, 16 (1).

Messer, Ellen and Kathryn E. May. 1988. *Back Rooms: An Oral History of the Illegal Abortion Era.* NY: Simon and Schuster.

Morris, Jenny. 1991. "The chance of life." *Pride Against Prejudice: Transforming Attitudes to Disability.* Philadelphia, PA: New Society Publishers.

Muraskin, Roslyn. 1993. "Abortion: is it abortion or compulsory childbearing?" Pp. 291-302 in *It's A Crime: Women and Justice,* edited by Roslyn Muraskin and Ted Alleman. Englewood Cliffs, NJ: Regents/Prentice Hall.

Petchesky, Rosalind Pollack. 1990. *Abortion and Woman's Choice: the State, Sexuality, and Reproductive Freedom,* rev. ed. Boston: Northeastern University Press.

Rothman, Barbara Katz. 1987. *The Tentative Pregnancy: Prenatal Diagnosis and the Future of Motherhood.* NY: Penguin.

Velez-I., Carlos G. 1980. "The nonconsenting sterilization of Mexican women in Los Angeles." Pp. 235 - 248 in *Twice a Minority: Mexican American Women,* edited by Margarita B. Melville.

White, Evelyn C. (ed.). 1990. *The Black Women's Health Book: Speaking for Ourselves.* Seattle, WA: Seal Press.

Women's Action Coalition (WAC). 1993. "Abortion/Birth Control." Pp. 7 - 10 in *WAC Stats: The Facts About Women.* NY: The New Press.

VIII. ORGANIZATIONS

Catholics for a Free Choice. 1436 U Street NW, Suite 301, Washington, D.C. 20009. (202) 986-6093.

Chicago Abortion Fund. P.O. Box 578307 Chicago, IL 60657.
Client Services: (773) 248-4541   Administration: (773) 248-4807.

Emergency Clinic Defense Coalition. P.O. Box 1634, Evanston, IL 60204. (847) 845-6838.

Mujeres Latinas En Acción (Latin Women in Action). 1823 West 17th St. Chicago, IL 60608. (312) 226-1544.

National Latina Health Organization/Organización Nacional de la Salud de la Mujer Latina. P.O. Box 7567, Oakland, CA 94601. (415) 534-1362.

Planned Parenthood Information and Referral Hotline. 14 E. Jackson Blvd., Chicago, IL 60604. (312) 427-2275.

Women of All Red Nations (WARN). 4511 N. Hermitage Ave., Chicago, IL 60640. (773) 493-2791.

WOMEN AND SOCIAL ACTION: CLASS 14
Religion

 Before you read this Chapter of the Study Guide
Read Andersen, Chp. 8, "Women and Religion"

I. INTRODUCTION

JOURNAL
ASSIGNMENT

> If you have a religious affiliation, describe it, the role of women in your religious organization, the role of women in the clergy, and changes in this religious organization concerning women in the time you have been involved. If you do not have a religious affiliation, describe your observations of the role of religion in other's lives and the impact religion has on women.

Andersen begins her summary of the chapter on "Women and Religion" with the contradiction we face in talking about women and religion: religion is a key institution in the oppression of women while it has also has been a foundation for inspiring social change. In considering the elements of religion which contribute to the subordination of women, feminist theologians have examined a range of religious beliefs and practices, including the language of religious texts, the negative images of women in religious thinking, discrimination against women in the clergy and in other religious positions, the lack of recognition and value for women's contributions to religious life, the central tenets of religious philosophy, and systems of religious organization.

Feminist theologians differ in their approach to social change. The approach most familiar to the general public focuses on increasing women's numbers in the clergy, eliminating sexist language in religious texts, and removing religious images demeaning to women. This approach is similar to other social change strategies which focus on changing laws and getting more women into political positions.

A less publicized approach is based on the conviction that what we know as religion is essentially patriarchal and, therefore, depends upon the oppression of women's power and experience for its maintenance and depends upon the exploitation of women's volunteer labor to exist (Daly, 1973; Reuther, 1979, 1986). From this point-of-view, women must reject traditional religions and create systems of spiritual expression and practice rooted in women's power and experience.

We will find in Class 14 that many women, including myself, see traditional religious institutions as oppressive, but we also see many women who are nourished and supported by their religious convictions. In Class 14, we will explore how women in the laity and women in the clergy struggle with the contradictions they encounter within traditional religious organizations. Our guest Ellen Cannon is a feminist and a devout member of a traditional Jewish religious organization. We will hear how she manages what are to me disparate identities and how her religious faith has provided a powerful foundation for her commitment to social justice and social change.

II. CLASS THEMES

- The role of religion in women's lives
- Ways in which women challenge traditional religious beliefs about women
- Ways in which women are transforming the role of women in the clergy and religious organizations
- Ways in which religion is a foundation for women's commitment to transforming society

III. VIDEOTAPE SYNOPSIS

- Introduction to the topic of religion and women
- Class discussion of the role of religion in their lives
- Video visit with Rev. Cheryl Pero, Crossings Ministry (Lutheran), Harold Washington College Campus Ministry, Chicago and Rabbi Ellen Dreyfus, Congregation Beth Sholom, Park Forest, Illinois
- Interview and class discussion with Ellen Çannon, Ph.D., Northeastern Illinois University

IV. VIDEOTAPE COMMENTARY

A. Introduction to the topic of religion and women

I give an overview of the themes of Class 14 and briefly discuss the role of religion in my life.

B. Class discussion of the role of religion in their own lives

Class members identify ways in which religion has provided inspiration or limitation in their lives. Some class members have been members of religious organizations since they were young and have continued into adulthood. For example, Jan, Trenace, Janet, and Phyllis compare their childhood and adulthood experiences. Ada talks about her reasons for developing a religious affiliation as an adult. Claudia, Judith, Joan, and Janet raise issues they have with religious organizations. As you listen to the different experiences class members discuss, make a list of things they identify as inspirational and those things they identify as oppressive or cause for conflict in their lives. Also note how the role of women plays a part in the concerns raised.

C. Video visit with Rev. Cheryl Pero, Crossings Ministry (Lutheran), and Rabbi Ellen Dreyfus, Congregation Beth Sholom

We first heard from Rev. Cheryl Pero in Class 13 "Abortion and Reproductive Issues." Rev. Pero has served as an Associate Pastor in a congregation and, most recently, been involved with campus ministry. In addition, her strong commitment to social justice issues and her experience as an African-American pastor in a predominately white congregation give her a strong foundation for reflecting on the complex barriers women face in the clergy, such as sexism and racism, and effective leadership approaches for women in the clergy.

Rabbi Ellen Dreyfus was ordained in 1979 and has served at the Congregation Beth Sholom since 1987. As the first woman rabbi in Illinois, Rabbi Dreyfus has had numerous occasions to reflect on women in Judaism and on women in the rabbinate.

In the videotape, Rev. Pero and Rabbi Dreyfus give examples of ways they see they have approached their role differently from their male counterparts and the effects this has on their congregations. Rev. Pero also offers thoughts about the sources of resistance women clergy face. As you watch the videotape, think about the concept of centerwoman we discussed earlier in the course and identify ways their approaches to leadership do and do not fit within the definition. Also consider sources of resistance Rev. Pero identifies and then add your own.

D. Interview and class discussion with Ellen Cannon, Professor of Political Science Northeastern Illinois University

In addition to addressing the role of religion in women's lives and the experiences of women as clergy, a theme of Class 14 is to explore the role religion plays in women's commitment to social change. Ellen Cannon is an excellent example of someone for whom religion has been a deep inspiration for her dedication to social change. Ellen Cannon is a political scientist, but she is our guest because she is committed to feminism, traditional Judaism, and social justice. As part of this work, Ellen serves as the chairperson of the American Jewish Congress' Midwest Region Commission for Women's Equality.

In Ellen's opening comments, she tells us of her growing up in a community deeply immersed in Judaism. What are examples of this immersion? In her discussion of the work she is now doing, she draws heavily on the inspiration of Judaism for her social justice work. What are her key points about the foundation Judaism plays in her life?

In response to a question from Helen about the tension between social and personal commitments, Ellen draws parallels between Judaism and Christianity. What are the commonalities she notes? Ada asks Ellen to explain the ways in which women are visible in Judaism. Ellen places her answer in the context of the demographics of the Jewish population in the United States. She identifies the ways in which women are included in religious rituals and the variety of ways Jewish feminism is expressed. Helen and Peg continue Ada's quest for more information about the role of women. Ellen addresses the struggle Jewish feminists have with some aspects of religious practice and how different women deal with these practices. What is your understanding of the varieties of Jewish feminism and the different ways that women are challenging religious practices?

 Now watch the videotape.

V. REVIEW QUESTIONS

1. In what ways can religion serve to oppress as well as liberate women?

2. What are sociological perspectives on religion?

3. According to Andersen, how was the persecution of women as witches used to control women?

4. According to Andersen, what influence did the Second Great Awakening and the widespread belief in the cult of domesticity have on the development of the feminist movement?

5. What are key images of women in religion? What variations are there across religious groups?

6. How are religious beliefs and gender related?

7. What are women's roles in religious institutions?

8. What are variations in women's participation in the clergy? in the laity?

9. How does the role of the clergy differ if a religious organization is group-centered or if it is leader-centered? Give examples from Rev. Pero and Rabbi Dreyfus.

10. According to Andersen, what is the role of the church in African-American communities?

11. According to Andersen, what are roles of women in African-American churches?

12. How are religion and social justice issues related?

13. How are religion and anti-feminist issues related?

14. Compare and contrast feminist efforts for religious reform and radical feminist theology.

VI. INTERVIEW EXCERPT

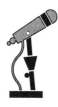

Because of the importance of religious experience in people's lives, many feminists who have rejected traditional religious organizations have developed women-centered religious images and practices. Feminist spirituality is a very important effort to create empowering religious experiences for women. Sometimes the inspiration for empowering images and practices comes from observations of historical or cross-cultural religious communities in which women were or are highly valued. Andrea Smith, Women of All Red Nations, expresses concerns about individuals and groups (not just feminists) who incorporate traditional Native American beliefs and practices into religious ceremonies.

 Andrea Smith:

We've been trying to publicize the issues of Indian spiritual exploitation because nowadays it's really a fashion to be Indian and everybody's great, great, great, great grandmother is Indian and everybody wants to take part in Indian spiritual practices. They want to incorporate Indian spiritual practices into their Christian things or whatever and so we find this all very problematic. First of all there's a misunderstanding about the way Indian spiritual practices operate. It's not like Christianity where Christians want to spread the word and want everybody to see the light. There isn't an Indian religion. Each tribe has their own practices and they're all very land-based and community-based and consequently people who practice our tradition don't think that what they practice would make sense for anybody else besides themselves. And many times you're not even allowed to talk about who the spirits of the tribe are. And second of all most of what is being passed off as Indian is just totally inaccurate. Also, this is a racist phenomenon because there's the idea that we have nothing better to do with our time than to educate white people on our religion. There's also the problem that it creates a stereotype and perpetuates a stereotype that we're always spiritualistic guru types and nobody sees our real issues or sees us as real people because all they see is this stereotype of somebody who passes off wise sayings to all the white followers. The other problem is that we find it ironic that everybody wants Indian religions when we ourselves have a hard time practicing them when recent Supreme Court decisions have said that we don't have any right to protection under the Indian Religion Freedom Act. If the U.S. government has any "compelling" interests then it's always more important than our right to practice our religions so we find it very ironic that everybody else wants to do this and we ourselves can't do it. And we think that, considering everybody's taken everything from us, and this is the one thing that we have left, we feel that it's very important to maintain integrity of Indian traditions because that's what keeps us together as a people and keeps our resistance going.

VII. SOURCES AND FURTHER READING

Thanks to Ellen Cannon and Jeanne Wirpsa, each of whom provided an extensive list of recommendations for further reading.

Allen, Paula Gunn. 1986. *The Sacred Hoop: Recovering the Feminine in American Indian Traditions.* Boston: Beacon Press.

Beck, Evelyn Torton (ed.). 1982. *Nice Jewish Girls: A Lesbian Anthology.* Watertown, MA: Persephone Press.

Brooks, Evelyn. 1980. "The feminist theology of the black Baptist church, 1880 - 1900." Pp. 31 - 59 in *Class, Race, and Sex: The Dynamics of Control*, edited by Amy Swerdlow and Hanna Lessinger. Boston: EK Hall and Company.

Crow Dog, Mary. 1991. *Lakota Woman.* NY: Harper and Row.

Daly, Mary. 1973. *Beyond god the father: Toward a Philosophy of Women's Liberation.* Boston: Beacon Press.

Christ, C.P. and J. Plaskow (eds.). 1979. *Womanspirit Rising.* NY: Harper and Row.

Daly, Mary. 1978. *Gyn/Ecology the Metaethics of Radical Feminism.* Boston: Beacon Press.

Eck, Diana L. and Devaki Jain (eds.). 1987. *Speaking of Faith: Global Perspectives on Women, Religion, and Social Change.* Philadelphia, PA: New Society Publishers.

Fabella, Virginia and Mercy Amba Oduyoye (eds.). 1988. *With Passion and Compassion: Third World Women Doing Theology.* NY: Orbis Books.

Fishman, Sylvia. 1993. *A Breath of Life: Feminism in the American Jewish Community.* NY: Free Press.

Gilkes, Cheryl Townsend. 1985. "Together and in harness: women's traditions in the sanctified church." *Signs:Journal of Women in Culture and Society.* 10 (Summer): 678-699.

Heschel, Susannah (ed.). 1983. *On Being a Jewish Feminist.* NY: Schocken.

Hungry Wolf, Beverly. 1982. *The Ways of My Grandmothers.* NY: Quill.

Isasi-Diaz, Ada Maria and Yolanda Tarango. 1988. *Hispanic Women: Prophetic Voice in the Church.* NY: Harper and Row.

Kingston, Maxine Hong. 1977. *The Woman Warrior: Memoirs of a Girlhood Among Ghosts.* NY: Random House.

Marshall, Paule. 1984. *Praisesong for the Widow.* NY: E.P. Dutton.

The Mudflower Collective. 1985. *God's Fierce Whimsy: Christian Feminism and Theological Education.* NY: The Pilgrim Press.

Not Mixing Up Buddhism: Essays on Women and Buddhist Practice. 1987. Fredonia, NY: White Pine Press.

Plaskow, Judith. 1990. *Standing Again at Sinai: Judaism from a Feminist Perspective.* San Francisco: Harper and Row.

Plaskow, Judith and Carol P. Christ (eds.). 1989. *Weaving the Visions.* NY: Harper and Row.

Reuther, Rosemary. 1979. " Mother earth and the megamachine: a theology of liberation in a feminine, somatic, and ecological perspective." Pp. 43 - 51 in C.P. Christ and J. Plaskow (eds.) 1979. *Womanspirit Rising.* NY: Harper and Row.

Reuther, Rosemary R. and R.S. Keller (eds.). 1986. *Women and Religion in America.* NY: Harper and Row.

Russell, Pui-lan, Isasi-Diaz, and Cannon (eds.). 1988. *Inheriting Our Mother's Gardens: Feminist Theology in Third World Perspective.* Philadelphia, PA: The Westminster Press.

Walker, Alice. 1973. "Diary of an African nun." *In Love and Trouble.* NY: Harcourt, Brace, and Jovanovich Publishers.

VIII. ORGANIZATIONS

American Jewish Congress Commission of Women's Equality, Midwest Region. 22 W. Monroe, #1900, Chicago, IL 60603. (312) 332-7355.

Women of All Red Nations (WARN). 4511 N. Hermitage Ave. Chicago, IL 60640. (773) 493-2791.

WOMEN AND SOCIAL ACTION: CLASS 15
Work

 Before you read this Chapter of the Study Guide

Read   Andersen, Chp. 5, "Women at Work"

I. INTRODUCTION

JOURNAL
ASSIGNMENT

Describe a work experience you have had. Describe the work itself, the working conditions, the division of labor in the work setting, how decisions were made about the work people did, and the rewards of the work.

Consider if there were any gender differences in the type of work people did, the conditions under which people worked, the decision-making process, and the rewards of the work.

We can look at the issue of work from many different angles. Each angle reveals a different set of issues and possible actions. One approach is to examine the **economic political system** within which people live and the impact this has on women's experience. For example, our current economic structure depends upon a significant amount of unpaid labor (e.g. volunteer work, housework, child care, shopping). Typically this work is done by women and is invisible and/or devalued. Feminists have proposed and debated a variety of responses, including challenging capitalism, instituting wages for housework, and recognizing and valuing unpaid work. Our current economic system is also part of a global economy dependent upon the labor of women and children worldwide. Feminists have, therefore, examined women's work beyond national borders and advocated a global perspective on women's work.

Another approach to women and work focuses on the **structure of the work world.** For example, extensive debate and activism have focused on occupational segregation by gender and race, the distribution of power by gender in the workplace, gender inequities in pay, women's unemployment, and the feminization of poverty. A variety of social change strategies have been developed and debated, including instituting comparable worth, creating collective work environments, expanding opportunities for women in the labor force, and changing the gender and race division of labor for housework and domestic responsibilities.

There has also been concern about the impact the structure of the work world has on women's experiences of work, family life, and other aspects of women's lives. For instance, scholars and activists have considered how sexual harassment, stress, low salaries, minimal benefits, low status, technology, and unhealthy or dangerous working conditions affect women. Additionally, attention has been directed to work and family interrelationships as well as changes in the structure of work and families.

In Class 15, we will focus on women's experience of work and organizational efforts to support and advocate for women workers. As you watch the videotape, consider ways in which our experiences and strategies have been shaped by global and national politics and economics as well as the structure of the work world.

II. CLASS THEMES

- The interrelationship between gender socialization and gender stratification in work choice and experience
- How work status affects prestige, power, and privilege
- Support systems needed for resocialization and resistance
- Strategies for networking, mentoring, and advocacy for women workers

III. VIDEOTAPE SYNOPSIS

- Overview of women and work
- Class discussion of work choices and experiences
- Video visit with Melissa Josephs, Policy Associate, and Sheila Rogers, Director of Participant Services, Keys to Success Program, Women Employed
- Interview and class discussion with Eileen Kreutz, Training Coordinator, Chicago Women in Trades

IV. VIDEOTAPE COMMENTARY

A. Overview of women and work

In my introduction to women and work, I mention areas of work feminist scholars have examined. I identify the focus for Class 15 and give some examples of ways my work choices were affected by gender socialization and stratification.

B. Class discussion of socialization and work experiences

Sharon, Ada, Linda, Mary, and Peg give examples of the limited options they were presented by parents, teachers, or employers and how this influenced their education and work choices. What were these options? How similar is this to options suggested to you or women you know?

Trenace points out the similarities in the messages she and Ada received about going to college. She suggests this is an example of a way in which sexism and racism are interrelated. What other ways can you identify? Ada, Trenace, and Phyllis offer examples of ways in which their abilities have been recognized and utilized, but not rewarded. Have you noticed similar experiences?

Linda, Judy, Mary, Phyllis, and Peg identify reasons why professional positions are appealing to them. What reasons are identified? Which of these are reasonable expectations for any job? Phyllis and Peg discuss the importance of mentors. In what ways are mentors helpful? Debbie briefly describes her mother's success in the business world and ponders why her mother did not encourage her to enter the business world also. What are ways that parents can support their daughters?

C. Video visit with Melissa Josephs, Policy Associate, and Sheila Rogers, Director of Participant Services, Keys to Success Program, Women Employed

For almost twenty years, Women Employed has provided advocacy and service to women workers. Women Employed advocacy work has included efforts to enforce equal opportunity laws at the federal, state, and local level. Women Employed testified before Congress, worked to implement the Civil Rights Act of 1991, and worked for passage of the Illinois Family and

Medical Leave Act. Women Employed services include career counseling, networking services, and listings of job opportunities.

On the videotape, Women Employed staff members Melissa Josephs and Sheila Rogers give us an overview of the mission of Women Employed and some of its programs. What issues do they identify that women commonly face? Melissa identifies problems with some job training programs. What do her comments suggest about the kind of job training support women need? What strategies does Sheila suggest for getting women interested in work that has not traditionally been open to women workers?

D. Interview and class discussion with Eileen Kreutz, Training Coordinator, Chicago Women in Trades

Eileen Kreutz is the Training Coordinator for Chicago Women in Trades. She draws upon her experience in carpentry (she has been a carpenter since the early 1970s), extensive networking skills, and a deep commitment to supporting other women. Her experience with housing has been mostly in building low-income housing. She also does furniture projects and renovations. Through her teaching with Chicago Women in Trades, she provides opportunities and support for other women to develop skills and experiences in the trades. She is in the process of developing a self-esteem training program for Chicago Women in Trades.

On the videotape, Eileen tells us about her background and how she became a carpenter. What similarities and differences do you see in her experience and the experience women in the class described earlier? Eileen gives us an overview of the training session she conducts. What are the elements of the training? What role does self-esteem building play? How does Eileen relate the need for a support network and the percentage of women currently in the trades?

Ada, Joe, and Gunther raised questions about men's reactions to women in the trades. What ideas did they and Eileen explore? Trenace raises a key issue that parents often face: how best to encourage your child when you know she or he will encounter discrimination and resistance? What does Eileen suggest?

Judy raised a question about harassment. Eileen gave examples as did Peg in an earlier comment. What types of harassment do women encounter? In response to a question Peg raised about job discrimination, what strategies did Eileen suggest for becoming a valued crew member? Judy's question about unions gave Eileen an opportunity to talk about women's role in unions and how the training program offered by Chicago Women in Trades relates to union pre-apprentice programs. What reasons does Eileen give for the need for preliminary training for women? Eileen also tells us about the beginnings of Chicago Women in Trades. How did it begin? What does this example tell us about the importance of networking? In response to Jan's comment about trades in the 50s and 60s, Eileen talks about some of the changes that have occurred which are beneficial to women. What are these key changes? What examples of advocacy work does Eileen give in her concluding comments?

 Now watch the videotape.

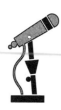

1. Compare and contrast the role of women in a family-based economy, family-wage economy, and family-consumer economy. How has the definition of womanhood changed as the economy has changed?

2. How do individualistic and sociological perspectives differ on work?

3. What is meant by work? How do conventional definitions of work affect women?

4. What is meant by gender stratification? How does it relate to gender socialization? How do they affect work choices and experiences for women?

5. How do race, class, and gender stratification intersect to shape women's work experiences? How does the type of work women do affect their work experience?

6. How do women and men compare in terms of labor-force participation, occupational distribution, and income?

7. How do human capital theory and dual labor market theory differ in their explanations of women's status in the workplace?

8. What is meant by the political economy of housework?

9. What are support systems needed to prepare women for jobs from which women have traditionally been excluded?

10. Identify strategies for networking and advocacy for women workers.

VI. INTERVIEW EXCERPT

> Mrs. Hallie Amey, President, Resident Management Council, has done volunteer work in her community for over thirty years. She talks about how decisions get made, how the work gets done in a volunteer organization, and why she thinks it is predominately women involved in volunteer work in her community. She also identifies some of the rewards of her work.

 Martha: Could you talk about how all these decisions get made and how the work gets done?

Mrs. Amey: What we do in our committees is we talk about issues, we talk about problems that we, and we alone, have to solve. If we need directions from somebody, we'll try to get us some directions. And when we get the direction, we proceed to do what we have to do to accomplish our goals for survival.

Martha: Talk about why you think it's mostly women involved in community work at Wentworth Gardens.

Mrs. Amey: Well, many, many, many years ago we had several active men. But as years go by, some of them moved out, some of them became discouraged because nothing is done overnight. For these accomplishments that we have made it has taken years. And another thing, see, with myself, I have been on a budget through social security with the passing of my husband and I had time with the seeing after my children, but I had an income. I did not have to go out and work and I could give time here in the community. Many people become frustrated and discouraged when things are not done quickly. They become discouraged when there are no jobs so that has had a lot of effect too for many of the workers.

Martha: You've been involved here in the community for 40 years and 30 some years in community work. What have been some of the rewards?

Mrs. Amey: In my work, and with me it's a real reward to get to where we are now. Things that we thought we'd never have; an office here that's at our disposal, we have a key; the laundromat, and we have a key; the store, and we have a key. All of those things, step by step. We have come a long way. When I think back from the beginning, we had so little. Nobody had faith in us, the CHA didn't have faith in us, but they do know now that there is a group who will stand for the community—not personally—but for the community.

VII. SOURCES AND FURTHER READING

Almquist, Elizabeth M. 1987. "Labor market gender inequality in minority groups." *Gender & Society* 1 (4): 400-414.

Bookman, Ann. 1988. "Unionization in an electronics factory: the interplay of gender, ethnicity, and class." Pp. 159 -179 in *Women and the Politics of Empowerment,* edited by Ann Bookman and Sandra Morgen. Philadelphia, PA: Temple University Press.

Brandow, Karen, Jim McDonnell, and Vocations for Social Change, 2nd edition. 1981. *No Bosses Here! a manual on working collectively and cooperatively.* Boston MA: Alyson Publications and Vocations for Social Change.

Costello, Cynthia B. 1988. "Women workers and collective action: a case study from the insurance industry." Pp. 116 - 135 in *Women and the Politics of Empowerment,* edited by Ann Bookman and Sandra Morgen. Philadelphia, PA: Temple University Press.

Daniels, Arlene. 1988. *Invisible Careers.* Chicago, IL: University of Chicago Press.

Dill, Bonnie Thornton. 1988. "'Making your job good yourself:' domestic service and the construction of personal dignity." Pp. 33 -52 in *Women and the Politics of Empowerment,* edited by Ann Bookman and Sandra Morgen. Philadelphia, PA: Temple University Press.

Edmond, Wendy and Suzie Fleming. 1975. *All Work and No Pay.* Bristol, England: Power of Women Collective and Falling Wall Press.

Eisenstein, Zillah R. (ed). 1979. *Capitalist Patriarchy and the Case for Socialist Feminism.* NY: Monthly Review Press.

Epstein, Cynthia Fuch . 1970. *Woman's Place: Options and Limits in Professional Careers.* Berkeley, CA: University of California Press.

Feldberg, Roslyn. 1984. "Comparable worth: toward theory and practice in the United States." *Sign: Journal of Women in Culture and Society* 10 (2): 311-328.

Frank Fox, Mary and Sharlene Hess-Biber. 1984. *Women at Work.* Palo Alto CA: Mayfield Publishing Company.

Hall, Marny. 1993. "Private experiences in the public domain: lesbians in organizations." Pp. 167 -173 in *Women's Studies: Essential Readings*, edited by Stevi Jackson. Washington Square, NY: New York University Press.

Hartmann, Heidi. 1976. "Capitalism, patriarchy, and job segregation by sex." *Signs: Journal of Women in Culture and Society*, 1, (3): 137-169.

Hartmann, Heidi. 1985. *Comparable Worth: New Directions for Research.* Washington, D.C.: National Academy Press.

Hochschild, Arlie. 1989. *The Second Shift: Working Parents and the Revolution at Home.* NY: Viking-Penguin.

Hoffman, Nancy and Florence Howe (ed.). 1974. *Women Working: An Anthology of Stories and Poems.* Old Westbury, NY: The Feminist Press.

James, Selma. 1972. *A Woman's Place.* Bristol, England: Falling Wall Press.

Kanter, Rosabeth Moss. 1977. *Men and Women of the Corporation.* NY: Basic Books.

Kessler-Harris, Alice. 1982. *Out to Work: A History of Wage-Earning Women in the United States.* Oxford: Oxford University Press.

Lamphere, Louise and Guillermo J. Grenier. 1988. "Women, unions, and 'participative management': organizing in the sunbelt." Pp. 227 - 256 in *Women and the Politics of Empowerment,* edited by Ann Bookman and Sandra Morgen. Philadelphia, PA: Temple University Press.

Lopata, Helena Z. 1971. *Occupation: Housewife.* NY: Oxford University Press.

Mainardi, Pat. 1970. "The politics of housework." Pp. 447-554 in *Sisterhood is Powerful,* edited by Robin Morgan (ed.). NY: Vintage.

Pearce, Diana. 1985. "Toll and trouble: women workers and unemployment compensation." *Signs: Journal of Women in Culture and Society* 10: 439-59.

Peña, Devon. 1993. "Between the lines: a new perspective on the industrial sociology of women workers in transnational labor processes." Pp. 77 -95 in *Chicana Voices: Intersections of Class, Race, and Gender.* Albuquerque, NM: University of New Mexico Press.

Oakley, Ann. 1976. *Woman's Work: The Housewife, Past and Present.* NY: Vintage.

Rollins, Judith. 1985. *Between Women: Domestics and Their Employers.* Philadephia PA: Temple University Press.

Romero, Mary. 1992. *Maid in the U.S.* NY: Routledge.

Ruiz, Vicki L. 1987. *Cannery Women, Cannery Lives.* Albuquerque, NM: University of New Mexico.

Russo, Nancy Felipe and Mary A. Jansen. 1988. "Women, work, and disability: opportunities and challenges." Pp. 229 - 244 in *Women with Disabilities: Essays in Psychology, Culture, and Politics*, edited by Michelle Fine and Adrienne Asch. Philadelphia, PA: Temple University Press.

Sacks, Karen Brodkin and Dorothy Remy (eds.). 1984. *My Troubles Are Going to Have Trouble With Me: Everyday Trials and Triumphs of Women Workers.* New Brunswick, NY: Rutgers University Press.

Seguara, Denise A. 1989. "Chicana and Mexican immigrant women at work: the impact of class, race, and gender on occupational mobility." *Gender & Society*, 3 (March): 37-52.

Seguara, Denise A. 1993. "Chicanas and triple oppression in the labor force." Pp. 47 - 65 in *Chicana Voices: Intersections of Class, Race, and Gender.* Albuquerque, NM: University of New Mexico Press.

Sochen, June. 1989. "Some observations on the role of American Jewish women as communal volunteers." *American Jewish History* 70 (Sept): 23 - 34.

Stallard, Karin, Barbara Ehrenreich, and Holly Sklar. 1983. *Poverty in the American Dream: Women and Children First.* Boston: South End Press.

Ward, Kathryn (ed.). 1990. *Women Workers and Global Restructuring.* Ithaca, NY: Cornell University.

Women's Action Coalition (WAC). 1993. *"Work." WAC Stats: The Facts About Women.* NY: The New Press.

Werthheimer, Barbara M. and Anne H. Nelson. 1989. "'Union is power': sketches from women's labor history." Pp. 312 - 328 in *Women: A Feminist Perspective,* fourth edition., edited by Jo Freeman. Mountain View, CA: Mayfield Publishing Company.

Weston, Kathleen and Lisa B. Rofel. 1984. "Sexuality, class, and conflict in a lesbian workplace." *Signs: Journal of Women in Culture and Society* 9 (4): 623 - 646.

Woo, Deborah. 1992. "The gap between striving and achieving: the case of Asian American women." Pp. 191- 200 in *Race, Class, and Gender: An Anthology*, edited by Margaret L. Andersen and Patricia Hill Collins. Belmont, CA: Wadsworth Publishing Company.

Zavella, Patricia. 1988. "The politics of race and gender: organizing Chicana cannery workers in Northern California." Pp. 202- 224 in *Women and the Politics of Empowerment*, edited by Ann Bookman and Sandra Morgen. Philadelphia, PA: Temple University Press.

VIII. ORGANIZATIONS

Chicago Women in Trades. 37 S. Ashland Ave, Chicago, IL 60607. (312) 942-1444.

Habitat for Humanity-Uptown. 3225 W. Foster Ave, Chicago, IL 60625. (773) 509-6034.

Midwest Women's Center. 828 S. Wabash, Chicago, IL 60605. (312) 922-8530.

Wentworth Resident Management Council. 252 W. 39th Street, Chicago, IL 60609. (773) 548-8453 or (773) 548-7512.

Women Employed. 22 W. Monroe Ave, Suite 1400, Chicago, IL 60603. (312) 782-3902.

WOMEN AND SOCIAL ACTION: CLASS 16
Sexual Harassment

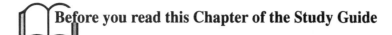 **Before you read this Chapter of the Study Guide**

Read Andersen, pp. 133-136 "Work Environments for Women"
"Sexual Harassment: A Sociological Perspective," Appendix B, Study Guide

I. INTRODUCTION

**JOURNAL
ASSIGNMENT**

Describe a situation in which you or someone you know has been sexually harassed in an educational or work setting. Write about the positions the people involved in the experience held in the organization, the behavior of the harasser, the response of the person sexually harassed, and the consequences for the people involved. Reflect on ways that power relationships and the institutional environment might have influenced what happened.

In the late 1970s, I was attending a party held during a professional society meeting when a well-known sociologist drunkenly stumbled toward me asking if I preferred if he grabbed my ass or my breasts. I told him to keep his hands off me and all the other women in the room. He quickly moved away. At a session on women's issues the next morning, I mentioned my experience. There had been several parties the night before and we discovered as we talked at least one woman had been sexually harassed at every party that had been held .

Though all of us present were aware of the extensiveness of sexual harassment, the public unfolding of a pattern of unwanted and unwelcome behavior in which men relegated female colleagues to sexual objects was a shock. This pattern of sexual harassment was discussed at the board of the professional society, a letter was sent to the dean of one of the harassers, and the women's caucus of the organization planned in the future to sponsor a yearly party guaranteed to be harassment-free. What weighed on the minds of many of us was what was happening on college campuses where these harassers were in the classroom with women who did not have the resources that my colleagues at this professional society meeting had.

Much has changed since I attended that particular professional meeting. Legal interpretations of Title VII of the 1964 Civil Rights Act and Title IX of the Education Amendments of 1972 (1976) clearly make sexual harassment illegal. Employers and educational institutions are responsible for responding to complaints of sexual harassment and for creating a work and educational environment that inhibits sexual harassment. Institutions have developed policies and grievance procedures. Many corporations and institutions of higher education have developed sexual harassment prevention programs to develop awareness of sexual harassment. Lawsuits have been settled in women's favor.

Even though sexual harassment is clearly illegal, women on campuses and in the workplace continue to face inappropriate behavior from supervisors, teachers, and peers. Even though formal and informal grievance procedures have been developed and publicized, women rarely use formal mechanism for reporting sexual harassment. More often, women ignore the behavior, avoid the harasser, or verbally object.

In Class 16, we explore sexual harassment, the impact it has on women, how it reflects gender stratification and power differentials between women and men. We also suggest strategies for directly challenging sexual harassment.

II. CLASS THEMES

- Background on sexual harassment
- Sexual harassment and sexual expression
- Changes in the law, gender roles, sex-based occupational segregation, and bureaucratic procedures and policies
- Individual, legal, and institutional strategies for challenging sexual harassment

III. VIDEOTAPE SYNOPSIS

- Overview of sexual harassment
- Class discussion of sexual harassment experiences
- Video visit with Randall Gold, attorney with Lawrence, Kamin, Saunders, and Uhlenhop in Chicago
- Class discussion of video visit with Randall Gold
- Video visit with Mary Mittler, Vice-President for Student Affairs, Oakton Community College, Skokie, Illinois
- Class discussion of video visit with Mary Mittler
- Interview and sexual harassment scenarios with Joe Connelly, Instructor, Self Empowerment Group

IV. VIDEOTAPE COMMENTARY

A. Overview of sexual harassment

After I give an overview of the session, I tell a story my mother told me while she was watching the Clarence Thomas and Anita Hill hearings on television. What does my mother's story illustrate about the effects of sexual harassment on women? What does my mother's experience and the graphics on factory workers and Louisa Mae Alcott tell us about the history of sexual harassment?

B. Class discussion of sexual harassment experiences

Christine, Debbie, and Ada tell us about experiences they have had with sexual harassment. Christine's example shows quick thinking and action on her part. What are the things she did that effectively stopped a sexual assault? Debbie's example illustrates the deep feelings associated with sexual harassment. What is the key feeling she identifies? Ada introduces another important part of sexual harassment: collusion by others. What could others have done to support Ada?

In summarizing this section of our class, I briefly define sexual harassment and identify factors which contribute to its existence. What are those factors?

C. Video visit with Randall Gold, attorney with Lawrence, Kamin, Saunders, and Uhlenhop in Chicago

Randy Gold has done numerous presentations to a variety of groups about the law and sexual harassment in the workplace. He is personally and professionally committed to people developing an understanding of sexual harassment, their rights, and their responsibilities. He gives us the legal definition of harassment, identifies different types of harassment, discusses the scope of the problem and awards in lawsuits, and tells us how his own observations of sexual harassment contributed to his commitment to stopping it. Make sure you can briefly summarize each of the topics he discusses.

D. Class discussion of video visit with Randall Gold

Debbie and Judy have different questions about the meaning of the large awards in sexual harassment cases. Debbie focuses on the message to harassers; Judy has concerns about the consequences for women who win lawsuits. What do you think about the issues they raise?

E. Video visit with Mary Mittler, Vice-President for Student Affairs, Oakton Community College, Skokie, Illinois

Mary Mittler is a dedicated educator and advocate for students, teachers, and staff . She has worked on sexual harassment issues for over 15 years locally, regionally, and nationally. Mary is often the first administrator on her campus a student approaches about a sexual harassment experience. Mary tells us about the complex feelings women report when they have been sexually harassed in an educational setting. She reviews the options that students have and how their harassers respond. She also offers us her insights into the impact the Anita Hill and Clarence Thomas hearings have had on sexual harassment reporting. As you listen to Mary, note the different feelings she identifies that people have around this issue and what she has to say about how sexual harassment is related to positions of power. Identify also the strategies she sees as effective for stopping sexual harassment.

F. Class discussion of video visit with Mary Mittler

Carlos, Jan, Gunther, and Sharon offer reactions to the videotape and comments from others. Carlos talks about developing a heightened awareness. What is Carlos doing to encourage increased awareness about sexual harassment issues? Gunther expresses concern about contradictions he sees in talking about sexual harassment. Sharon suggests that it is not a contradiction, but a matter of having a label. What do you see as the issues? Jan raises a question about the difference between joking and sexual harassment. Based on the discussion here, how would you distinguish sexual harassment from joking and from sexual expression?

G. Interview and sexual harassment scenarios with Joe Connelly, Instructor, Self Empowerment Group

Joe Connelly is a martial artist and self-defense instructor who is dedicated to providing opportunities for women to practice skills which will increase their ability to stop sexual harassment and sexual assault. Joe tells us about his background and motivation for doing this work. How have the experiences of women in his life influenced Joe?

Joe offers us an overview of what factors contribute to the success of harassers. What are those factors? He also offers us three tips for what to do in a situation in which we or someone else might be sexually harassed. Identify those three ideas and imagine how you might use them in an actual situation. To demonstrate the importance of practicing these skills, Joe takes on the role of a harasser and Christine, Phyllis, and Joan respond. Though they had volunteered to participate in these demonstrations, they had no idea what the harasser would say to them. You are seeing unrehearsed responses. Joe points out what each of them did to deter the harasser. What were those behaviors? Were there other behaviors you saw that they used to stop the harassment? What would you have done in each of these situations?

 Now watch the videotape.

V. REVIEW QUESTIONS

1. What is sexual harassment? What factors contribute to its existence?

2. What are the EEOC sexual harassment guidelines? What do quid pro quo and hostile environment mean in this context?

3. How would you distinguish sexual harassment from sexual expression? from friendly joking?

4. What are common myths associated with sexual harassment? What is known about the frequency of sexual harassment? What effects does sexual harassment have on women?

5. What is known about the reporting of sexual harassment? What are barriers to reporting sexual harassment?

6. What are individual strategies for challenging sexual harassment?

7. What are legal and institutional strategies for challenging sexual harassment?

VI. INTERVIEW EXCERPT

Melissa Josephs, Policy Associate at Women Employed, talks about the calls they get concerning sexual harassment and the role she sees Women Employed plays in supporting women who have been harassed.

 Melissa Josephs:

The mission of Women Employed in a nutshell is that we're a not-for-profit membership organization and we work to increase career and economic opportunities for women. Some of the issues that we are addressing, and I'll start with one I personally address, are sexual harassment and pregnancy discrimination on the job. And those two things have a great and an unfortunate impact on women's ability to get ahead in the workplace and just to work safely and productively in the workplace. I'm sure everyone's familiar with the Anita Hill and Clarence Thomas hearings that took place in 1991. But even before that, Women Employed has been around for 20 years, and for the 20 years we've always received calls about sexual harassment. Even after the Thomas/Hill hearings, people still call wanting to know if what's happening to them is sexual harassment, what they have to stand for, what they can do about it, what they should do about it. There are still a lot of people who are afraid to come forward, to complain about it because as Anita Hill shows, a lot of times women are not believed or if they are believed and something's done, they're retaliated against. And so a lot of times people just weigh the odds and what their choices are and they'll say well forget it, that's just the way it is or this is the way it's going to be and I don't want to risk losing my job. That's unfortunate because it doesn't stop the situation, it has a negative impact on the woman both at her job, and a lot of times emotionally, that goes beyond the job that if she's not believed, that she is treated as less than an individual. She's not treated as a worker, but as a sex object. Then unfortunately on the harasser's end, he — it's usually "he" about 90% of the cases of harassment — the harasser goes on to harass other people and so that's a huge problem that employers are now beginning to address. A lot of times it's because of the Thomas/Hill hearings or because they're becoming more sensitive to it or it's the bottom line of economics. If because some women are coming forward and filing charges, employers see that they're going to have to pay, the bottom line is economics, that's a reason to change. Just so that the point is made that it's wrong and that it's illegal and it should be stopped, that it's not just a joke.

Sometimes it's enough just telling people that what's happening to them is wrong, is illegal, and that there are things that can be done about it. But even if someone's not ready to do something about it, just being there to say to someone, yeah, that's wrong. Oftentimes, especially in the case of these illegal issues like sexual harassment, people have to hear something more than once before they're ready to take the step to change something. And so if I'm that first person or the second or the third person, just to give her confidence. Just to have let her know that it's wrong. That there's someone else that agrees with her, cause oftentimes in the case of harassment, women talk to other people who don't agree with her. And so that's certainly a reward. But the bottom line is making the changes. And it's one of the reasons why I feel that every day, by talking to people, I can be making some small change.

VII. SOURCES AND FURTHER READING

Thanks to Mary Mittler for her list of recommendations for further reading.

Allen, Deborah and Judy Bessai Okawa. 1987. "A counseling center looks at sexual harassment." *Journal of the National Association of Women Deans, Administrators, and Counselors* 51 (1): 9 - 16.

Baker, Douglas D., David E. Terpstra, and Bob D. Cutler. 1990. "Perceptions of sexual harassment: a re-examination of gender differences." *The Journal of Psychology* 124 (July): 409 - 416.

Benson, Donna J. and Gregory E. Thomson. 1982. "Sexual harassment on a university campus: the confluence of authority relations, sexual interest, and gender stratification." *Social Problems*, 29: 236 - 251.

Bernays, Anne. 1989. *Professor Romeo.* NY: Penguin Books.

Brandenburg, J. B. 1982. "Sexual harassment in the university: guidelines for establishing a grievance procedure." *Signs*, 8 (2): 320 - 334.

Bravo, Ellen. 1992. *The 9 to 5 Guide to Combatting Sexual Harassment: Candid Advice from 9 to 5, the National Association of Working Women.* NY: John Wiley and Sons.

Bravo, Ellen. 1992. "Sexual harassment: what to do if it happens to you?" *Women in Business* 44 (Sept/Oct): 22.

Brewer, Marilyn B. and Richard A. Berk (eds.). 1982. "Beyond nine to five: sexual harassment on the job, special issue on sexual harassment. *Journal of Social Issues,* 38.

Carroll, Jeffrey. 1992. "Freshman: confronting sexual harassment in the classroom." *Composition Studies/Freshman English News* 20 (2): 60 - 70.

Crocker, Phyllis. 1983. "An analysis of university definitions of sexual harassment." *Signs: Journal of Women in Culture and Society* 8: 696 - 707.

Decker, Robert H. 1989. "Can schools eliminate sexual harassment?" *Education Digest* 54 (January): 59 - 63.

Dziech, Billie Write. 1992. "Sexual harassment: everybody's problem." *NACADA Journal* 12 (1): 48 - 55.

Dziech, Billie Wright and L. Weiner. 1984. *The Lecherous Professor.* Boston: Beacon Press.

Fisher, Anne B. 1993. "Sexual harassment: what to do." *Fortune* 128 (August):84.

Gibbs, Nancy. 1991. "Office crimes." *Time* 138 (October 21): 52 .

Gruber, James E. 1989. "How women handle sexual harassment: a literature review." *Sociology and Social Research* 74 (October): 3 - 9.

Henley, Nancy and Jo Freeman. "The sexual politics of interpersonal behavior." Pp. 457 - 469 in Jo Freeman (ed.). *Women: A Feminist Perspective,* fourth edition. Mountain View, CA: Mayfield Publishing Company.

Hoffman, Frances. 1986. "Sexual harassment in academia: feminist theory and institutional practice." *Harvard Educational Review*, 56 (2): 105 -120.

Johnson, Catherine B., Margaret S. Stockdale, and Frank E. Saal. 1991. "Persistence of man's misperceptions of friendly cues across a variety of interpersonal encounters." *Psychology of Women Quarterly* 15 (Sept): 463-475.

Langelan, Martha J. 1993. *Back Off! How to Confront and Stop Sexual Harassment and Harassers.* NY: Simon and Schuster.

Lanpher, Katherine. 1992. "Reading, 'riting, & 'rassment." *Ms. Magazine* 2 (May/June): 90.

Lewis, Anne C. 1992. "Gender issues." *Education Digest* 57 (May): 50.

Livingston, Jay. 1982. "Responses to sexual harassment on the job: legal, organizational, and individuals actions." *Journal of Social Issues*, 38: 5 - 22.

MacKinnon, Catherine A. 1979. *The Sexual Harassment of Working Women: A Case of Sex Discrimination.* New Haven: Yale University Press.

Martin, Susan Ehrlich. 1989. "Sexual harassment: the link joining gender stratification, sexuality, and women's economic status." Pp. 57 -75 in Jo Freeman (ed.) *Women: A Feminist Perspective*, 4th ed. Mountain View, CA: Mayfield Publishing Company.

McCormack, Arlene. 1985. "The sexual harassment of students by teachers: the case of students in science." *Sex Roles*, 13: 21 - 32.

McKinney, K, C. Olson, and A. Satterfield. 1988. "Graduate students' experiences with and responses to sexual harassment." *Journal of Interpersonal Violence*, 3: 319- 325.

Moskal, Brian S. 1991. "Sexual harassment: an update." *Industry Week* 240 (Nov 18): 37.

Niven, Daniel, et al. 1992. "Case of the hidden harassment." *Harvard Business Review* 70 (March/April): 12.

Saal, Frank E. 1989. "Friendly or sexy? It may depend on whom you ask." *Psychology of Women Quarterly* 13 (Sept): 263 -276.

Safran, Claire. 1976. " What men do to women on the job: a shocking look at sexual harassment." *Redbook*, November: 149, 217 - 223.

Sandler, B. R. 1983. *Writing a Letter to the Sexual Harasser: Another Way of Dealing with the Problem.* Washington, D.C.: Association of American Colleges.

Schneider, Beth E. 1982. "Consciousness about sexual harassment among heterosexual and lesbian women workers." *Journal of Social Issues*, 38: 75 - 97.

"Sexual Harassment," special feature. 1991. *Journal of Counseling and Development,* 69 (July/August).

"Sexuality after Thomas/Hill," Roundtable. 1992. *Tikkun*, 7 (1): 25 - 30, 96.

Thacker, Rebecca. 1992. "Preventing sexual harassment in the workplace." *Training and Development* 46 (2): 50 - 53.

Toobin, Jeffrey. 1993. "The burden of Clarence Thomas." *The New Yorker*, September 27: 38 - 51.

Truax, Anne, et al. 1989. "Sexual harassment in higher education." *Thought & Action* 5 (1): 25 - 52.

Webb, Susan L. 1991. *Step Forward: Sexual Harassment in the Workplace, What You Need to Know!* NY: Mastermedia.

Women's Action Coalition (WAC). 1993. "Sexual harassment." Pp. 53 - 54 in *WAC Stats: The Facts About Women.* NY: The New Press.

VII. ORGANIZATIONS

American Sociological Association. 1722 N. Street NW, Washington, D.C. 20036. (202) 833-3410.

Self Empowerment Group. 6219 N. Sheridan, Chicago, IL 60660. (773) 338-4545.

U.S. Equal Employment Opportunities Commission (EEOC). Check your local phone book.

Women Employed. 22 W. Monroe Ave., Suite 1400, Chicago, IL 60603. (312) 782-3902.

WOMEN AND SOCIAL ACTION: CLASS 17
Low-income Resistance

Before you read this Chapter of the Study Guide

Read   Andersen, pp. 129 - 133 "Poverty and Welfare"
Feldman, Roberta M. and Susan Stall. "Resident Activism in Public Housing:
A Case Study of Women's Invisible Work of Building Community."
Appendix C

I. INTRODUCTION

JOURNAL ASSIGNMENT

> Write about an experience in which you or someone you know had less income or fewer resources than others. Describe how you felt about the experience and yourself. Reflect on what you learned or are learning from this experience.

What images come to your mind when you think of women with low income and limited resources? Do you think of women living in public housing, in the hills of Appalachia, in small Southern towns, in migrant labor camps, in the rural midwest, in the streets of major U.S. cities?

What images come to your mind when you think of people trying to improve the lives of women with low income and limited resources? Do you think of middle-class, educated, idealistic women and men teaching in farm labor camps, working in soup kitchens, taking baskets of food and clothing to the needy, working in literacy programs in the basement of local churches?

The few times women with limited resources are portrayed in the media, we typically see women with tired, haggard faces; women who can't read; women who have given up battling the violence of poverty; women with lots of children and little time; women who are isolated and demoralized; women who are helpless and hopeless. When we see people trying to alter conditions of limited resources, we often see people from outside the situation coming in to turn things around.

In contrast, we will see in Class 17 strong, able people who now have or have had limited resources. We will see women defining their own problems, analyzing factors which contributed to their circumstances, and working on solutions relevant to themselves and their situation.

In the opening class discussion, we will hear a number of members of our class talk about their own experience with limited resources. We will hear that the stereotypes, barriers, and limits imposed by others were typically what was devastating to self-esteem, not the lack of resources themselves.

In the videotape of residents at Wentworth Gardens in Chicago, we will visit a few of the women who have been engaged in ongoing activism to improve living conditions in public housing in Chicago. We will see women who are part of a larger group of activists who have supported each other, who have worked collectively for the betterment of their community, and who are role models for all of us.

We will talk with Susan Stall, a sociologist who along with Roberta Feldman, an architect and environmental psychologist, has studied the activities of the women at Wentworth. We will hear how the women of Wentworth engage in often invisible, but ongoing acts of political resistance through their appropriation of space in public housing.

II. CLASS THEMES

- The impact of low income and few resources on women
- Women's resistance to barriers, stereotypes, and limits imposed by others
- Participatory research as social action and social science
- Appropriation of space as resistance
- Modest struggles and social change

III. VIDEOTAPE SYNOPSIS

- Overview of Class 17
- Class discussion of experience with low income or limited resources
- Video visit with Hallie Amey, Beatrice Harris, and Andrea Henley, Wentworth Gardens, Chicago
- Interview and class discussion with Susan Stall, Assistant Professor of Sociology and Women's Studies, Northeastern Illinois University

IV. VIDEOTAPE COMMENTARY

A. Overview of Class 17

To open Class 17, I share my own experience with limited income and resources. What does my example show about how others' stereotypes can affect one's self-esteem?

B. Class discussion of experience with low income or few resources

Christine, Gail, Trenace, Ada, Judy, Virginia, Mary, Helen, and Joe tell us about their experiences with low income or few resources. Christine's story illustrates the distinction between absolute and relative deprivation. In a situation of absolute deprivation, we do not have adequate food or shelter to sustain our bodies. In a situation of relative deprivation, we have enough to get by, but in relationship to others we have considerably less. What did Christine learn from her experience?

Gail's example raises the issue of conflicting social statuses and the impact this conflict can have on self-esteem and behavior. What was the struggle she faced? Ada's story illustrates the impact of well-intentioned but demeaning advice from others. What could her neighbor have done differently?

Trenace and Judy's examples illustrate how an adult's decision to return to school may affect her or his relationship to others. Trenace talks about others' seeing her as more dependent. Judy discusses family members feeling they are deprived of resources. How might these perceptions undermine someone's returning to school? What have Trenace and Judy done to combat these perceptions?

Virginia's story about her mother shows that people may continue to use survival strategies for coping with low income long after it is no longer necessary for economic reasons. Her example illustrates how what was once a good coping strategy for those with low income is now a good environmental strategy. Can you think of other examples whereby a coping strategy for economizing has other benefits?

Mary's story illustrates the gap between our own and others' perceptions. What was rich about her life as the spouse of a cowboy that had nothing to do with money? Helen's example shows the humiliation that often accompanies charity. What ideas do you have for ways to offer help to others that are empowering not degrading?

C. Video Visit with Wentworth Gardens resident activists:
   Mrs. Hallie Amey, President, Resident Management Council
   Mrs. Beatrice Harris, President, Local Advisory Council and Resident Management Council Board Member
   Mrs. Andrea Henley, Director, Boys and Girls Club

Wentworth Gardens is a lowrise public housing development on the southside of Chicago. Its boundaries include Comisky Park (the White Sox Stadium), the Dan Ryan Expressway, an industrial park, and a limited commercial strip. In the 1960s when the Chicago Housing Authority (CHA) began to reduce provision of services, upkeep of the physical plant, and elimination of programs, Wentworth Gardens resident activists organized to take care of their homes and community. The many accomplishments of Wentworth Gardens resident activists include: the development of a preschool program, fieldhouse youth programs, an onsite Boys and Girls Club, a resident owned and operated laundromat and grocery store, and renovation of the playground area. Wentworth Gardens resident activists have done this work with a limited number of people and limited resources. I talked with three women activists who on behalf of the larger group of resident activists tell us about the accomplishments of Wentworth Gardens.

Mrs. Hallie Amey, an outstanding example of a centerwoman, tells us about the beginnings of their organizing, the development of the laundromat, the fieldhouse, and the gardens. Mrs. Beatrice Harris, a longtime committed resident activist, tells us about her experience in working in the laundromat, her pride in their accomplishments, and the development of the new playground area. Mrs. Andrea Henley, an enthusiastic resident activist, tells us about the Boys and Girls Club and their activities.

What do we learn about the challenges the resident activists of Wentworth have faced? What do we learn about the rewards of maintaining and improving their community?

D. Interview and class discussion with Susan Stall, Assistant Professor of Sociology and Women's Studies, Northeastern Illinois University

Susan is a social activist, a sociologist, and a feminist. In the time I've known Susan she has worked on many research and social action projects. In her teaching, her research, and her social action, Susan continually demonstrates a commitment to empowerment and social justice. She uses her considerable skills as a centerwoman to facilitate an exciting interchange between academics and activists. In the work she discusses here, she provides a model of what participatory research is all about.

Susan tells us about her background in working with public housing residents and what participatory research is. What does she say about participatory research and how it is different from other types of research?

She also tells us about her work with Women United for a Better Chicago and Chicago Housing Authority Residents Taking Action (CHARTA). What did she do with these organizations? How did this experience influence her and her colleague, Roberta Feldman, architect and environmental psychologist, to work with the women at Wentworth Gardens?

Susan tells us that developing the laundromat, grocery store, fieldhouse, and center courtyard at Wentworth Gardens were political acts of resistance. How does she see the appropriation of space as a political act of resistance in public housing? She also introduces the concept of modest struggles. What does she mean by this concept? Give an example from Wentworth Gardens. How does Susan tie in the concepts of centerwoman and group-centered leadership?

In response to a question from Joe about small and large goals, Susan discusses how the modest goals of a laundromat and grocery store were a foundation for challenging the building of the Sports Stadium south of Comiskey Park. What do you see as the relationship between modest and large goals?

Gail raises a question about the influence the type of housing has on organizing. Susan adds the issue of density as another consideration. How does Susan recommend organizers work with different types of space and density?

Trenace's question about how many people are involved gives Susan an opportunity to talk about different levels of participation. What are some of the things which distinguish leadership, work on projects, and participation in events?

In response to Joan's question about changes in public housing, Susan tells us about key concerns. What are the key issues facing public housing residents that Susan identifies?

Christine raises a question concerning publicity about the lawsuit against the City of Chicago and the White Sox. When was there lots of publicity? Why do you suppose there is not much now?

Ada expresses concern about the racial stereotypes associated with low income and public housing. Susan tells us about scattered site housing for white public housing residents and briefly mentions the ways in which public housing has been used for racial segregation. What do you see as the relationship between racial stereotypes, racial segregation, and public housing?

 Now watch the videotape.

V. REVIEW QUESTIONS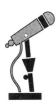

1. What is meant by the feminization of poverty? How is it related to unemployment and the job market?

2. What are myths and realities concerning women and poverty?

3. How are racial politics related to the public housing crisis in Chicago?

4. What are problems that organizers in public housing face?

5. What are some accomplishments of activists at Wentworth Gardens?

6. What is meant by appropriation of space as a political act of resistance?

7. What is meant by modest struggles?

8. How do the concepts of centerwomen and group-centered leadership apply to resident activism in public housing?

VI. INTERVIEW EXCERPT

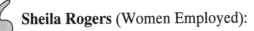

> Increasingly, women and their children are the majority of the poor. Households headed by women are more likely to be poor than households headed by men. Sheila Rogers, Director of Participant Services, Keys to Success Program at Women Employed, talks about the support the Keys to Success Program provides women who have been out of the workplace for an extended period of time and who then become responsible for providing financially for themselves and their families.

Sheila Rogers (Women Employed):

The Keys to Success Program is an organization that provides women who have been out of the workplace for an extended period of time an opportunity to prepare themselves to return to the workplace. We work with women who have been traditional homemakers, responsible for taking care of their families on a full-time basis and, therefore, were unable to work outside of the home. While they were taking care of their families on a full-time basis, they were provided for financially by another person or spouse. Perhaps this person died or perhaps there's been a divorce, separation, or the spouse has become permanently disabled. Now the woman needs to return to the workplace or perhaps work for the first time because she needs to provide income for herself and her family. But because she has not worked in a number of years or perhaps has never worked, she needs help in making that transition. So we offer a program that helps people prepare themselves to look for employment. We help women to assess what their skills are. Many women feel that because they've been homemakers for a number of years, they lack the skills. That's not true. It takes many skills in order to run a household efficiently and often women do other things in addition to taking care of their homes. They might be very active in their community in some manner or active in their child's school. We use all of those life experiences to draw up a list of their skills and find out what there is that they possess and what they can offer to an employer. We help them to sharpen their interview techniques, we help them to put together a resume, feel more confident. It's a sense of empowering women to let them know that they do have the skills that are necessary in order to make that transition if they wish. If they want to get into a field for which they do not have the skill or education, what we do is we help identify where they can get job training, or where they can go to continue their education. So we help many women to identify various job training programs that they can enroll into. We really encourage women to look at nontraditional fields of training, where they can earn high wages and that way they have a better chance at being able to provide for themselves and their family in an adequate way. I've been involved with that for over five years. I've been involved with the organization for over 10. And I like what I'm doing because I see results. It's amazing the results that I see with women in a matter of three weeks. Women come in and they feel that they're the only ones in this situation, perhaps they've been trying on their own to find employment and they've been unsuccessful, they've been rejected every place they go, they don't know what they're doing wrong. They come here and they finally find a place where, number one, they are with other women who understand what it is that they're going through because they're in it themselves or have gone through it. And they also find a way in which they can look at how to overcome these barriers. So we do see a remarkable sense of change in the women in that program. Their change in self-esteem is enormous. So it gives me and other people at the program great satisfaction.

VII. SOURCES AND FURTHER READING

Thanks to Susan Stall for her list of recommendations for further readings.

Ackelsberg, M. A. "Communities, resistance, and women's activism: some implications for a democratic polity." Pp. 297 - 313 in *Women and the Politics of Empowerment*, edited by Ann Bookman and Sandra Morgen. Philadelphia, PA: Temple University Press.

Bonacich, Edna. 1992. "Inequality in America: the failure of the American system for people of color." Pp. 96 - 110 in *Race, Class, Gender: An Anthology*, edited by Margaret L. Andersen and Patricia Hill Collins. Belmont, CA: Wadsworth Publishing.

Dujon, Diane, Judy Gradford, and Dottie Stevens. 1992. "Welfare mothers up in arms." Pp. 259 - 266 in *Race, Class, Gender: An Anthology*, edited by Margaret L. Andersen and Patricia Hill Collins. Belmont, CA: Wadsworth Publishing.

Evans, Sara and Harry Boyte. 1981. "Schools for action: radical uses of social space." *Democracy*, Summer: 55 - 65.

Garland, Anne Witte. 1988. "Gale Cincotta: *We found the enemy.*" *Women Activists: Challenging the Abuse of Power.* NY: The Feminist Press.

Hayden, Dolores. 1984. "*Redesigning the American Dream:The Future of Housing, Work, and Family Life.* NY: W.W. Norton and Company.

Hertz, Susan H. 1977. "The politics of the welfare mothers' movement: a case study." *Signs: Journal of Women in Culture and Society* 7 (3): 600 - 611.

Hooks, Bell. 1990. *Yearning: Race, Gender, and Cultural Politics.* Boston, MA: South End Press.

Kotlowitz, Alex. 1991. *There Are No Children Here: The Story of Growing Up in the Other America.* NY: Doubleday.

Krause, Celene. 1983. "The elusive process of citizen activism." *Social Policy*, Fall: 50 -55.

Lawson, Ronald and Stephen E. Barton. 1990. "Sex roles in social movements: a case study of the tenant movement in New York City." Pp. 41 - 56 in *Women and Social Protest,* edited by Guida West and Rhoda Lois Blumberg. NY: Oxford University Press.

Lefkowitz, Rochelle and Ann Withorn (eds.). 1986. *For Crying Out Loud: Women and Poverty in the United States.* NY: Pilgrim.

Lewis, Gwendolyn, Patricia Holland, and Kathleen Kelly. 1992. "Working-class students speak out." *Radical Teacher*, Fall: 10 - 12.

Morgen, Sandra and Ann Bookman. 1988. "Rethinking women and politics: an introductory essay." Pp. 3 -29 in *Women and the Politics of Empowerment,* edited by Ann Bookman and Sandra Morgen. Philadelphia, PA: Temple University Press.

Mudrick, Nancy R. 1988. "Disabled women and public policies for income support." Pp. 245 - 268 in *Women with Disabilities: Essays in Psychology, Culture, and Politics*, edited by Michele Fine and Adrienne Asch. Philadelphia, PA: Temple University Press.

Myrdal, Gunnar. 1962. *An American Dilemma.* NY: Harper.

Payne, Charles. 1989. "Ella Baker and models of social change." *Signs: Journal of Women in Culture and Society*, 14 (4): 885-899.

Payne, Charles. 1990. "'Men led, but women organized': Movement participation of women in the Mississippi delta." Pp. 156 -165 in *Women and Social Protest,* edited by Guida West and Rhoda Lois Blumberg. NY: Oxford University Press.

Pearce, Diana M. 1989. "Farewell to alms: women's fare under welfare." P p. 493 - 506 in *Women: A Feminist Perspective*, fourth edition, edited by Jo Freeman. Mountain View, CA: Mayfield Publishing Company.

Pope, Jackie. 1990. "Women in the welfare rights struggle: the Brooklyn Welfare Action Council." Pp. 57 - 74 in *Women and Social Protest,* edited by Guida West and Rhoda Lois Blumberg. NY: Oxford University Press.

Rappaport, Julian. 1981. "In praise of paradox: a social policy of empowerment over prevention." *American Journal of Community Psychology*, 9 (1): 1 - 25.

Sacks, Karen Brodkin. 1988. "Gender and grassroots leadership." Pp. 77 - 94 in *Women and the Politics of Empowerment,* edited by Ann Bookman and Sandra Morgen. Philadelphia, PA: Temple University Press.

Seifer, Nancy. 1976. *Nobody Speaks for Me! Self-Portraits of American Working Class Women.* NY: Simon and Schuster.

Shortridge, Kathleen. 1989. " Poverty is a woman's problem." Pp. 485 - 506 in *Women: A Feminist Perspective*, fourth edition, edited by Jo Freeman. Mountain View, CA: Mayfield Publishing Company.

Sidel, Ruth. 1986. *Women and Children Last: The Plight of Poor Women in Affluent America.* NY: Viking Penguin.

Smith, Dorothy E. 1987. "The everyday world as problematic: a feminist methodology." *The Everyday World as Problematic: A Feminist Sociology.* Boston, MA: Northeastern University Press.

Stack, Carol B. 1974. *All Our Kin: Strategies for Survival in a Black Community.* NY: Harper and Row, 1974.

Terkel, Studs. 1967. "Lucy Jefferson." *Division Street: America.* NY: Pantheon.

Thomas, Sherry. 1981. *We Didn't Have Much, But We Sure Had Plenty: Stories of Rural Women.* Garden City, NY: Anchor Books.

Zinn, Maxine Baca. 1992. "Family, race, and poverty in the eighties." Pp. 71 - 91 in *Rethinking the Family: Some Feminist Questions*, edited by Barrie Thorne with Marilyn Yalom. Boston: Northeastern University Press.

VIII. ORGANIZATIONS

Chicago Housing Authority Residents Taking Action (CHARTA). (now dissolved)

Environmental Design Research Association. P.O. Box 24083, Oklahoma City, OK 73124.

Wentworth Resident Management Council. 252 W. 39th Street, Chicago, IL 60609.
(773) 548-8453 or (773) 548-7512.

Women Employed. 22 W. Monroe Ave, Suite 1400, Chicago, IL 60603. (312) 782-3902.

Women for Economic Security. 200 S. Michigan Avenue, Suite 1400, Chicago, IL 60604.
(312) 663-3574.

Women United for a Better Chicago. (now dissolved)

II. CLASS THEMES

- The impact of homelessness on women and children
- Causes of homelessness for women and children
- The relationship of homelessness to other issues
- Empowerment and homeless women

III. VIDEOTAPE SYNOPSIS

- Introduction to the topic of homelessness
- Class discussion of homelessness
- Video visit with homeless women
- Class discussion of reasons for homelessness
- Video visit with women who serve as shelter representatives on the Coordinating Committee of the Women's Empowerment Project
- Interview and class discussion with Della Mitchell, Coordinator, Chicago Coalition for the Homeless Empowerment Project for Homeless Women with Children

IV. VIDEOTAPE COMMENTARY

A. Introduction to the topic of homelessness

In this brief introduction I give an overview of an experience I have had with homelessness and raise a question about what the phrase a "woman's place is in the home" means for homeless women.

B. Class discussion of homelessness

Virginia, Ada, and Jan talk about their experiences in working with shelters or programs in which homeless women and children were involved. What are some of the issues they raise that may be interrelated with homelessness? What role might violence play in contributing to women's homelessness? Ada uses the term "throwaways." What does that term mean?

Debbie, Mary, and Judy talk about their own experiences with not having a home. What psychological effects do they mention? What longterm impact does Debbie think her experience had on her? What role does Judy see material things play in maintaining individual identity?

C. Video visit with homeless women

To get a sense of the immediate impact of homelessness on women, we wanted to talk with women who are currently homeless. Della Mitchell suggested we attend one of the biweekly meetings held at one of the participating shelters. Women who attended had spent the previous night at the shelter and were coming to their first meeting of the Women's Empowerment Project. What reasons do the women give for their current situation? Mrs. Campbell is the director of the shelter we visited and has been homeless herself. How does she describe the help others have given to her and why she is doing this work?

D. Class discussion of reasons for homelessness

Carlos, Gail, Christine, Ada, Janet, and Trenace talk about their reactions to the video visit. What reasons do they observe as reasons for the women's homelessness? What does Janet note about Mrs. Campbell's desire to pay back for the help she got?

In response to class comments, I briefly talk about the concept of empowerment. What does this concept mean? Trenace observes the tendency of women to blame themselves. As you watch the next video visit, notice the difference between assuming blame and taking responsibility.

E. Video visit with women who serve as shelter representatives on the Coordinating Committee of the Women's Empowerment Project

To see the results of the Women's Empowerment Project, we attended one of the meetings of the Project's Coordinating Committee. At each meeting, one of the women talks indepth about her own experience with homelessness. What challenges has the woman featured faced? What do you see as the relationship between violence, sexual abuse, substance abuse, and homelessness? What were her initial reservations about the Project? How does she describe the support of the Project ?

F. Interview and class discussion with Della Mitchell, Coordinator, Chicago Coalition for the Homeless Empowerment Project for Women with Children

When the Chicago Coalition for the Homeless hired Della Mitchell for the Women's Empowerment Project, the Coalition thought it was a near impossible task to organize homeless women, but a worthy dream. We have seen for ourselves that Della and the women she is working with have made the dream a reality. Della Mitchell's business card reads "Della Mitchell, organizer." What volumes that one word speaks! To me it simultaneously represents her humility, her vision, and her actions. The Women's Empowerment Project is an exemplary project and Della Mitchell is an exemplary organizer.

In listening to Della Mitchell talk about her work with the Women's Empowerment Project, what do you see as the role building trust, caring, and nonjudgemental support play in women's empowerment? What are some of the key services of the Empowerment Project? Della identifies the number one cause of homelessness as lack of affordable housing. What other causes does she see? What role does she see other issues playing?

In response to Judy's question about programs for preventing homeless, Della tells us about the role the Project plays and also introduces the idea of the hidden homeless. What does she mean by that concept? Della also tells us about taking groups of homeless women to Springfield and Washington, D.C. to influence the press and legislators and women working with businesses and banks to develop housing alternatives. What are some specific ways the Project supports women who do this work?

Trenace raises concerns about homeless women having the primary responsibility for their children. She wonders where the men are and what they are doing (see Sidel under "Sources and Further Reading). Della ties in the importance of women having control over their own bodies as well as addressing the complicated rules of shelters which divide families and discourage men from having responsibility for their children. Why do you suppose shelters have these rules? What impact do you think these rules have on children?

Gunther asks about the possibility of women taking care of each other's children. Della talks about the rules and legal liabilities of the shelters as well as the protectiveness homeless women feel toward their children. What does she identify as reasons for this protectiveness? Christine comments on the importance of affordable housing that provides an adequate living space. Ada follows up with concerns about the quality of affordable housing.

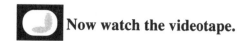 **Now watch the videotape.**

V. REVIEW QUESTIONS

1. What are key findings about homeless families in Chicago?

2. What are major causes of homelessness among women? What is meant by the term "the hidden homeless"?

3. What types of shelters are available?

4. How do shelter rules about children affect families?

5. What are some of the accomplishments of the Chicago Coalition for the Homeless Women's Empowerment Project?

6. What are some of the problems the Empowerment Project has faced?

7. What are strategies the Empowerment Project uses to support participants?

8. What are some of the changes which occur for women who participate in the project?

9. What does the term "throwaways" mean?·

10. What is meant by empowerment? How do you see it illustrated in the Women's Empowerment Project?

VI. INTERVIEW EXCERPT

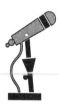

Judy Vaughan and Dihya Al Kahina, National Coordinating Team, National Assembly of Religious Women (NARW), talk about ways their organization has worked in solidarity with homeless women.

 Judy Vaughan:

Part of our understanding of solidarity is that people who are being oppressed by the system have the right and the responsibility to set the direction for their own liberation.... We are an action-oriented organization so not only are we grassroots community based but many of our members are in fact women with limited incomes, who are being economically exploited. We work together, kind of a national platform for their voices to be heard.

Martha: Can you give an example?

Dihya Al Kahina: At the first meeting of the homeless committee, they invited the homeless women to come and sit in on this meeting and make suggestions and take part in the planning of what they were doing around Presidential Towers. At this first meeting, the people who were already on the committee were sitting around the tables and the homeless women were sitting in chairs in back of tables and so forth. So after the meeting was over we asked the women, the homeless women, how they liked the meeting. And they didn't, they didn't seem to appreciate the fact that they weren't sitting at the table with the other people. So the next meeting we asked them to come a little early and we had them sit around the table and the other people sat around the outside of the table and that meeting went very well.

Judy Vaughan: It's kind of a concrete symbol for us—shifting the power equation—from where voices can't be heard, where one's input is not respected, where even people are made invisible by the system. Where you move to a collective effort where everyone around the table is respected, whose voice is significant, important and needs to be heard in order to both have an adequate sense of how critical the problems are as well as to be able to offer the solutions and really work together for change. We hold on to that as one kind of concrete image for us and how our commitment has really shifted geography to change the system, to change the power equation of our present society and world. And it's also true for our work in terms of institutional turf structures where certainly women's voices are not heard, we're not even at the table. So how do we push and organize to have a place at that table so that we can co-create with one another what happens in this institution that is really fundamentally ours.

VII. SOURCES AND FURTHER READING

Thanks to Renny Golden for a list of recommendations for further reading.

Bessuk, Ellen L. 1991. "Homeless families." *Scientific American*, December.

Birch, E.L. 1985. *The Unsheltered Woman: Women and Housing in the 80s.* New Brunswick NJ: Center for Urban Policy Research.

Brickman, Philip, Vita Carulli Rabinowitz, Jurgis Karuza, Dan Coates, Ellen Cohn, and Louise Kidder. 1982. "Models of helping and coping." *American Psychologist*, 37 (4): 368 - 384.

Hirsch, Kathleen. 1990. *Songs from the Alley.* NY: Doubleday.

Katz, Michael B. 1989. *The Undeserving Poor: From the War on Poverty to the War on Welfare.* NY: Pantheon.

Kieffer, C.H. 1984. "Citizen empowerment: a developmental perspective." Pp. 9 -36 in *Studies in Empowerment: Steps Toward Understanding Action,* edited by J. Rappaport, C. Swift, and R. Hess. NY: Haworth.

Kozol, Jonathan. 1988. *Rachel and Her Children: Homeless Families in America.* NY: Fawcett Columbine.

Liebow, Elliott. 1993. *Tell Them Who I Am: The Lives of Homeless Women.* NY: Free Press.

McCourt, Kathleen and Gwendolyn Nyden. 1990. *Promises Made, Promises Broken...The Crisis and Challenge: Homeless Families in Chicago.* Report Prepared for and with The Chicago Institute on Urban Poverty Travelers and Immigrant Aid. Chicago, IL.

Polakow, Valerie. 1993. *Lives on the Edge: Single Mothers and Their Children in the Other America.* Chicago: University of Chicago Press.

Rappaport, Julian. 1981. "In praise of paradox: a social policy of empowerment over prevention." *American Journal of Community Psychology,* 9 (1): 1 - 25.

Rousseau, Ann Marie. 1981. *Shopping Bag Ladies.* NY: Pilgrim Press.

Ryan, William. 1971. *Blaming the Victim.* NY: Pantheon Books.

Sidel, Ruth. 1986. "But where are the men?" *Women and Children Last: The Plight of Poor Women in Affluent America.* NY: Viking Penguin.

Swift, Carolyn and Gloria Levin. 1987. "Empowerment: an emerging mental health technology." *Journal of Primary Prevention,* 8 (1 and 2): 71 - 94.

Torrey, E. Fuller. 1989. *Nowhere to Go: The Tragic Odyssey of the Homeless Mentally Ill.* NY: Harper.

Vanderstaay, Steve. 1992. *Street Lives: From Destitution to Community Building.* Philadelphia, PA: New Society Publishers.

Women's Action Coalition (WAC). 1993. "Homelessness." Pp. 28-29 in *WAC Stats: The Facts About Women.* NY: The New Press.

Weisman, Leslie Kanes. 1992. *Discrimination by Design: A Feminist Critique of the Man-Made Environment.* Urbana, IL: University of Illinois Press.

VIII. ORGANIZATIONS

Chicago Coalition for the Homeless Empowerment Project for Homeless Women with Children, 1325 S. Wabash, Suite 205, Chicago, IL 60605-2504. (312) 435-4548.

For a list of the cooperating shelters, please contact the Chicago Coalition for the Homeless (see above).

National Assembly of Religious Women (NARW). 529 S. Wabash, Room 404, Chicago, IL 60605. (312) 663-1980.

WOMEN AND SOCIAL ACTION: CLASS 19
Connecting the Issues

 Before you read this Chapter of the Study Guide

Read Sharon Hartman Strom, "Florence Luscomb, for Suffrage, Labor, and Peace," in Ellen Cantarow, Chp. 1, **Moving the Mountain**

I. INTRODUCTION

JOURNAL ASSIGNMENT

> Select any three issues we have addressed in this class and discuss the interrelationships you see among these issues. Briefly discuss a social action in which you have participated or could participate which would deal in some way with these three issues.

Florence Luscomb was a dedicated, committed social activist who worked on many social issues during her lifetime. In reading about her life, we get a glimpse of the combination of factors which give rise to and sustain social activism. Though Florence Luscomb worked on a variety of issues, all her work represented a passion for social justice. Florence Luscomb, like many of her activist contemporaries, was committed to understanding the larger picture and seeing connections among issues.

We see this same dedication to understanding the larger picture in different eras of the women's movement. In the "Declaration of Sentiments and Resolutions" of the first Woman's Rights Convention in Seneca Falls, New York in July 1848, the convention members linked women's oppression to laws, the electoral process, marriage, divorce, work, morality, government, property, education, religion, and self-respect.

Early manifestos of the women's liberation movement also identified multiple issues facing women. For example, in the Redstockings Manifesto of 1969 the roots of women's oppression were seen in women's exploitation as workers, mothers, sex objects, and housewives. The Manifesto identified the need to challenge class, race, education, and other social statuses which divide women. The Southern Female Rights Union Program for Female Liberation of the late 1960s outlined a program for ending sexism which would deal with issues, such as childcare, education, health care, wages, discrimination in employment, self-defense, birth control, and the media. Older Women's Liberation (OWL) demanded a series of programs including wages for housework, divorce referral, transitional communes, job training, employment services, child care, and health care.

Flora Davis (1991) gives an overview of the issues feminists have worked on into the 1990s, including abortion, politics, education, health, heterosexism, family, violence, work, and poverty. In "Women and Social Action, we see the additional issues of leadership, socialization, child care, body image, food, motherhood, sterilization abuse, religion, sexual harassment, housing, homelessness, crime, prostitution, and self defense.

The connections made among these issues vary within political frameworks as do the goals and methods of social change. A way that I have connected all these issues in my political framework has been to explain their relationship to the oppression and transformation of women's bodies. My work in self-defense is the most recent example of a way I have found to link these issues and to work to create opportunities for women to change the conditions of their lives.

The goal for this session is not to advocate a particular political analysis, but to encourage each of you to seek an understanding of the ways in which one issue is related to others and to figure out how this understanding will influence your choice of social actions. The idea is to find a starting point for connecting issues that makes sense for you; to see issues in relationship to each other; and to make choices for social action that offer a manageable way to challenge the many forces that maintain women's oppression.

II. CLASS THEMES

- Exploring ways to connect issues
- Choosing issues on which to work
- Dealing with multiple issues through social action

III. VIDEOTAPE SYNOPSIS

- Overview of connecting the issues
- Discussion of Florence Luscomb and connecting issues
- Video visit with Dihya Al Kahina and Judy Vaughan, National Coordinating Team, National Assembly of Religious Women
- Interview and class discussion with Maha Jarad, Director of Women in Organizing Project, Women United for a Better Chicago and Program Development Coordinator, Union of Palestinian Women's Association

IV. VIDEOTAPE COMMENTARY

A. Overview of connecting the issues

I give a quick overview of the multiple issues we have addressed in this course so far and review the key themes for Class 19.

B. Class discussion of Florence Luscomb and connecting issues

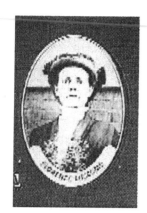

"There is nothing in the world that is so transitory and fragile as a snow-flake, and there is nothing so irresistible as an avalance, which is simply millions of snowflakes.

So that if each one of us, little snowflakes, just does our part, we will be an irresistible force."

Florence Luscumb

We open this discussion with a look at Florence Luscomb's comment about the power of many. What do you see as the key ideas reflected in the quote in the graphic?

Joe, Ada, Judy, and Sharon comment on the important contributions Florence Luscomb makes to

138

our understanding of ways to connect issues. Joan noted that Florence Luscomb devoted her whole life to organizing. She asks what we each can do in our own lives. What do we learn from Florence Luscomb that offers some insights into Joan's question?

Claudia raises a question about the label "suffragette." Mary, Helen, and Ada comment on their perception of what the term means. As a follow-up to the class, I found that the term "suffragette" was used by the media of the day to trivialize the suffrage movement in Great Britain. Christabel Pankhurst and other women in the suffrage movement claimed it as a symbol of pride (Kramarae and Treichler, 1992).

C. Video visit with Dihya Al Kahina and Judy Vaughan, National Coordinating Team, National Assembly of Religious Women (NARW)

The National Assembly of Religious Women is a social justice organization which works on multiple issues with a goal of making connections among issues. Whether their particular focus is on homelessness, economic justice, sexual harassment, religious oppression, or other concerns, they make connections among issues and challenge sexism, racism, and heterosexism.

Dihya and Judy give us an overview of the National Assembly of Religious Women, an example of one of their projects, and the rewards and challenges of their work. What are the key ideas you hear in their comments? Judy mentions the impact the phrase "stuck like a washrag in your throat" had on her figuring out what issues on which to work. What does this phrase mean to you?

D. Interview and class discussion with Maha Jarad, Director of Women in Organizing Project, Women United for a Better Chicago and Program Development Coordinator, Union of Palestinian Women's Association

Maha Jarad has over a decade of organizing experience on multiple issues, multiple levels, and with multiple groups. In her work as the Director of Women in Organizing Project for Women United for a Better Chicago as well as the Program Development Coordinator for the Union of Palestinian Women's Association, Maha works to bring diverse groups of women together to work on a variety of issues. In particular, she works with a variety of groups advocating for a just and lasting peace in the Middle East. Her own life and work are an excellent example of connecting issues.

Maha tells us about her background in communications and organizing. How did her early work in student government introduce her to the importance of seeing connections among issues? How has her experience as a Palestinian woman influenced her in seeing connections among issues? Maha briefly addresses the importance of offering programs in the communities you want to reach. What issues does she identify as influencing women's participation in social action?

Maha tells us about her perspective on the relationship between the personal and the political. Helen asks Maha to develop this idea more by commenting upon the role of women in Islam. Maha connects Islam, political authority, and social change in her response. What do you see as her perspective on "the personal is political"?

In response to Peg's question about why Maha is one of the 100 women in Chicago to watch and what her work for Women United is, Maha again covers myriad issues. A theme throughout is connecting ways to do educational work and political work in diverse communities on multiple issues. What are some of the issues she addresses? What connections do you see among these issues. She also addresses the issue of burnout. How does she see working to connect issues as a way to avoid burnout?

Maha also gives us a brief background on the history of Women United for a Better Chicago. We learn that connecting issues was a central idea of this organization. What do we learn about the political climate within which Women United was developed?

Mary asks Maha to tell us about how she decides to what to give her time. What does Maha tell us about her decision-making process? Jan, Phyllis, Helen, and Janet raise questions for Maha concerning her views and experience as a Palestinian woman. In response to their questions, we hear how she was expelled from the West Bank and how that felt to her. We hear her views on foreign policy and ideas about how to talk with others about the Palestinian people. Since Maha met with us, there have been major developments in the Middle East. Based on what she said here, what reactions do you think she might have to these changes?

Maha's wide-ranging discussion demonstrates the complexity of connecting issues, the need to consider individual as well as global issues, and the importance of beginning with our own life circumstances.

 Now watch the videotape.

V. REVIEW QUESTIONS

1. What issues has Florence Luscomb tackled in her organizing work?

2. What are key themes in Florence Luscomb's work?

3. What are some examples of her work that demonstrate her ability to make connections among issues?

4. What were important experiences and influences in her life?

5. Identify ways to connect issues through social action.

6. Identify suggestions for how to choose issues on which to work.

7. How does the sociological imagination or the idea of "the personal is political" relate to the ability to connect issues?

8. What does it mean to begin social action where you are?

VI. INTERVIEW EXCERPT

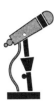

How we connect one issue to another is influenced by historical, social, and political factors. Irene Campos Carr, Coordinator of Women's Studies at Northeastern Illinois University, addresses several issues and how they are influenced by point-of-view. She first discusses how the social and political context influences whether the descriptor Latino, Hispanic, or a specific national origin is used. She then compares issues of class and color and patriarchy and machismo in Latin America and the United States.

Irene Campos Carr:

Most people who are not Latino wonder, okay so what's "Latino" or "Hispanic?" Both "Latino" and "Hispanic" are umbrella words, I like to call them, generics, in order to encompass all of the people who have a Latin-American origin; that is the Caribbean and Latin America. Latin America, of course, comprising Mexico on down to Argentina and Cuba and then the Caribbean Islands. So that "Latino" is preferred by many of us simply because it is was a name that we've more or less adopted ourselves. "Hispanic' is a word that was adopted by the government in order to build a political block that could be counted during the census. Now most of us prefer, of course, our own nationalities. I'm Nicaraguan by origin. My parents are Nicaraguan and I was born in Chicago but grew up in Nicaragua and El Salvador so that you know I'm Central American. Then we have the Chicano — Mexican-American. "Chicano" is a term that developed in the Southwest and the West. However, here in the Midwest you can find very few people, either men or women, who call themselves Chicanos because that connotes something more militant and it isn't something that they would label themselves. But the rest of Puerto Ricans, Nicaraguans, Cubans and so on among ourselves, we use our own national label but for the society at large we say why yes, we're Latinos.

At times Latin Americans that come to this country are upper middle-class professionals and will not understand Latino issues. Then there is certainly a conflict because Mexican-Americans and Puerto Ricans have had a completely different experience in coming from Latin America so that indeed there can be conflict. If we have someone, a Latin American, who presumes to take over, then it's a class difference.

In Latin America structured class differences are of the most profound importance. I think in the United States we tend to think that there are no class differences. It would be foolish to think that there aren't; however, cutting across classes is much easier here than in Latin America. Over here we want the classic Cinderella story, you know, the young woman growing up in a poor neighborhood who marries a wealthy person. That's kind of a fairy tale anyhow, but nevertheless we see a lot more cross-overs, from working class families to upper-middle class families—through marriage, through professional associations, etc. In Latin America I've always said that class supercedes color, whereas in the United States color supercedes economics, class, and everything else. In Latin America, class affects structures so that the poor would be in one category, the lower-middle class would be another category, and certainly upper-middle class would be a different one. I will admit to having grown up in an upper-middle class environment, not knowing much about the suffering of the people in my country. I had to come to the United States to awaken, to have a true consciousness-raising as to what the community was all about and the prejudice in the United States against people of Latin American origin. But the class consciousness in Latin America is extraordinary, that's why socialism is what we all talk about. And class struggle is what we talk about, because what we need is to do away with the class system which rules the population.

Another issue is patriarchy. I think that "patriarchy" is the word for the whole world. In Latin America for instance, the manifestation of our culture is the so-called "machismo"; however, "macho" and "machismo" are widely misunderstood in the United States. To begin with, let's define what the word "macho" means. In Spanish the word "macho" is simply a male animal. In English we don't have that word. In Latin America it means virility and, boy, I doubt if you will find a female in Latin America or one who has come here recently who's not going to say "I like my men really macho." What they mean is somebody virile and masculine. I'm not saying that to be macho is positive, I'm simply saying that there is a sexism inherent in Latin American society that is probably much more visible; however, here in the United States we have many subtle ways of being very macho. And we have such a macho society here in the United States but we pretend often that we don't. We like to ascribe all of the evils of machismo to the Mexicans and Puerto Ricans. But a Senator addressing women who come to testify before the Congress and who says "Well, how are you lovely ladies and what do you have to say about yourselves?" is just as utterly sexist as any macho Latin American who says "Well, you know where you belong."

VII. SOURCES AND FURTHER READING

Adamson, Nancy, Linda Briskin, and Margaret McPhail. 1988. "Constructing a Framework," Section II. *Feminists Organizing For Change: The Contemporary Women's Movement in Canada.* Toronto: Oxford University Press.

Beck, Evelyn Torton. 1992. "From 'kike' to 'jap': how misogyny, anti-semitism, and racism construct the 'Jewish American Princess.'" Pp. 88 - 95 in *Race, Class, and Gender: An Anthology*, edited by Margaret L. Andersen and Patricia Hill Collins. Belmont, CA: Wadsworth Publishing Company.

Blood, Peter, Alan Tuttle, and George Lakey. 1992. "Understanding and fighting sexism: a call to men." Pp. 134 - 140 in *Race, Class, and Gender: An Anthology,* edited by Margaret L. Andersen and Patricia Hill Collins. Belmont, CA: Wadsworth Publishing Company.

Chow, Esther. 1987. "The development of gender consciousness among Asian American women." *Gender & Society*, 1(September): 4 - 10.

Collins, Patricia Hill. 1989. "The social construction of black feminist thought." *Signs*, 14 (4): 745 - 773.

Cordoba, Teresa. 1993. *Chicana Voices: Intersections of Class, Race, and Gender*. Austin: CMAS.

Davis, Angela. 1989. *Women, Culture, and Politics*. NY: Random House.

Davis, Barbara Hillyer. 1984. "Women, disability, and feminism: notes toward a new theory." *Frontiers* VIII (1): 1 - 5.

Divine, Donna Robinson. 1985. "Palestinian Arab women and their reveries of emancipation." Pp. 57 -83 in *Women Living Change*, edited by Susan C. Bourque and Donna Robinson Divine. Philadelphia, PA: Temple University Press.

Essed, Philomena. 1990. *Everyday Racism: Reports from Women of Two Cultures.* Alameda, CA: Hunter House Inc. Publishers.

Haj, Samira. 1992. "Palestinian women and patriarchal relations." *Signs:Journal of Women in Culture and Society* 17: 761 - 778.

Higginbotham, Elizabeth. 1992. "We were never on a pedestal: women of color continue to struggle with poverty, racism, and sexism." Pp. 183 - 190 in *Race, Class, and Gender: An Anthology*, edited by Margaret L. Andersen and Patricia Hill Collins. Belmont, CA: Wadsworth Publishing Company.

Kramarae, Cheris and Paula A. Treichler (eds.). 1992. "Suffragette." *Amazons, Bluestockings, and Crones: A Feminist Dictionary.* London: Pandora Press.

McIntosh, Peggy. 1992. "White privilege and male privilege: a personal account of coming to see correspondence through work in women's studies." Pp. 70 - 81 in *Race, Class, and Gender: An Anthology,* edited by Margaret L. Andersen and Patricia Hill Collins. Belmont, CA: Wadsworth Publishing Company.

Smith, Barbara. 1993. "Homophobia: why bring it up?" Pp. 99 -109 in *The Lesbian and Gay Studies Reader*, edited by Henry Abelove, Michèle Aina Barale, David M. Halperin. NY: Routledge.

Stephens, Richard C., George T. Oscar, and Zena Smith Blau. 1980. "To be aged, Hispanic, and female." Pp. 249 -258 in *Twice a Minority: Mexican American Women,* edited by Margarita B. Melville. St. Louis: The C.V. Mosby Company.

Susser, Ida. 1988. "Working-class women, social protest, and changing ideologies." Pp. 257 - 271 in *Women and the Politics of Empowerment,* edited by Ann Bookman and Sandra Morgen. Philadelphia, PA: Temple University Press.

Tanner, Leslie B. 1970. *Voices from Women's Liberation.* NY: New American Library.

West, Guida and Rhoda Lois Blumberg. 1990. "Reconstructing social protest from a feminist perspective." *Women and Social Protest.* NY: Oxford University Press.

Whitt, Shirley Hill. 1984. "Native women today: sexism and the Indian woman." Pp. 23 - 31 in *Feminist Frameworks,* second edition, edited by Allison Jaggar and Paula Rothenberg. NY: McGraw-Hill.

VIII. ORGANIZATIONS

National Assembly of Religious Women (NARW). 529 S. Wabash, Room 404, Chicago, IL 60605. (312) 663-1980.

Union of Palestinian Women's Association. 3148 W. 63rd Street. Chicago, IL 60629. (773) 436-6060.

Women United for a Better Chicago. (now dissolved)

Women's Studies Program, Northeastern Illinois University. 5500 N. St. Louis Ave., Chicago, IL 60625. (773) 583-4050, ext. 3308.

WOMEN AND SOCIAL ACTION: CLASS 20
Violence Against Women

 Before you read this Chapter of the Study Guide

Read Andersen, "Violence in the Family," pp. 174 -178; "Women as Victims of Crime," pp. 266 -274.

JOURNAL
ASSIGNMENT

> In recent years public awareness of violence in family and interpersonal relationships has increased. Awareness has also increased about the high incidence of rape. Describe your fear of violence or actual experience of violence and how this fear or experience has affected other life experiences.

I. INTRODUCTION

It was 1964. I was in high school. I returned to school one day because I had left a book I needed in my locker. As I rounded the corner of a darkened hallway to go to my locker, I saw one of my friends reeling against the wall from a strike she had just taken from her boyfriend. They both turned as I gasped. She soundlessly whispered, "It's all right." I turned and fled down the steps. I never told anyone and we never talked about it. Even as I write these words, I ask myself, "Did I really see him hit her?" "Did I really turn and leave her?" "Did I really never say a word?"

My response reflects the microcosm of challenges we face in talking about violence against women. Horrible acts of violence are committed by ordinary men and, therefore, we may question their existence. Even when we see violence with our own eyes or experience violence to our own bodies, many of us remain silent rather than seek support, offer help, or intervene.

In Class 20, we explore the scope of violence against women. We look at statistics concerning rape, battery, and incest. We look at statistics about perpetrators and see that we are talking about crimes against women committed by men. We see these crimes are often committed by men who are the husbands, boyfriends, fathers, brothers, uncles, and grandfathers of the women they attack. We see that women seldom report these crimes and even more rarely are men convicted. We see that experiencing violence has longterm and negative consequences for women. We also see that the fear of violence shapes women's lives in many ways, including the hours and places women may choose to work, the leisure activities women engage in, how women walk down the street, what clothes women choose to wear, and women's actions in their own homes. We hear that violence against women is embedded in language, social institutions, and social relationships.

Facing the reality of violence against women is an important step toward ending violence. In addition to developing theories, research, and educational programs about violence, activists have worked to change social structures and social ideologies which perpetuate violence against women and to provide support and concrete services for women who have experienced violence. Efforts have included: rewriting laws about rape, battery, and incest; working with police departments, the courts, and hospitals to advocate for women who are victims of violence; developing rape crisis centers, battered women shelters, and underground networks to provide direct services for victims of violence; examining prostitution and pornography; and developing self-defense programs. In later sessions we will focus on prostitution, the clemency movement for battered women imprisoned for killing their attackers, and the self-defense movement.

In Class 20, we will focus on shelters for battered women and the holistic services women and children need. Ranjana Bhargava and Lee Maglaya will also address the challenges facing immigrant women who are in violent relationships and the multi-cultural services needed to provide adequate support for all women.

II. CLASS THEMES

- The difficulties in recognizing and discussing the scope of violence against women
- Understanding different perspectives on violence against women
- Actions to deal with and to challenge violence against women

III. VIDEOTAPE SYNOPSIS

- Overview of the issue of violence against women
- Class discussion of experiences and perspectives on violence against women
- Video visit with Stephanie Riger, co-author of *The Female Fear*, Coordinator of Women's Studies, University of Illinois in Chicago
- Interview and class discussion with Ranjana Bhargava and Lee Maglaya, Apna Ghar, Chicago

IV. VIDEOTAPE COMMENTARY

A. Overview of the issue of violence against women

I open Class 20 with acknowledgement of the range of feelings people may experience as we discuss violence against women. To set the stage for our discussion, I review statistics about the extent of violence, perpetrators, reporting and conviction rates, and longterm consequences of violence against women.

B. Class discussion of experiences and perspectives on violence against women

Claudia leads off our discussion with a comment she heard a prominent politician make about rape. Judy, Gunther, and Gail offer their interpretations of how this comment condones rape. What is your reaction to the comment?

Gunther makes a comment regarding the "sickness" of violence. He and Debbie offer different views on whether people are or society is "sick." How do their viewpoints reflect contrasting perspectives on the roots of violence? Where do you stand? What are the benefits and limits of using the concept of "sickness" to describe violence against women?

Joe, Peg, and Christine offer differing ideas about sources of violence. Is it lack of punishment, cultural glorification of violence, or lack of education? Think about how these differing viewpoints suggest different social actions. Jan raises a question about cross-cultural differences in rates of violence. Mary offers a viewpoint on these statistics that suggests they may not reflect an accurate picture of violence. What are possible cross-cultural variations that might affect statistical data?

Christine and Gail discuss their own experiences with violence. What have they done to educate others about date rape? Ada raises other issues about how cultural definitions concerning sexuality and responsibility affect our views of rape. Think about your own views on sexuality and responsibility. How do they relate to your views on rape?

C. Video visit with Stephanie Riger, Coordinator of Women's Studies at University of Illinois in Chicago and co-author of *The Female Fear*

Margaret Gordon and Stephanie Riger investigated a previously neglected topic: women's fear of rape. Through surveys and extensive indepth interviews of women and men in U.S. cities, they carefully and systematically documented the pervasive and longterm effects of fear on women's lives. Their groundbreaking research showed that women's full participation in society is limited by their experience and fear of rape.

Stephanie Riger gives us an overview of their research. What did they find about women's fear of crime and rape? How does this affect women's experience? Stephanie also talks about the ways rape is built into our culture and what women need to have a sense of safety. What does she identify as the basics women need?

D. Interview and class discussion with Ranjana Bhargava, Executive Director, and Lee Maglaya, Board Member, Apna Ghar, a shelter for victims of domestic violence

Apna Ghar was founded in 1989 as the first residential shelter in the U.S. serving women of Asian origins who are victims of domestic violence. Along with Prem Sharma, Kanta Khipple, and Frances Kung, Ranjana Bhargava and Lee Maglaya founded Apna Ghar. Apna Ghar comes from a Hindi-Urdu phrase meaning "Our Home." Apna Ghar developed in response to increased reports about violence occurring in Asian American immigrant families. In addition to the temporary shelter for women and children who are seeking protection from violence, Apna Ghar offers a 24-hour crisis hotline, peer support groups, multi-lingual and multi-cultural counseling and referral service, social service advocacy, and legal advocacy. Apna Ghar also offers broad community services and advocacy, including: educational and public awareness programs on domestic violence, research and internship programs, volunteer opportunities, networking, a progressive voice within the Asian American community, and cultural sensitivity trainings.

Lee Maglaya, in addition to serving on the Apna Ghar Board, is Race Relations, Research and Advocacy Coordinator for Asian Human Services of Chicago. She gives us a brief overview of experiences which inspired Apna Ghar. What does she mean by "underground safe homes?" Ranjana elaborates on the experiences which inspired Apna Ghar and tells us about the founders of Apna Ghar and the response they received when they brought the issue of domestic violence to the Asian American community. What does she tell us about that response and the struggle for setting up the shelter? How did they take matters in their own hands?

In response to a question Ada raised about deaths from battery, Ranjana talked about dowry deaths and an organization in India called "Helping Hands." What do we learn about dowry deaths and the Helping Hands strategy?

Gail asks about the support Ranjana and Lee receive from the men in their lives for their work with Apna Ghar. What do we learn about the ways in which men can support women activists? In response to Lee's comment about immigrant women receiving a booklet of their civil rights when they arrive in the United States, Judy asks for information about the legalities facing

147

women who marry in another country and are divorced here. What do we learn about the particular challenges facing immigrant women who are abused?

In response to Peg's questions about how people hear about Apna Ghar and Gunther's comments about their bittersweet successes, Ranjana and Lee talk about public speaking, volunteers, and new programs. What do you learn about Apna Ghar's community connections and commitments from their comments?

In summary, I identify some key areas to consider when thinking about violence against women and social action. What are these key areas?

 Now watch the videotape.

V. REVIEW QUESTIONS

1. How has violence been used to control women?

2. What are the pitfalls of gender neutral language when talking about violence?

3. What are some common characteristics in families where incest occurs?

4. How do data on rape show the connection between rape and women's status in society?

5. What are some key findings concerning date rape?

6. Compare and contrast theories of rape: psychological theories, subculture of violence, gender socialization theory, and political economic theory. Illustrate with examples from comments of class members, Stephanie Riger, Ranjava Bhargava, and Lee Maglaya.

7. What are key findings about the scope of violence in U.S. society, perpetrators of violence, reporting and conviction rapes, and long-term consequences of violence against women? What are some limitations with statistical evidence about violence?

8. What are the benefits and limits of shelters for victims of domestic violence? What is meant by a holistic approach?

9. How are religion, culture, and the law involved in perpetuating violence against women?

10. What are ways that Apna Ghar benefits the larger community?

VI. INTERVIEW EXCERPT

> Pam Wilson, Office Manager at the time of the interview, and Radhika Sharma, Legal Advocate/Community Educator, Apna Ghar, both work directly with women who have been abused. They each talk about the challenges and rewards in doing anti-violence work.

A. Interview with Pam Wilson

Martha: What are some of the challenges in working with women who have been battered?

Pam: It's very emotionally exhausting. When I first worked here I was the only staff member for three months and it seemed like I kept taking my work home with me. You always start thinking about the clients, you start thinking, "I wonder if she's okay," especially if they go back to their husbands. I know I was having nightmares about a girl who did go back to her husband so I find that it is very challenging. You're always wanting to make their lives better but you can't make their decisions for them. You have to give them different solutions and different ways that they can handle it but they have to make the decision in the end. And it's always hard to distance yourself from them and say okay, it's her decision. I think that's one of the parts that's challenging and another thing is, since we are such a small staff, we end up doing a lot of things whether it be paper work, administrative work as well as counseling so it's all rolled up in one. You can't make distinct job descriptions so that it takes a toll on you—it does.

Martha: What are some of the rewards?

Pam: There are quite a bit. When you see a woman who came to you all shattered and had no self-esteem and now she's got her own job, she's got a place to stay. Some are even working two jobs, going to school and seeing that they're on their own. They usually don't come back to you very often after that; except to tell you when something good happens to them and that really is good. And we're very close to the children. The children love coming here and we love watching them grow. Many still feel a great bond with the staff members.

B. Interview with Radhika Sharma

Martha: What have been some of the challenges that you've faced since you've been involved here?

Radhika: There are a number of challenges for those of us working at Apna Ghar. There are community challenges. We're having to face sexism which is deeply, deeply ingrained in our culture. We come from a culture which for many reasons discriminates against females. We come from a culture which at one point practiced infanticide on female babies. We come from a culture where a daughter has a very different role than the son in the family in terms of her position of power and prestige; where violence is considered all right in some families; where even if it's disapproved of, people aren't going to speak out against it. We come across a lot of ingrained sexism within our culture. Women who are afraid to speak out. Women who are sometimes victimized by other women; a daughter-in-law by a mother-in-law, often there's a power struggle there, that's something that we've had to face. We have to deal not with just the individual. When you marry into an Asian family, you marry a family, you just don't marry an individual. So it gets even larger and more complex. We also have to deal with a larger system which poses a number of challenges. At this point, many women feel as though the legal system is stacked against them. It's very difficult to obtain the protection that you need. Right now there's nothing, there's no protection, there's no actual physical barrier which will prevent a man from abusing her. And I refer to this as a man against a woman because 95% of the domestic violence cases are perpetrated by a man against a woman. An order of protection can be somewhat effective but it's really limited. So we face cultural as well as systemic challenges in trying to assist our clients and/or clients trying to help themselves.

Martha: What have been the rewards for you?

Radhika: The rewards are multiple. One client with whom we worked very closely has found a great sense of empowerment and involvement since she has chosen to leave her abuser and has stepped away from the abuse and has helped herself and her child. She's a nurse and she's been able to speak out against injustices that she sees, not just domestic violence related, but even on her own job which is very affirming to see; the sense that I can take some control and I can speak out against injustice on a personal level. Children who can finally sleep. They're still plagued by memories of the violence. There's one boy who wrote a poem and he said now my beautiful mother can finally sleep peacefully at night. There are women who gain a sense of independence which they were denied by their abuser; women who are now going on to pursue an education and a career which they were not allowed to do by their abuser. So those are some of the rewards we see, people whose lives are changed and are improved and who touch again that sense of joy and independence which they were denied.

VII. SOURCES AND FURTHER READING

Thanks to Shelley Bannister for her list of recommendations for further reading.

Armstrong, Louise. 1987. *Kiss Daddy Goodnight: Ten Years Later.* NY: Simon and Schuster.

Barry, Kathleen. 1979. *Female Sexual Slavery.* Englewood Cliffs, NJ: Prentice Hall.

Bart, Pauline. 1979. "Rape as a paradigm of sexism in society—victimization and its discontents." *Women's Studies International Quarterly,* 2: 347 - 357.

Bart, Pauline, Patricia Y. Miller, Elizabeth Moran, and Elizabeth Stanko (eds.). 1989. "Special Issue: Violence Against Women." *Gender & Society* 3 (4).

Bass, Ellen and Laura Davis. 1988. *The Courage to Heal: A Guide for Women Survivors of Sexual Abuse.* NY: Harper and Row.

Belknap, Joanne. 1992. "Perceptions of woman battering." *The Changing Role of Women in the Criminal Justice System,* second edition, edited by Imogene L. Moyer. Prospect, IL: Waveland Press.

Burt, Martha R. 1980. "Cultural myths and supports for rape." *Journal of Personality and Social Psychology* 38:217-230.

Cantrell, Leslie. 1986. *Into the Light: A Guide for Battered Women.* Edmonds, WA: The Charles Franklin Press.

Davis, Angela. 1975. *Violence Against Women and the Ongoing Challenge to Racism.* NY: Women of Color Press.

Davis, Flora 1991. " Violence Against Women;" chapter 15. *Moving the Mountain: The Women's Movement in America Since 1960.* NY: Touchstone.

Dobash, R.E. and R. Dobash. 1979. *Violence Against Wives.* NY: Free Press.

Dworkin, Andrea. 1974. *Woman Hating.* NY: E.P. Dutton.

Dworkin, Andrea and Catherine A. MacKinnon. 1988. *Pornography and Civil Rights: A New Day for Women's Equality.* To order, send $5.00 to Organizing Against Pornography, 734 East Lake Street, #300 West, Minneapolis, MN 55407.

Frieze, I.H. 1983. "Investigating the causes and consequences of marital rape." *Signs* 8 (Spring): 532- 553.

Gordon, Linda. 1992. "Family violence, feminism, and social control." Pp. 262 - 286 in *Rethinking the Family: Some Feminist Questions*, second edition, edited by Barrie Thorne with Marilyn Yalom. Boston: Northeastern University Press.

Gordon, Margaret T. and Stephanie Riger. 1989. *The Female Fear.* NY: Free Press.

Griffin, Susan. 1979. *Rape: The Power of Consciousness.* NY: Harper and Row.

Grothaus, Rebecca S. 1985. "Abuse of women with disabilities." Pp. 124 - 128 in *With the Power of Each Breath: A Disabled Women's Anthology*, edited by Susan E. Browne, Debra Connors, and Nanci Stern. Pittsburgh, PA: Cleis Press.

Kishwar, Madhu and Ruth Vanita (eds.). 1984. *In Search of Answers: Indian Women's Voices from Manushi.* London: Zed Press.

Kokopeli, Bruce and George Lakey. 1992. "More power than we want: masculine sexuality and violence." Pp. 443 - 449 in *Race, Class, and Gender: An Anthology*, edited by Margaret L. Andersen and Patricia Hill Collins. Belmont, CA: Wadsworth Publishing Company.

Lerner, Gerda. 1972. "The rape of black women as a weapon of terror." Pp. 172 - 193 in Gerda Lerner (ed) *Black Women in White America: A Documentary History.* NY: Vintage.

Levy, Barrie (ed.). 1991. *Dating Violence: Young Women in Danger.* Seattle, WA: Seal Press.

Lobel, Kerry. 1986. *Naming the Violence: Speaking Out About Lesbian Battering.* Seattle, WA: Seal Press.

Martin, Del. 1983. *Battered Wives.* NY: Simon and Schuster.

Martin, Patricia Yancey and Robert A. Hummer. 1992. "Fraternities and rape on campus." Pp. 413 - 429 in *Race, Class, and Gender: An Anthology*, edited by Margaret L. Andersen and Patricia Hill Collins. Belmont, CA: Wadsworth Publishing.

Muraskin, Roslyn and Ted Alleman (eds.). 1993. "Women: Victims of Violence," Section 7. *It's A Crime: Women and Justice.* Englewood Cliffs, NJ: Regents/Prentice Hall.

Radford, Jill and Diana E.H. Russell (eds.). 1992. *Femicide: The Politics of Woman Killing.* NY: Twayne.

Russell, Diana E. 1986. *The Secret Trauma: Incest in the Lives of Girls and Women.* NY: Basic Books.

Sanday, Peggy Reeves. 1990. *Fraternity Gang Rape: Sex, Brotherhood, and Privilege on Campus.* NY: New York University Press.

Schechter, Susan. 1982. *Women and Male Violence: The Struggles of the Battered Women's Movement.* Boston: South End Press.

Scully, Diana. 1991. *Understanding Sexual Violence: A Study of Convicted Rapists.* London: Harper Collins Academic.

Stanko, Elizabeth. 1990. *Everyday Violence: How Women and Men Experience Sexual and Physical Danger.* London: Pandora Press.

"Violence Against Women." 1992. Pp. 131 - 150 in Boston Women's Health Book Collective. *The New Our Bodies, Ourselves: a Book by and for Women.* NY: Simon and Schuster.

Walker, Lenore E. 1979. *The Battered Woman.* NY: Harper and Row.

Warshaw, Robin. 1988. *I Never Called It Rape: The Ms. Report on Recognizing, Fighting, and Surviving Date and Acquaintance Rape.* NY: Harper and Row.

White, Evelyn. 1985. *Chain Chain Change: Black Women Dealing with Physical and Emotional Abuse.* Seattle, WA: Seal Press.

Women's Action Coalition (WAC). 1993. "Rape," "Sex industry," "Sexual harassment," and "Violence." Pp. 49 - 58 in *WAC Stats: The Facts About Women.* NY: The New Press.

Yllo, Kersti and Michele Bograd (eds.). 1988. *Feminist Perspectives on Wife Abuse.* Newbury Park, CA: Sage.

VIII. ORGANIZATIONS

Apna Ghar ["Our Home"]. 4753 N. Broadway, Suite 502, Chicago, IL 60640. (773) 334-4663

Asian Human Services of Chicago, Inc. 4753 N. Broadway, Suite 632, Chicago, IL 60640. (773) 728-2235.

Before you read this Chapter of the Study Guide

Read Andersen, "Women, Crime, and Deviance," chapter 9

JOURNAL
ASSIGNMENT

Describe a situation in which you or someone you know has been defined as deviant. Reflect on ways that gender expectations influenced this labeling process.

I. INTRODUCTION

A man who did odd jobs in my neighborhood seemed unusually despondent one day. As I talked with him about how things were going, he revealed the source of his deep depression. He had been walking down the street with his 10 year old daughter when a well-dressed man approached them and offered him $50 for an hour with his daughter. His outrage was overshadowed by his despair at how vulnerable his children were because of their poverty.

Like the movie of the same name, this was an "indecent proposal," but one that did not romanticize the buying of female bodies. The $50 "opportunity" he refused could have fed his family for a few days, could have gained them temporary shelter, or could have purchased clothes and supplies for his daughter to go to school. Though he believed he could protect them while they were young, he was deeply worried that his children had too little in their lives for them to resist the smiles and money of strangers.

In Class 21, we will focus on aspects of women's experience that are simultaneously romanticized and despised: prostitution, the killing of an abuser, and prison. Whether the image is of an independent, sassy, shameless woman thumbing her nose at rigid social conventions or a dependent, subservient, shameful woman getting herself into an awful mess, popular images of women who land in prison, kill their abusers, or sell sex are as off the mark as other popularized images of women.

In Class 21, we will look at these experiences through the eyes of women who have a realistic and complex understanding of prostitution, killing a batterer, and prison. We will see that a comprehensive understanding of women's experience of prostitution, murder, and prison cannot be gained without considering the social ideologies and social structures which perpetuate gender, race, and class inequality.

Jean Lachowitz, Executive Director of Genesis House, will tell us of the social systems which draw women into prostitution and make it difficult for them to leave. She will tell us of ways Genesis House creates support for women to leave prostitution. Leslie Brown, Director of Support Advocates for Women, will give us insight into the social factors which contribute to women killing their abusers. Shelley Bannister, Illinois Clemency Project for Battered Women, will address the social myths and structures which perpetuate gender, race, and class inequality in the criminal justice system and ways that the Illinois Clemency Project for Battered Women is attempting to override the system. As always, students in"Women and Social Action" will share their insights, questions, and comments to enhance our understanding of women in prostitution and women in prison.

II. CLASS THEMES

- Women in prostitution and in the jails are not "the other"
- Prostitution and the criminal justice system are influenced by systems of gender, race, and class
- Actions to deal with and challenge women's experience in prostitution and the criminal justice system

III. VIDEOTAPE SYNOPSIS

- Overview of women in prostitution and in prison
- Class discussion of social definitions of female deviancy and women's experience
- Video visit with Jean Lachowitz, Executive Director of Genesis House
- Class discussion of prostitution
- Video visit with Leslie Brown, Director, Support Advocates for Women... Both Inside and Outside Prison (S.A.W.)
- Interview and class discussion with Shelley Bannister, Illinois Clemency Project for Battered Women and Associate Professor of Criminal Justice and Women's Studies, Northeastern Illinois University

IV. VIDEOTAPE COMMENTARY

A. Overview of women in prostitution and women in prison

I make a brief statement about what it means to see women in prostitution and in prison as "the other." What does this mean to you? How does seeing prostitution and prison through the eyes of women differ from treating women as "the other?" What do the statistics about prostitution tell us?

B. Class discussion of social definitions of female deviancy and women's experience

How do Sharon and Judy define deviance and female deviancy? Claudia raises a question about why prostitutes get arrested and not the men who are involved. Gunther draws a comparison between prostitution and drug dealing. Claudia's and Gunther's comments stimulate a lively discussion. How do Judy, Mary, and Gail respond? Where do you stand?

C. Video visit with Jean Lachowitz, Executive Director, Genesis House,Chicago

Founded by Edwina Gateley in 1984, Genesis House is dedicated to offering hospitality and nurturing to all adult women in prostitution and to provide a place where they can make choices about whether or not to continue in prostitution. Genesis House assists those who want to leave prostitution by providing support and holistic services. Genesis House offers a residential program for four to five women on a long-term basis; a non-residential program offering a range of services; an outreach program to provide AIDS and health education and information about Genesis House to women on the streets and in the criminal justice system; a drop-in space for food, coffee, and talking; a pantry for food and clothing; and community education on prostitution.

Jean Lachowitz, Executive Director, gives us an overview of issues women in prostitution face, makes distinctions between legalization, decriminalization, and criminalization of prostitution, and discusses why prostitution is a feminist issue.

What are the major issues women in prostitution face? What are the distinctions between legalization, decriminalization, and criminalization of prostitution? What makes prostitution a feminist issue?

D. Class discussion of prostitution

Joe and Gunther make comments about where to place the blame for prostitution. What are differences in blaming individual female prostitutes, individual male customers, or the culture which perpetuates prostitution? Gail talks about a woman she knew who was a "call girl." What differences do you hear in her discussion in contrast to Jean Lachowitz's comments about the experiences of women in prostitution who work the streets?

E. Video visit with Leslie Brown, Director, Support Advocates for Women... Both Inside and Outside Prison (S.A.W.)

Leslie Brown served over ten years in prison for her involvement in the killing of her husband who battered her for years. Leslie tell us about her experience of being beaten and being imprisoned. Leslie was one of the first women in Illinois who was granted clemency for her involvement in the killing of her batterer. While serving time in prison, Leslie dedicated herself to helping women in prison while inside and once they got out. She is currently the Director of Support Advocates for Women. The mission of S.A.W. is to provide advocacy, transportation, referrals, and counseling for incarcerated and formerly incarcerated women and for their children. S.A.W. provides transportation for children to visit their mothers when they are in prison. [See the "Interview Exerpt" for more about Leslie Brown.]

What do we learn about the barriers women face in getting out of a battering relationship when there is no social support to do so?

F. Interview and class discussion with Shelley Bannister, Illinois Clemency Project for Battered Women and Associate Professor of Criminal Justice and Women's Studies, Northeastern Illinois University

Shelley Bannister is a highly dedicated attorney and teacher. She uses her extensive legal, academic, networking, and activist skills to advocate for justice for women. The Illinois Clemency Project for Battered Women is a network of attorneys and law students who do the legal research and advocacy needed to petition the governor for clemency.

Shelley gives us an overview of her background and tells us about the clemency process and what it requires. She also comments upon our discussion of women in prison and in prostitution. What do we learn about the clemency process? How has Shelley used her commitment and dedication on behalf of women?

Phyllis asks follow-up questions about Leslie Brown. Jan and Judy ask Shelley questions about self-defense in the case of battering. What do we learn about the different factors that judges consider? What is Shelley's view on the ways in which gender affects judges' decision-making?

In response to Gunther's comment about the source of the problem, Shelley talks about actions men need to take. What is Shelley's key point here? What does Shelley tell us in response to Janet's comment about what women do when their children are threatened with abuse? Carlos raises a question about programs available for women in prison. What do we learn from Shelley?

In response to Joe's question about differential penalties for women depending on the weapon they used to defend themselves against their abuser, Shelley addresses ways in which race, class, and how much it looked like self-defense influence the criminal justice process. How do race, class, and how much women's actions looked like self-defense influence the criminal justice process?

Gail and Debbie raise questions concerning women as victims and individual responsibility. Phyllis addresses the issue of what boys are taught. What point does Shelley make about learning to be victims and victimizers? In closing, Shelley addresses specific actions we can each take right now in our own lives to stop violence against women. What are the key actions she identifies?

 Now watch the videotape.

V. REVIEW QUESTIONS

1. What does Andersen mean by deviance? by a social labeling process? by crime?

2. What are conventional assumptions about female deviants that feminist scholars critique?

3. How does gender influence what happens in the courts? in the juvenile justice system? in the experience of prison?

4. What does it mean to see women in prostitution and in prison as "the other?" What does it mean to study prostitution through the eyes of prostitutes? to study women in prison through the eyes of women in prison?

5. What are the major issues women in prostitution face?

6. How do legalization, decriminalization, and criminalization of prostitution differ?

7. What makes prostitution a feminist issue? How does female socialization support prostitution and violence against women?

8. What is the clemency process? How does it work in the case of battering?

9. What are the implications for social action if we focus on individual responsibility, on culture, or on a combination of individual responsibility and culture to explain women in prostitution and in prison?

10. What are actions we can take right now to challenge the myths and experiences of women in prostitution and in prison?

V. INTERVIEW EXCERPT

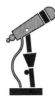

In the video visit with Leslie Brown, we heard her talk about the circum-stances that led to her imprisonment. In the interview excerpt below, Leslie talks about being in prison and her ongoing work with women inside and now outside of prison.

" Leslie Brown:

While I was sitting there in the Cook County Jail I had a chance to think about my life and as I sat there I contemplated suicide. I had just bought this building, I thought about my little chil-dren, my baby was only 4 months old and my other baby was 1. My only daughter at that time was 3. My other son was 8 and my oldest son was 9. I said those are my children, I never, ever have been separated from them. I've always been a mother. I've always been there and I said how is it going to feel for them to wake up and not have a mother there and not be there to comfort them when they cry, not be there to put them to bed, not be there to hug them. How are they going to understand that I'm not there? And I did contemplate suicide. I really did. And the Lord allowed my life to flash before me. He said you know, Leslie, when he hit you in the head with a pipe and tried to throw you off the third floor porch, I was there. He said when he took that knife and cut your coat and tried to stab you, he said I was there. He said I didn't allow him to take your life. He said you are unfortunate, yes, you're in jail, yes, you're away from the children but I spared your life for a reason. He said one day you'll be reunited with your chil-dren. He said just trust me. This gave me hope. At that moment my whole life changed. I fell on my knees and I asked God to forgive me. Forgive me for the thoughts that I had and at that time I became different in my thinking.

I was sentenced to 20 years in prison. And while I was in prison, God wouldn't allow me to have a pity party. He gave me strength. He told me to help others and reach out and I did. While I was there, when the women would come in on intake, I would share with them the things that I had. God blessed me to always have excess deodorant, soap and everything. And I would share with them that there is hope and I would invite them to come to church. It was fulfilling for me. Also while I was there I led an aerobics class for a year. I even started a class called CAT—Christian Action Team—and I would start going to the mental health unit and ministering to the women there. Sometimes the staff would even join in with us. We would sing songs and read scripture. Also while I was there I earned my license in cosmetology. I also earned 30 credit hours toward my bachelor's degree. It's not that I was happy with being away, it's just that I made a human error. Life goes on. You can't undo the past. You can only look forward to a better future. I knew one day I would be reunited with my children and I knew that I wanted to do something more than what I was doing before. And I also knew that women needed help, needed assistance and so the Lord made me strong so that I could reach out to someone else. And as I stressed to the women, it's our attitude as we go through. Sure it's painful, no one likes being away from their children. Any mother would know how painful it is to be away from her children, but we can't drown ourselves in self-pity. We should reach out and think about the future.

A lady referred me to Sister Margaret Allen Tracksler, she's the founder and executive director of the Institute of Women Today. I sat down and wrote her a letter stressing to her that my mother has all 6 of my children, and my mother's health is beginning to fail. Also that I felt it was time for me to do something legally to be reunited with my children. I also expressed to her that I had no funds and I would like to file for a clemency. She called the Institute, talked to some of the staff about me and she wrote me and said yes. I will send a lawyer to talk to you and she will help you. The lawyer's name is Peggy Burn. Peggy came and talked to me. She said, now Leslie I have to be very honest with you. Your chance of clemency is 1 out of a million. She said no one has received clemency for years and years and years. And I looked at her and I said, Peggy, I said if you would just do the paper work, my God will do the rest. After I was home, I received a call from the former warden. She called me to her office to see if I could establish a good relationship between mothers in prison and their children. Through God's grace and mercy we now transport the children once a month to see their mothers. Communication is so essential between a mother and child. Also we worked with the former prisoners to help find jobs and housing once they're released. We also work with the caregivers. We help the caregivers financially, and we give moral support. Last Thanksgiving we were able to take Thanksgiving baskets to the families that we transport and we will be doing that again this Thanksgiving. I'm also the former executive director of a shelter for homeless women and children. Many of the women, once they're released from prison, have nowhere to go. They have no one to go to. Many return back to prison because they go into the same environment. But they come to Maria's shelter where they can start their lives over. I thank God for the work that he is doing and that he is allowing me to reach out to others because that's really what life is all about. Not just self, but reaching out, and helping someone else.

VI. SOURCES AND FURTHER READING

Thanks to Shelley Bannister for recommendations for further reading.

Bannister, Shelley A. 1993. "Battered women who kill their abusers: their courtroom battles." Pp. 316 - 333 in *It's A Crime: Women and Justice*, edited by Roslyn Muraskin and Ted Alleman. Englewood Cliffs, NJ: Regents/Prentice Hall.

Barry, Kathleen. 1979. *Female Sexual Slavery*. Englewood Cliffs, NJ: Prentice-Hall.

Bergsmann, Ilene. R. 1991. "The forgotten few: juvenile female offenders. " Pp 496 - 507 in *The Dilemmas of Corrections: Contemporary Readings*, edited by Kenneth C. Hass and Geoffrey P. Alpert. Prospect Heights, IL: Waveland Press.

Browne, Angela. 1987. *When Battered Women Kill*. NY: Free Press.

Campbell, Anne. 1986. *The Girls in the Gang*. NY: Basil Blackwell.

Chesney-Lind, Meda and Randall G. Shelden. 1992. *Girls: Delinquency and Juvenile Justice*. Pacific Grove, CA: Brooks/Colege Publishing Company.

Chilton, Roland and Susan K. Datesman. 1987. "Gender, race, and crime: an analysis of urban arrest trends," 1960 - 1980. *Gender & Society* 1 (June): 152 - 171.

Gillespie, Cynthia K. 1989. *Justifiable Homicide: Battered Women, Self-Defense, and the Law.* Columbus, OH: Ohio State University Press.

Greene, Kenneth M. and Cathleen E. Chadwick. 1991. "Talking with incarcerated teens about dating violence." Pp. 142 - 150 in *Dating Violence: Young Women in Danger*, edited by Barrie Levy. Seattle, WA: Seal Press.

Harris, Jean. 1988. *They Always Call Us Ladies: Stories from Prison.* NY: Zebra Books/ Kensington Publishing.

Hass, Kenneth C. and Geoffrey P. Alpert (eds.). 1991. *The Dilemmas of Corrections: Contemporary Readings.* Prospect Heights, IL: Waveland Press.

Immarigeon, Russ and Meda Chesney-Lind. 1993. "Women's prisons: overcrowded and overused." Pp. 242 - 257 in *It's A Crime: Women and Justice*, edited by Roslyn Muraskin and Ted Alleman. Englewood Cliffs, NJ: Regents/Prentice Hall.

Jenness, Valerie. 1993. *Making It Work: The Prostitutes' Rights Movement in Perspective.* Hawthorne, NY: Aldine de Gruyter.

LeBlanc, Adrian Nicole. 1993. "I'm a shadow: the true story of a teenage prostitute." *Seventeen*, March: 212 - 218.

Lovelace, Linda. 1980. *Ordeal.* NY: Berkeley Books.

MacKinnon, Catherine. 1987. *Feminism Unmodified: Discourses on Life and Law.* Cambridge, MA: Harvard University Press.

Miller, JoAnn L. 1991. "Prostitution in Contemporary American Society." Pp. 45 - 57 in *Sexual Coercion: A Sourcebook on its Nature, Causes, and Prevention*, Elizabeth Grauerholz and Mary A. Koralewski, editors. Lexington, MA: Lexington Books.

Miller, Eleanor. 1986. *Street Women.* Philadelphia: Temple University Press.

Peacock, Carol Antoinette. 1981. *Hand-Me-Down Dreams.* NY: Schoclan Books.

Scheffler, Judith A. (ed.). 1986. *Wall Tappings: An Anthology of Writings by Women Prisoners.* Boston, MA: Northeastern University Press.

Shrage, L. 1989. "Should feminists oppose prostitution?" *Ethics* 99: 347 - 361.

Silbert, M.H. 1988. "Compounding factors in the rape of street prostitutes." Pp. 75 - 90 in *Rape and Sexual Assault*, edited by A. W. Burgess. NY: Garland Publishers.

Simon, Rita. 1975. *Women and Crime.* Lexington, MA: Lexington Book.

Walker, Lenore E. 1989. *Terrifying Love: Why Battered Women Kill and How Society Responds.* NY: Harper and Row.

Women's Action Coalition (WAC). 1993. "Prison" and "Sex industry." Pp. 46 - 48; 51 - 54 in *WAC STATS: The Facts About Women.* NY: The New Press.

VII. ORGANIZATIONS

Genesis House. 911 West Addison, Chicago, IL 60613. (773) 281-3917. Satellite Drop-in Center. 743 S. Sacramento, Chicago, IL.

Illinois Clemency Project for Battered Women. P.O.Box 257292, Chicago, IL 60625.

Maria Shelter. 7320 S. Yale Ave., Chicago, IL 60621. (773) 994-5350.

Support Advocates for Women...Both Inside and Outside Prison (S.A.W.). 9453 S. Ashland Avenue, Suite 14, Chicago, IL 60620.

Women's Action Coalition (WAC). P.O. Box 1862, Chelsea Station, New York, NY 10011. (212) 967-7711, ext. WACM (9226).

WOMEN AND SOCIAL ACTION: CLASS 22
Rape and Self-Defense

Before you read this Chapter of the Study Guide

Read "NCASA Guidelines for Choosing a Self-Defense Course,"
Appendix E, Study Guide

JOURNAL
ASSIGNMENT

Describe an experience you or someone you know has had with sexual assault. Describe what you or that person did to survive the assault, stop it, or prevent it. What recommendations would you make to women about preventing, stopping, or surviving a sexual assault?

I. INTRODUCTION

Among the first issues to emerge from the contemporary women's movement was recognition of the widespread incidence of rape and the need for self-defense. Over the last twenty years, researchers have documented women's and children's risks and fears of sexual assault. In response to the immediate needs of women and children to protect themselves, columnists, entrepreneurs, community groups, police officers, martial artists, and others have offered women advice about the best way to defend themselves from rape. However, the advice is often conflicting and confusing. Here is a sampling of the range of advice found in product advertisements, newspaper and magazine columns, and rape prevention brochures.

"Tired of being afraid of the dark? Tired of not being able to go out at night?"
"Tired of wondering who else might be in your home? Don't get a man. Get a
Dober-man."

"Those who get caught in a rape situation might discourage a rapist by
employing 'the big three' tactics—vomiting, defecating, and urinating."

"Scream and yell 'fire' to attrack quick attention."

"The all new pepper gas key ring. The best self-defense weapon for civilians."

"Purchase...a tiny device that can be concealed in an undergarment and is
totally sealed and odor-proof. If you are attacked the device can be instantly
activated, releasing a skunk essense so powerful the attacker is instantly
repelled."

"The best way to avoid being raped is to travel in groups."

"Carry a police whistle at all times."

"If attacked, eat grass so you will vomit."

"Always park over mud puddles so an attacker can't hide under your car."

Any of these products or tips may work in particular situations for some people, but how do you decide if these are for you or a situation you might find yourself in? Should you take a self-defense course or not? If you take a course, which one? Should you carry a device? If so, what is better; a gun, an alarm, a whistle, pepper gas? If you are attacked, what should you yell? If you are attacked, should you fight back? The questions and possible scenarios are endless. In Class 22 we will look at women's experiences with rape and self-defense. We will hear students in "Women and Social Action" talk about their experiences, their fears, and concerns about self-defense. We will hear from Pauline Bart, co-author of *Stopping Rape*, about the research she and Patricia O'Brien did on rape-avoidance. We will hear from Nancy Lanoue, a martial artist and self-defense instructor, talking about the range of life skills we can draw upon and use in our own defense. We will see women fighting in simulated rape scenarios against a padded assailant in IMPACT, a self-defense course for women and hear them talk about what effect self-defense training has had on them. I hope that Class 22 on Rape and Self-Defense will give you a framework for making your own decisions about self-defense.

II. CLASS THEMES

- Developing a broad definition of self-defense
- Developing an understanding of and appreciation for women's ability to defend themselves
- Understanding factors which contribute to effective self-defense
- Exploring the relationship between self-defense, martial arts, and the anti-violence movement

III. VIDEOTAPE SYNOPSIS

- Overview of self-defense
- Video visit with students in IMPACT: Self-Defense for Women
- Class discussion of self-defense
- Video visit with Pauline Bart, co-author of **Stopping Rape: Successful Survival Strategies,** Department of Psychiatry, University of Illinois at Chicago.
- Interview and class discussion with Nancy Lanoue, Co-director of Thousand Waves: Martial Arts and Self-defense for Women and Children

IV. VIDEOTAPE COMMENTARY

A. Overview of self-defense

I open the class session with the purposes of the class and a story about one of my experiences with self-defense. How do I define self-defense? Why do I say my story is an illustration of successful self-defense?

B. Video visit with students in IMPACT: Self-Defense for Women

We see the final class session of an IMPACT self-defense course which I was involved in teaching. During 24 hours of coursework, women have the opportunity to learn and practice self-defense skills in an emotionally supportive and physically safe environment. Women have an opportunity to practice their skills in simulated rape scenarios with a padded attacker.

We see several women successfully defending themselves in attacks which begin from behind, from the front, and on the ground. Elaine, Carol, and Allison, students in the IMPACT self-defense course, talk about what this self-defense course meant to them. What do you hear as their key ideas? Steve Rehrauer, a male instructor who has the dual role of teacher and attacker, talks about the reasons he does this work and what he sees taking place in the course. What are his major points?

C. Class discussion of self-defense

Virginia, Judy, Peg, and Joe ask questions about the course. What do you learn about the simulated attacks and the effective elements of the course? Claudia comments on what she learned as well as shares a misperception she had about self-defense because of vague information given to her. What is her key point about legs?

Virginia, Mary, and Gunther comment upon what they saw the women doing in IMPACT that was effective. What do they identify as effective self-defense strategies?

D. Video visit with Pauline Bart, co-author of *Stopping Rape: Successful Survival Strategies*, Department of Psychiatry, University of Illinois at Chicago.

Pauline Bart and Patricia O'Brien, authors of *Stopping Rape: Successful Survival Strategies*, did groundbreaking research in their study of women who avoided and didn't avoid rape. Bart and O'Brien's research challenged conventional notions that women were incapable of defending themselves and were likely to be harmed further if they did. Through in-depth interviews comparing women's experiences with avoiding and not avoiding rape, they documented effective self-defense strategies used by women.

Pauline Bart is a feminist and a sociologist whose scholarly and political commitment to understanding rape as well as other forms of violence against women has been inspired by the real-life experiences of women for whom she cares deeply.

Pauline tells us what she and Patricia found to be effective strategies for avoiding rape. She also identifies childhood and adulthood socialization experiences which were related to rape-avoidance. Can you identify these strategies and factors?

E. Interview and class discussion with Nancy Lanoue, Co-director of Thousand Waves: Martial Arts and Self-Defense for Women and Children

Nancy Lanoue, a fourth degree black belt in Seido Karate, is the Co-director of Thousand Waves: Martial Arts and Self-Defense for Women and Children. Nancy is highly regarded in the women's self-defense movement, the anti-violence movement, and the martial arts community. Nancy has been involved since the late 1970s in developing self-defense programs and teaching self-defense to women and children, first in New York City and later in Chicago. Nancy has been instrumental in bringing together martial artists, self-defense instructors, and activists in the anti-violence movement.

Nancy tells us of her background in teaching self-defense and the importance Pauline Bart and Patricia O'Brien's work had for the women's self-defense movement. What does she identify as a tension between her work and the work of women providing support services for rape victims? What does she identify as important about Pauline and Patricia's research?

Nancy gives us an overview of her approach to teaching self-defense. What do you see as key aspects of her approach? Nancy also explains the difference between martial arts and self-defense. How would you characterize the differences? Why are the eyes, throat, knees, and groin vulnerable as self-defense targets? Sharon and Joe ask Nancy questions about self-defense programs for children and in colleges. What are the key issues for Nancy in developing age appropriate programs?

Peg shares an experience when she was attacked and the feelings stirred up by our discussion. How does Nancy see self-defense training affecting women's fears?

In response to Helen's question about images of women in the media and the effect they have on us, Nancy talks about the importance of hearing self-defense success stories. What does Nancy mean by a testing process by potential rapists?

In response to Jan's concern about education for boys and men, Nancy describes an experience in teaching high school students through role-playing. What do we learn about the different perceptions of girls and boys? What does this experience suggest for self-defense?

Mary raises an ethical concern with perpetuating violence. How has Nancy resolved this issue for herself? What is your position? Following up on comments by Gunther and Mary, Nancy talks about the effect of self-defense training on women's feelings of rage. What effects does Nancy note?

In conclusion, I briefly summarize key ideas and note that self-defense training can also contribute to healing from past assaults. Why do you think this might be the case? What have you learned from Class 22 about self-defense?

 Now watch the videotape.

V. REVIEW QUESTIONS

1. According to Andersen, in what ways do gender, race, and class influence victimization for crime?

2. What does research show about the relationship between rape and women's isolation in society?

3. What is date or acquaintance rape? How does the climate on college campuses contribute to date rape?

4. According to Andersen, what are the key ideas in each of the following theoretical explanations of rape: psychological, subculture of violence, gender socialization, and political-economic status of women?

5. What is self-defense?

6. What are key principles of a good self-defense program?

7. What behaviors and attitudes contribute to effective self-defense?

8. What are similarities and differences between self-defense and the martial arts?

9. In the early history of the anti-violence movement, what were tensions between women doing self-defense work and women involved in providing support services for rape victims?

10. How do rapists test potential victims? What insights does this awareness offer for self-defense strategies? (Also, consider the strategies discussed with sexual harassment).

VI. SOURCES AND FURTHER READING

Bart, Pauline B. and Patricia O'Brien. 1985. *Stopping Rape: Successful Survival Strategies.* Elmsford, NY: Pergamon Press.

Beneke, Timothy. 1982. *Men on Rape.* NY: St. Martin's Press.

Caignon, Denise and Gail Groves. 1987. *Her Wits About Her: Self-Defense Success Stories by Women.* NY: Harper and Row.

Delacoste, Frederique and Felice Neweman (eds.). 1981. *Fight Back: Feminist Resistance to Male Violence.* Minneapolis, MN: Cleis Press.

Elgin, Suzette Haden. 1980. *The Gentle Art of Verbal Self-Defense.* Englewood Cliffs, NJ: Prentice Hall.

Gordon, Margaret T. and Stephanie Riger. 1989. *The Female Fear.* NY: Free Press.

Kidder, Louise H., Joanne L. Boell, and Marilyn J. Moyer. 1983. "Rights consciousness and victimization prevention: personal defense and assertiveness training." *Journal of Social Issues* 39 (2):155-170.

"Kids who rape." 1990. *Redbook*, April:136-137.

Klein, Marty. 1988. "Stopping rape: women, read this to men." *Utne Reader*, Nov/Dec: 109-111.

Lueng, Debbie. 1991. *Self-Defense: The Womanly Art of Self-care, Intuition, and Choice.* Tacoma, WA: R & M Press.

Martin, Laura C. 1992. *A Life Without Fear: A Guide to Preventing Sexual Assault.* Nashville, TN: Rutledge Hill Press.

Morgan, M.K. 1986. "Conflict and confusion: what rape prevention experts are telling women." *Sexual Coercion & Assault* 1: 160-168.

Nelson, Joan M. 1991. *Self-Defense: Steps to Success.* Champaign, IL: Leisure Press.

Pava, W.S., P. Bateman, M.K. Appleton, and J. Glascock. 1991. "Self-defense training for visually impaired women." *Journal of Visual Impairment and Blindness,* December: 397-401.

Prentkey, Robert Alan, Ann Wolbert Burgess, and Daniel Lee Carter. 1986. "Victim responses by rapist type." *Journal of Interpersonal Violence* 1:73-98.

Scully, Diana. 1991. *Understanding Sexual Violence: A Study of Convicted Rapists.* NY: Harper Collins.

Smith, Susan. 1986. *Fear or Freedom.* Racine, WI: Mother Courage Press.

Thompson, Martha E. 1991. "Self-defense against sexual coercion: theory, research, and practice." Pp. 111 - 121 in *Sexual Coercion*, edited by Elizabeth Grauerholz and Mary A. Koralewski. Lexington, MA: Lexington Books.

Quinsey, Vernon L., Gabriel Marion, Douglas Upfold, and Kenneth T. Popple. 1986. "Issues in teaching physical methods of resisting rape." *Sexual Coercion & Assault* 1 (4): 125-130.

Ullman, Sarah E. and Raymond A. Knight. 1993. "The efficacy of women's resistance strategies in rape situations." *Psychology of Women Quarterly* 17: 23 - 38.

Ullman, Sarah E. and Raymond A. Knight. 1992. "Fighting back: women's resistance to rape." *Journal of Interpersonal Violence* 7: 31-43.

Wiley, Carol A. (ed.). 1992. *Women in the Martial Arts.* Berkley, CA: North Atlantic Books.

VII. ORGANIZATIONS

Chimera, Inc. 59 E. Van Buren, Chicago, IL 60605. (312) 939-5341.

IMPACT International, Inc. 701 Richmond Avenue, Silver Spring, MD 20910.
(301) 589-1349. IMPACT self-defense courses are offered by
      BAMM IMPACT. 1561 Industrial Way, San Carlos, CA 94070-4111. (415) 592-7300
      DC IMPACT. 701 Richmond Ave, Silver Spring, MD 20910. (301)589-1349
      IMPACT of Indianapolis. (317) 255-5881 or (317) 257-9527.
      IMPACT of Minnesota. P.O. Box 47052, Minneapolis, MN. (612)475-4008
      Self Empowerment Group. 6219 N. Sheridan, Chicago, IL 60660. (773)338-4545.

National Coalition Against Sexual Assault (NCASA). P.O. Box 21378, Washington, D.C.
20009.

National Women's Martial Arts Federation. c/o Melanie Fine, P.O. Box 4688, Corpus Christi,
TX 78469-4688.

Thousand Waves: Martial Arts and Self-Defense for Women and Children.
1220 W. Belmont, Chicago, IL 60657. (773) 472-7663.

WOMEN AND SOCIAL ACTION: CLASS 23
Perspectives on Social Change

 Before you read this Chapter of the Study Guide

Read Andersen, "Women and Social Reform: Liberal Feminism," Chp. 11
"Radical Alternatives: Socialist and Radical Feminism," Chp. 12

JOURNAL
ASSIGNMENT

Write about an experience you or someone else has had with participating in a collective action intended to bring about social change. Describe what the problem was, describe what the group decided were the roots of the problem and how to solve it, and describe what actions the group took and what the short-term and long-term consequences were.

I. INTRODUCTION

In "Women and Social Action," we have heard from many social activists who are highly dedicated to social change. While there have been some similarities, people have also differed on issues, approaches, goals, and methods. Some activists have focused on changing social institutions, such as the workplace, childcare, education, religion, health care and the legal system. Others have been primarily concerned with directly transforming women's experience of power, sexuality, health, motherhood, and reproduction. Still others have raised the possibility of creating women-only space for spiritual, emotional, mental, and physical development.

Some have talked about women's situation as unequal to men; others have framed women's experience within patriarchy; a few have drawn our attention to the interrelationships among race, class, and gender and how these systems are interwined with the political economy. Others have drawn our attention to the similarities in issues facing women while others have explored our differences in age, disability, ethnicity, occupation, race, religion, political background, sexual orientation, or social class.

We have not directly dealt with the role of men in social change, but a variety of perspectives has been implicit in our discussions. Some see men as harmed by gender stratification as much as women. Others see men as oppressors who learn to perpetuate women's oppression in their everyday life. For others, men can be allies, people who could benefit from women's oppression, but choose to join with women to challenge existing social institutions, social relationships, or oppressive social systems.

Some of the activists we have heard from work in large, hierarchical bureaucracies; others work within small informal political groups; still others work within their neighborhoods and communities; others are part of larger national and international organizations. We have heard from people who do their political work in a variety of ways, including, advocacy, coalition building, community building, counseling, demonstrations, direct service, experiential education, grantwriting, marches, meetings, legal work, networking, nontraditional roles or work, outreach, petitions, phone calls, religious practices, research, support groups, teaching, writing, or a combination of methods.

In Class 23, we will explore the perspective on social change implicit in "Women and Social Action." We will hear Marca Bristo, a feminist and disability rights activist, talk about the value of coalition building for bringing about social change. Renny Golden, a feminist and activist on Central American issues, will help us compare and contrast individualistic and collective models for social change. She will argue persuasively for the power of community in challenging systems of oppression. Reflect on your perspective on issues, goals, approach, and methods. Is your perspective more consistent with an individualistic or collective model?

II. CLASS THEMES

- Recognizing different perspectives on social change
- Perspectives on social change affect definition of problems, conceptualization of causes, and selection of social actions
- Community building is central to an empowerment process

III. VIDEOTAPE SYNOPSIS

- Introduction to perspectives on social change
- Class discussion of the perspective of "Women and Social Action"
- Video visit with Marca Bristo, President, Access Living, A Center for Service, Advocacy and Social Change for People with Disabilities
- Interview and Class Discussion with Renny Golden, Associate Professor of Criminal Justice and Women's Studies, Northeastern Illinois University

IV. VIDEOTAPE COMMENTARY

A. Introduction to perspectives on social change

We start out this session looking at a small collection of political buttons which reflect different perspectives on social change. Can you think of other buttons you have seen which reflect different views on what the important issues are, what the roots of the problems are, and what are the most effective social actions? Would you wear a political button? If so, what message would you want to proclaim?

B. Class discussion of the perspective of "Women and Social Action"

To ground our thinking about social change in concrete symbols, I ask members of "Women and Social Action" to think about what the hands seen in the opening credits of our course symbolize. Gail, Judy, Carlos, Felicia, Joan, Phyllis, Claudia, Ada, Debbie, Peg, Jan, Gunther, Helen, Mary, and Sharon suggest a variety of ways to think about the hands and what they tell us about the perspective of "Women and Social Action." Make a list of each person's comment. Look at the list and summarize the perspective of Women and Social Action as seen by participants in the course. How does this fit with your assessment of the perspective of the course?

I acknowledge that the perspective of this course is only one perspective on social change. Using the metaphor of one of our texts, **Moving the Mountain**, I ask class members to identify what are different ways of thinking about what the mountain is that has to be moved. Janet, Gail, Judy, Trenace, and Gunther suggest a variety of perspectives. What are the similarities and differences in what they identify as the problem?

C. Video visit with Marca Bristo, Executive Director, Access Living, A Center for Service, Advocacy and Social Change for People with Disabilities

Marca Bristo is one of the founders of the Independent Living Movement in Chicago. She is currently the President of Access Living, a non-residential center for Independent Living in Chicago. Marca is an outstanding example of someone whose perspective on social change emphasizes coalition and community building. For instance, she acknowledges the importance of the collective work of African-American, Latino-American, senior citizen, and feminist groups in supporting passage of the 1990 American Disabilities Act.

Marca tells us about her background and her involvement in the disability rights movement. She addresses the paradox of disability. What does she mean by this paradox? How do you see this paradox applying to other groups striving for social change? She also tell us about a growing movement of "disability pride." What does she mean by this?

Marca offers us a strategy for getting involved in social change? What is it? How would you describe Marca's perspective on social change? How does it fit with other perspectives we have read and discussed?

D. Interview and Class Discussion with Renny Golden, Associate Professor of Criminal Justice and Women's Studies, Northeastern Illinois University

Renny Golden is a poet, ethnographer, teacher, and activist. She is a dedicated and socially conscious teacher and writer. Renny has also been actively involved in Central American issues since the late 1970s. She was a key member of the Chicago Religious Network on Central America (now dissolved). She serves on the Boards of the Ecumenical Policy Institute in Central America (EPICA) and National Assembly of Religious Women (NARW).

Renny continues our earlier discussion of the symbolism of the hands seen in the opening credits of Women and Social Action. She suggests that linked and joined hands would best represent her perspective on social change. She then tells us a story which illustrates the power of a community joining together to challenge a military system of oppression. What do you understand as the key elements of her story?

Renny asks class members to compare and contrast a community versus a system of oppression. Gail, Judy, and Helen offer their ideas. What does Gail see as the responsibility of members of oppressed groups in their treatment of each other? What connection does Judy make with Florence Luscomb's image of the snowflakes? What moral contrast does Helen draw? In response to Judy's comment about the emphasis on individual activities in the United States, Renny asks us to consider who benefits from that emphasis. How would you answer her question?

Peg expresses her amazement at how courageous the women in Renny's story were even though they had such few resources. Renny asks us to think about different kinds of deprivation and how we are often deprived of a sense of community. She also places the notion of courage in a social context. What does she mean when she says that courage is a social gift that is a product of a liberation process?

Ada and Mary talk about ways that systems of oppression isolate us from each other. What are their key points? Judy, Janet, and Gail discuss the relationship between privilege and community. Renny contrasts a model of solidarity that is rooted in competitiveness and one that is rooted in community. What is the difference? Renny brings us back to exploring in more depth the differences between systems of oppression and community. How does the notion of struggle and crisis relate to community building?

 Now watch the videotape.

V. REVIEW QUESTIONS

1. What are the key ideas, goals, and methods of each of the following perspectives discussed by Andersen?
   a. women's right branch of the women's movement
   b. women's liberation branch of the women's movement
   c. liberal feminism
   d. radical feminism
   e. socialist feminism

2. How would you describe the key ideas, goals, and methods of this course? How similar and different are they to the perspectives you describe above?

3. How does Marca Bristo distinguish between equality and difference? How does this distinction apply to the disability rights movement? How would these concepts apply to the women's movement?

4. What is the difference between inequality and oppression?

5. What is the difference between attaining equal rights and liberation?

6. What is the difference between a community and a system of oppression? What is the difference between being a victim and a member of a community?

7. Compare and contrast individualistic and collective approaches.

8. What is meant by courage as a social gift? as a product of a liberation process?

VI. INTERVIEW EXCERPT

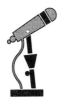

Della Mitchell, Coordinator for the Chicago Coalition for the Homeless Women's Empowerment Project, discusses the approach to social change on which the Women's Empowerment Project is based.

❝❝ Della Mitchell:

After a lot of research on working with the homeless we realized that the homeless can advocate for themselves a lot better than we can. They're experienced in this crisis and they know what it's doing to them. They know how devastating it is. We empathize and we have the time to work with them, but we really can't do it as well as they can do it. It's my job and my goal to get them to a point where they can indeed advocate for themselves and they're doing well. Since the project started, we have had three training sessions in basic organizing skills. We teach them how to choose an issue and how to develop the strategy to deal with that issue. How to sell the issue. How to network with others to get support for it. They have done some amazing things with women who really were at the lowest point in their lives and just didn't see any hope at all. They are now feeling a lot better about themselves. We still have a long way to go because they've asked us to do some training in self-esteem. But just actually getting out and beginning to advocate for oneself is empowering within itself. The women have participated in rallies down at Presidential Towers - that was the first big issue we took on. Presidential Towers are buildings downtown. They were built with federal dollars and any time you're using federal dollars you're suppose to set aside 20% of the units for lower income. And that didn't happen. So that was the first big project that they got involved in and they spoke at press conferences. We set up negotiating meetings to talk about the issue. Some of the women went to Washington to talk to Jack Kemp about the issue. And at this point we feel we've made some major accomplishments with that project, and with the homeless themselves. Whatever develops out of that project we have a proposal on the table now at the HUD office. Once this plan comes through, the homeless and especially the empowerment project can feel that they really had an impact in that decision. They made trips to Springfield to talk to the state legislators about the issues related to homelessness, whether it was budget cuts or just the need for more affordable housing. They've done a great job at that as well. The other lesson is understanding that if you do organize, how necessary it is to organize so that people do listen. You know, if you're one person and you go to CHA or to HUD to get something, you get shuffled from one person to another. But if you're a group, you're listened to. ❞❞

VII. SOURCES AND FURTHER READING

Thanks to Renny Golden for a list of resources for organizers.

Adamson, Nancy, Linda Briskin, and Margaret McPhail. 1988. *Feminist Organizing For Change: the Contemporary Women's Movement in Canada.* Toronto: Oxford University Press.

Anzaldúa, Gloria (ed.). 1990. "(De)Colonized Selves: Finding Hope Through Horror; Turning the Pain Around: Strategies for Growth," Section 3. *Making Face, Making Soul, Haciendo Caras.* San Francisco: Aunt Lute Foundation Book.

Blackwell-Stratton, Marian, Mary Lou Breslin, Arlene Byrnne Mayerson, and Susan Bailey. 1988. "Smashing icons: disabled women and the disability and women's movements." Pp. 306 - 332 in *Women with Disabilities: Essays in Psychology, Culture, and Politics*, edited by Michele Fine and Adrienne Asch. Philadelphia, PA: Temple University Press.

Browne, Susan E., Debra Connors, and Nanci Stern (eds.). 1985. "United We Stand, Sit, and Roll-Finding Each Other," Chapter 8. *With the Power of Each Breath: A Disabled Women's Anthology.* Pittsburgh: Cleis Press.

Cavin, Susan. 1990. "The invisible army of women: lesbian social protests, 1969 - 1988. Pp. 321 - 332 in *Women and Social Protest*, edited by Guida West and Rhoda Lois Blumberg. NY: Oxford University Press.

Chafetz, Janet Saltzman, Anthony Gary Dworkin, and Stephanie Swanson. 1990. "Social change and social activism: first-wave women's movements around the world." Pp. 302 - 320 in *Women and Social Protest*, edited by Guida West and Rhoda Lois Blumberg. NY: Oxford University Press.

Dauphinais, Pat Dewey, Steven E. Barkan, and Steven F. Cohn. 1992. "Predictors of rank-and-file feminist activism: evidence from the 1983 general social survey." *Social Problems* 39 (4): 332 -344.

Davis, Flora. 1991. *Moving the Mountain: the Women's Movement in America since 1960.* NY: Touchstone.

Echols, Alice. 1989. *Daring to Be Bad: Radical Feminism in America, 1967 - 1975.* Minneapolis, MN: University of Minnesota Press.

Faludi, Susan. 1991. *Backlash: The Undeclared War Against American Women.* NY: Anchor Books.

Fine, Michelle and Adriene Asch. 1988. *Women with Disabilities: Essays in Psychology, Culture, and Politics.* Philadelphia: Temple University Press.

Freeman, Jo. 1989. "Feminist organization and activities from suffrage to women's liberation." Pp. 541 - 555 in *Women: A Feminist Perspective*, 4th edition, edited by Jo Freeman. Mountain View, CA: Mayfield Publishing Company.

Freire, Paulo. 1968. *The Pedagogy of the Oppressed.* NY: Seabury Press.

Golden, Renny. 1991. *The Hour of the Poor, The Hour of Women: Salvdoran Women Speak.* NY: Crossroad.

Golden, Renny and Sheila Collins. 1982. *Struggle is A Name for Hope.* Minneapolis, MN: West End Press.

Golden, Renny and Michael McConnell. 1986. *Sanctuary: The New Underground Railroad.* Maryknoll, NY: Orbis Books.

Golden, Renny, Michael McConnell, Peggy Mueller, Cinny Poppen, and Marilyn Turkovich. 1991. *Dangerous Memories: Invasion and Resistance Since 1492.* Chicago, IL: The Chicago Religious Task Force on Central America.

Hooks, Bell. 1989. *Talking Back: Thinking Feminist, Thinking Black.* Boston: South End Press.

Katzenstein, Mary Fainsod and Carol McClurg Mueller, (eds.). 1987. *The Women's Movements of the United States and Western Europe: Consciousness, Political Opportunity, and Public Policy.* Philadelphia: Temple University Press.

Lamp, Sharon and Julie Marks-Walberer. 1991. "How we won wheels and rails." *The Creative Woman*, special issue on Swimming Upstream: Managing Disabilities 11(2): 11 -13.

McAdam, Doug. 1986. "Recruitment to high-risk activism: the case of Freedom Summer. *American Journal of Sociology* 92:64-90.

Morris, Jenny. 1991. "Fighting Back," Chapter 7. *Pride Against Prejudice: Transforming Attitudes Toward Disability.* Philadelphia, PA: New Society Publishers.

National Assembly of Religious Women. 1987. "'How to' skills with a feminist perspective." 1307 S. Wasbash, Chicago, IL 60605. (312) 663-1980.

Plutzer, Eric. 1988. "Work life, family life, and women's support of feminism." *American Sociological Review* 53:640-649.

Rich, Adrienne. 1980. "Compulsory heterosexuality and lesbian existence." *Signs* 5 (4): 631 - 660.

Rowland, Robyn. 1989. "Women who do and women who don't join the women's movement." Pp. 42 - 52 in Renate D. Klein and Deborah Lynn Steinberg (eds.) *Radical Voices: A Decade of Feminist Resistance from Women's Studies International Forum*. NY: Oxford Press.

Schoene, Lester P. and Marcella E. DuPraw. *Facing Racial and Cultural Conflict: Tools for Rebuilding Community.* $24 from the Program for Community Problem Solving. 915 15th St NW, Suite 600, Washington, D.C. 20005. (202) 783-2961.

Study Circles Resource Center. *A Manual for Study Circle Discussion Leaders, Organizers, and Participants.* Single copy is free from SCRC. PO Box 203, Pomfret, CT 06258. (203) 928-2616.

Theobalk, Robert. 1993. *Turning the century: personal and organizational strategies for your changing world.* $18.95 from Knowledge Systems Inc. 7777 W. Morris St., Indianapolis, IN 46209.

Wandersee, Winifred D. 1988. *On the Move: American Women in the 1970s.* Boston: Twayne Publishers.

West, Guida and Rhoda Lois Blumberg (eds.). 1990. *Women and Social Protest.* NY: Oxford University Press.

Westkott, Marcia. 1983. "Women's studies as a strategy for change: between criticism and vision." Pp. 210 -218 *Theories of Women's Studies*, edited by Gloria Bowles and Renate Duelli Klein. London: Routledge & Kegal Paul.

VIII. ORGANIZATIONS

Access Living of Metropolitan Chicago. 310 S. Peoria. Chicago, IL 60607. (312) 226-5900.

Chicago Coalition for the Homeless Empowerment Project for Homeless Women with Children, 1325 S. Wabash, Suite 205, Chicago, IL 60605-2504. (312) 435-4548.

The Chicago Religious Network on Central America. (now dissolved)

Ecumenical Program on Central America and the Carribean. 1470 Irving St. NW, Washington, D.C. 20010. (202) 332-0292.

National Assembly of Religious Women (NARW). 529 S. Wabash, Room 404, Chicago, IL 60605. (312) 663-1980.

National Organization for Women (NOW), Chicago chapter. 53 West Jackson Boulevard, #924, Chicago, IL 60604. (312) 922-0025.

WOMEN AND SOCIAL ACTION: CLASS 24
New Directions

Before you read this Chapter of the Study Guide

Read Andersen, "Conclusion: New Directions in Feminist Theory," p. 370 - 381

JOURNAL
ASSIGNMENT

Social change is often portrayed as resulting from the work of a few women at the center of power or on the fringes of society. Popular analyses of women and social change often limit themselves to women's roles in the family and the workplace. The goal for this course was for us to increase our awareness of ordinary women who are working collectively in diverse social settings to empower themselves and others. We've explored barriers women face, goals and strategies for social change, and the rewards and challenges of social action. For this assignment, look over your class notes, your other assignments, and think about class discussions and guests. Write about what you have learned this term that has been particularly meaningful to you, why it has been meaningful, and how what you have learned might influence you in the future.

I. INTRODUCTION

When most people think about women and social action, they focus on changes in laws and the advancement of women in politics, business, or the professions. For most women, however, the struggle for change begins not in boardrooms or courtrooms, but in their homes, communities, places of worship, schools, and workplaces.

The purpose of "Women and Social Action" has been to highlight the experiences of women who, through their beliefs and actions, demonstrate an understanding of the differences between "helping others" and "empowerment." When people are "helped," outsiders and experts define the problems, analyze their causes, and propose and implement courses of action. Analysis of causes may be limited to assessment of psychological sources or small group dynamics. Courses of action may be selected with little attention to their long-term effects or their relationship to the social roots of problems.

When an empowerment model is used, people define their own problems, draw upon their own insights and possibly those of outsiders and experts to analyze the sources of problems, and determine the course of action most appropriate for their circumstances. Empowerment often begins with a process of really talking and exploring the concrete issues facing people and the varied ways in which they affect different segments of the group. An understanding of the problems facing people is enhanced when compassion and empathy guide the exploration of commonalities and differences within the group.

While there is an understanding in an empowerment model that oppression can damage individuals and produce destructive relationships, people do not stop their analysis at the psychological, family, or community level. Analysis of the sources of problems points to an understanding of systems of power operating in the larger society. Courses of action are selected which not only deal with the immediate and specific problems facing a group of people, but move toward a transformation of these systems of power.

Though an empowerment process may be supported and facilitated by outsiders or experts, leadership in all phases comes from members of the group directly affected by the situation. For an empowerment process to move forward, everyone involved—outsiders, leaders, members—is accountable to the group and is open to being changed by the process.

In Class 24 we will hear what insights class participants have gained about empowerment, social action, and social change from their interviews of women activists and their experience in "Women and Social Action."

II. CLASS THEMES

- Recognizing the relationship between empowerment, social action, and social change
- Building community

III. VIDEOTAPE SYNOPSIS

- Class members' interviews of women activists
- Class discussion of what people learned in "Women and Social Action" and the new directions suggested by what was learned
- Class discussion of community building
- Celebrating "Women and Social Action"

IV. VIDEOTAPE COMMENTARY

A. Class members' interviews of women activists

Ada, Mary, Sharon, Jan, Janet, Phyllis, Joe, Laura, Joan, and Claudia offer brief summaries of the women activists they interviewed and what they learned from them. What is the significance to you of how many of them interviewed relatives and friends? What does that tell us about social action? Make a list of the key ideas each mentions that she or he learned from the women interviewed. How do these ideas fit within the framework of "Women and Social Action?"

B. Class discussion of what people learned in "Women and Social Action" and the new directions suggested by what was learned

Christine, Felicia, Linda, Trenace, Gunther, Debbie, Carlos, Helen, Peg, Caryn, and Jan tell us one of the things they learned from the course and how they think it will influence their future activities. Christine, Linda, Trenace, Gunther, and Caryn highlighted what they learned about how to work for social change. What are their key ideas? Felicia focused on the knowledge she gained. What did she learn? Debbie, Carlos, Joan, and Jan talked about insights they gained into themselves. What insights did they each gain? Helen and Peg focused on how the course reinforced and expanded their beliefs. What was most important to them?

C. Class discussion of community building for social change

Mary, Joe, Trenace, Ada, Claudia, and Peg identify some key elements of building community. Mary, Joe, and Trenace identify the need to reconceptualize social action in our everyday lives. What insights do they each offer? Mary, Ada, Claudia, and Peg identify the need for new models for social change. What insights do they each offer?

Celebrating "Women and Social Action"

In conclusion I briefly summarize the goals of "Women and Social Action" and ways they were met. David Ainsworth, Producer, and Margo Witkowsky, Graphics Designer, surprise us all with an opportunity to toast the success of our work together. Make sure you have a beverage on hand so you can join us.

V. REVIEW QUESTIONS

1. After reading Andersen, what do each of the following terms mean to you?
   a. feminist epistemology
   b. androcentric
   c. standpoint theory
   d. race/class/gender system
   e. post modernism

2. What is meant by integrating race, class, and gender into feminist thinking?

3. What are central elements of a community building process?

4. What are some of the key things people learned during "Women and Social Action?" How do these compare and contrast to what you have learned?

5. What are some of the ideas people offer for reconceptualizing social action and developing new models for social change?

6. What are the key elements of empowerment? How does empowerment differ from helping?

VI. SOURCES AND FURTHER READING

Ackelsberg, Martha A. 1988. "Communities, resistance, and women's activism: some implications for a democratic polity." Pp. 297 - 313 in *Women and the Politics of Empowerment*, edited by Ann Bookman and Sandra Morgen. Philadelphia, PA: Temple University Press.

Adamson, Nancy, Linda Briskin, and Margaret McPhail. 1988. "Conclusion." *Feminist Organizing for Change: The Contemporary Women's Movement in Canada.* Toronto: Oxford University Press.

Anzaldúa, Gloria (ed.). 1990. "If You Would Be My Ally," Section 6 and "'Doing' Theory in Other Modes of Consciousness," Section 7. *Making Face, Making Soul, Haciendo Caras.* San Francisco: Aunt Lute Foundation Book.

Belenky, Mary Field, Blythe McVicker Clinchy, Nancy Rule Goldberger, and Jill Mattuck Tarule. 1986. *Women's Ways of Knowing: The Development of Self, Voice, and Mind.* NY: Basic Books.

Bookman, Ann and Sandra Morgen. 1988. " 'Carry it on': continuing the discussion and the struggle." Pp. 314 - 321 in *Women and the Politics of Empowerment*, edited by Ann Bookman and Sandra Morgen. Philadelphia, PA: Temple University Press.

Boston Women's Health Book Collective. 1992. "Organizing for change: U.S.A." "Developing an international awareness." Pp. 699 - 732 in *The New Our Bodies, Ourselves.* NY: Touchstone.

Bourque, Susan C. and Donna Robinson Divine. 1985. *Women Living Change.* Philadelphia, PA: Temple University Press.

Christian, Barbara T. 1989. "We are the ones we have been waiting for: political content in Alice Walker's novels." Pp. 212 - 221 in *Radical Voices: A Decade of Feminist Resistance from Women's Studies International Forum,* edited by Renate D. Klein and Deborah Lynn Steinberg. Oxford: Pergamon Press.

Collins, Patricia Hill. 1989. "The social construction of black feminist thought." *Signs*, 14 (4): 745 - 773.

Combahee River Collective. 1981. "A black feminist statement." Pp. 210 - 218 in *This Bridge Called My Back: Writings by Radical Women of Color*, edited by Cherríe Moraga and Gloria Anzaldúa. Watertown, MA: Persephone Press.

de Valdez, T. Aragon. 1980. "Organizing as a political tool for the Chicana." *Frontiers.* 7 - 13.

Dill, Bonnie Thornton. 1987. "Race, class, and gender: prospects for an all-inclusive sisterhood." Pp. 204 -214 in *From Different Shores: Perspectives on Race and Ethnicity in America*, edited by R. Takaki. NY: Oxford University Press.

Driedger, Diane and Susan Gray (eds.). 1992. "Dealing with the World," Section V. *Imprinting Our Image: An International Anthology by Women with Disabilities.* Canada: Gynergy.

Elsasser, Nan, Kyle MacKenzie, and Yvonne Tixier Y Vigil. 1980. "A Lighted Fire," Section Four. *Las Mujeres: Conversations from a Hispanic Community.* Old Westbury, NY: The Feminist Press.

Faludi, Susan. 1991. "Epilogue." *Backlash: The Undeclared War Against American Women.* NY: Anchor Books.

Fine, Michele and Adrienne Asch. 1988. "Epilogue: research and politics to come." Pp. 333 - 336 in *Women with Disabilities: Essays in Psychology, Culture, and Politics,* edited by Michele Fine and Adrienne Asch. Philadelphia, PA: Temple University Press.

Giddings, Paula. 1984. "Outlook." *When and Where I Enter: The Impact of Black Women on Race and Sex in America.* Toronto: Bantam Books.

Gilkes, Cheryl Townsend. 1988. "Building in many places: multiple commitments and ideologies in black women's community work." Pp. 53 - 76 in *Women and the Politics of Empowerment*, edited by Ann Bookman and Sandra Morgen. Philadelphia, PA: Temple University Press.

Green, Rayna. 1992. "Culture and gender in Indian America." Pp. 510 - 518 in *Race, Class, and Gender: An Anthology*, edited by Margaret L. Andersen and Patricia Hill Collins. Belmont, CA: Wadsworth Publishing Company.

Gutierrez, Lorraine M. and Edith A. Lewis. 1992. "A feminist perspective on organizing with women of color." Pp. 113 - 132 in *Community Organizing in a Diverse Society*, edited by Felix G. Rivera and John L. Erlich. Boston: Allyn and Bacon.

Hyde, C. 1986. "Experiences of women activists: implications for community organizing theory and practice." *Journal of Sociology and Social Welfare* 13: 545 - 562.

Jackson, Donna. 1992. *How to Make the World a Better Place for Women in Five Minutes a Day.* NY: Hyperion.

Joseph, Gloria I. and Jill Lewis. 1981. *Common Differences: Conflicts in Black and White Feminist Perspectives.* Garden City, NY: Anchor Books.

Loo, C. and P. Ong. 1987. "Slaying dragons with a sewing needle: feminist issues for Chinatown's women." Pp. 186 - 191 in *From Different Shores: Perspectives on Race and Ethnicity in America*. NY: Oxford.

McCourt, Kathleen. 1977. *Working Class Women and Grass-roots Politics.* Bloomington, IN: Indiana University Press.

Morgan, Robin (ed.). 1984. *Sisterhood is Global: The International Women's Movement Anthology*. Garden City, NY: Anchor Books.

Morgen, Sandra and Ann Bookman. 1988. "Rethinking women and politics: an introductory essay." Pp. 3 - 29 in *Women and the Politics of Empowerment*, edited by Ann Bookman and Sandra Morgen. Philadelphia, PA: Temple University Press.

Rappaport, Julian. 1981. "In praise of paradox: a social policy of empowerment over prevention." *American Journal of Community Psychology* 9 (1): 1 - 25.

Raymond, Janice. 1989. "The visionary task: two sights-seeing." Pp. 182 -191 in *Radical Voices: A Decade of Feminist Resistance from Women's Studies International Forum,* edited by Renate D. Klein and Deborah Lynn Steinberg. Oxford: Pergamon Press.

Smith, Dorothy E. 1987. "Beyond methodology: institutionalization and its subversion." *The Everyday World as Problematic: A Feminist Sociology.* Boston: Northeastern University Press.

West, Guida and Rhoda Lois Blumberg. 1990. "Reconstructing social protest from a feminist perspective." *Women and Social Protest.* NY: Oxford University Press.

VII. ORGANIZATIONS

Think about the organizations you have learned about during this course and the organizations already familiar to you. Which ones best represent the "new direction" in which you would like to go? List them here. If you can't think of any that currently exist that match your vision, then note what such an organization might be named and what its goals and methods would be.

APPENDIX

A

Amy Blumenthal. 1990/91. "Scrambled Eggs and Seed Daddies: Conversations with My Son." *EMPATHY: Gay and Lesbian Advocacy Research Project.* 2 (2).

Since I made the decision seven years ago to become a parent through anonymous donor insemination, the question that others have asked most frequently is, "But how are you going to explain this to your child?" This has been asked by friends, family, and colleagues, regardless of their sexual orientation. My answer was and continues to be simple; I have told, and will continue to tell, my child the truth. The truth, however, is never simple; the complications come in trying to make that truth appropriate and understandable to a child whose emotional, physical, and intellectual development is constantly changing.

My son Jonathon is five years old. From the beginning, I have been the primary caretaker in his life-- a single mother in this sense, although I am not now "single." My son and I have always had a wonderful extended family made up of friends and relatives who have shared with us not only the birthday parties and trips to the zoo, but also the temper tantrums and two a.m. trips to the emergency room.

Jonathon first asked about his beginnings and the nature of our family when he was two and a half years old. His questions have usually come up in relation to specific situations and have revolved around why our family is different from many of the others he knows or hears about. My answers have focused on the notion that difference should not ignored or condemned, but should be understood and appreciated without fear or violence.

What follows are some of my journal entries from the last three years that relate to these explorations of difference, along with some later reflections. Of course, this must be seen as a work in progress which will change as my son and I continue to grow and change.

May 1986. During breakfast today, in the middle of a discussion about Velcro closings on shoes, Jonathon asked why he has only a mom and some people have a mom and a dad. I explained that there are all kinds of families in the world and gave lots of examples of those he knows: some with, some without kids; some big, some small. We talked about the fact that from the time I was fifteen, I just had a dad and no mom. I explained that there are no set rules for who family members can be; rather, families are people who love and are there for one another. Tonight I tried reading him one of those books that celebrate all kinds of families, but he managed to rip the cover in his attempts to get back to Dr. Seuss.

Looking back, I remember being surprised at how easy and comfortable this all was. I realize now that I had expected Jonathon to first ask this question with a touch of sadness or confusion or anger. Liberated as I think I am, I, too, had swallowed some of the view that Jonathon's realizations about his family's differences would be traumatic. However, simple, open curiosity seemed to be the overriding feeling. I did manage to stay in the present with my two and a half year old and resist the temptation to bring in lots of information that he wasn't asking for, like the biology/mechanics of different forms of conception or lesbian and gay rights.

March, 1987. In the car today Jonathon asked about where babies come from, or more specifically, how they start growing in a woman's body. I told him that women have eggs inside them ("scrambled eggs?", he asked amazed) and men have sperm and when the two get mixed together a baby can start growing. I explained that much of the time, and certainly in my case, people start babies growing because they want to be parents and know they will love that baby even before it's born. Jonathon then asked what I did before he was born, though I think he found it hard to believe that he didn't always exist. I, too, find this hard to fathom.

The thing I like most about this explanation is that it covers all forms of conception; in vitro, anonymous, and known-donor insemination, intercourse. Jonathon seemed very satisfied with this answer and didn't seem at all interested in learning about how the egg and sperm get together. Oh, to get into the head of a three year old! What image is there of the sperm and the egg and their meeting?

August, 1987. Jonathon's best buddy, Max, was angry at Jonathon and teased him by saying, "Well, you don't even have a Daddy!" Max immediately felt bad for what he had said, quickly adding, "You really do have a Dad, Jonathon. He just lives very, very far away." Jonathon asked if this were true, and I introduced the concept of the seed daddy — a man who is not really a parent, but one who helps a woman get a baby started. He got very excited and asked where he lived, what his name was... When I told him that we didn't know his seed daddy, he was disappointed and pouty, so I led the boys into a discussion of different families we know where the biological fathers are not known, including my first cousins who are adopted. I also tried to bring in the special relationships he has with adult friends who are our chosen family. After this, Jonathon seemed to remember some of our previous conversations and proudly informed Max that families are people that love each other, and that it doesn't matter how big your family is. I was prepared to continue talking about all the wonderful people in our lives and the ways that quality relationships are more important than biology, but both kids got bored and quickly changed the subject to the more pressing issue of which trucks were the biggest and noisiest.

This was the first discussion that upset me. I wanted to yell at Max and protect my boy from hurt and sadness. I had this flash of fear that Jonathon's life would always hold this touch of sadness, a fear that has so far not proven true. It seemed to help him to know that he was part of a larger group and wasn't the only one with an unknown biological father. To connect with others who are in similar situations is important. At the same time, all our discussions about accepting different types of families seem to have sunk in and seem well worth the time and effort.

January, 1988. Jonathon finally asked how the sperm and egg get together — this in relation to our neighbors, Susan and John, expecting another child and Susan being visibly pregnant. I explained two of the ways this can happen - how I went to a doctor who had sperm from the seed daddy in a little straw, and she put it in my vagina to start him growing. He nodded a lot, looking serious and pleased. But when I told about John's penis and Susan's vagina, he gasped and said, "But why didn't she just go to the doctor like you, Mama?" Oh, the look of horror and confusion on that boy's face. When I told this to Susan, she mentioned that her son Aaron had asked about Jonathon's daddy around the same time and also thought the doctor donor route made a lot more sense.

This reaction didn't surprise me much. After all, the doctor is always putting things in, taking things out. I suppose most children this age have a hard time imagining why anyone, especially their parents, would want to be sexual. Still, the conversation had made me nervous. Would Jonathon think this strange? Would he be angry at me for my decision? However, I soon realized that he was simply accepting and appreciative of this addition to his knowledge and understanding.

In my own questioning of what I should emphasize in these conversations, I realize that I want to focus on the fact that each situation must be evaluated openly without holding it up to the conventional standard of "right and wrong." However, Jonathon also needs to know what is out there in the world and be prepared for negative reactions. There is a fine balance that needs to be maintained between promoting a positive self-image in a child and preparing that young person for the all-too-real world.

March, 1988. In the bath tonight, Jonathon asked about marriage. "Does it have to be between a man and a woman? In school they said it does." I told him that some people thought that, but that many people, myself included, didn't think that way, and added that I thought the quality of a relationship was more important than ceremony or legal status. We had a fairly long conversation about freedom, choice, societal values, rituals, interracial marriage, people's fear of difference...I came to a thunderous conclusion by saying that people should be able to marry whomever they want. He ended the conversation by saying, "That's good, Mama, because when I grow up, I'm going to marry you!"

Gotcha!

June, 1988. In the supermarket today (very crowded) Jonathon said (loudly), "tell me again how come I don't have a daddy." Heads turned. Eyes widened. I managed to stall until we got to the car. When I again launched into the "different kinds of families..." response, he tuned out, said that wasn't what he meant. So I started talking about the different ways people love each other, the different kinds of relationships and commitments we make in our lives, and my self-definition as a lesbian, thinking that Jonathon was looking for the words to describe our family and my sexual orientation. He still looked bored, though. Finally, I asked what was really on his mind. "Could you go to the doctor and do that again, mom, so that I could have a brother or sister?" (His friend, Max, was then expecting a brother or sister). When I told him that I could, but didn't have any plans to, he was quiet, appearing both disappointed and relieved.

I, too, feel disappointed and relieved to be the mother of only one. Finances and time govern that decision. Initially, I had thought that Jonathon might be asking about my being a lesbian — something I had begun discussing with him although he hadn't been paying attention. This has simply been a given in our lives. How does one "come out" to someone who has grown up around more lesbians than heterosexual people? "Coming out" implies that an assumption of heterosexuality has existed, and there has never been any such assumption in our home.

I did not like feeling the need to stall until we were out of the grocery store, but there is still that pull to protect Jonathon from oppressive attitudes and behaviors, and I feared that he (and I) would hear either direct or indirect comments that would be offensive and hurtful. I need to put more conscious effort into teaching him the words, the strategies to deal with oppression, but I still want to let him take the lead in the asking his questions.

January, 1989. When I picked Jonathon up from pre-school today, three girls wanted to give him kisses before he left. He was flattered, it seemed, and each, in turn, gave and got a kiss. However, when Robert said that he also liked goodbye kisses, Jonathon informed him that he only kissed girls. Once in the car, I told Jonathon that it was okay for boys to kiss boys and girls to kiss girls. "I know. Peter and James kiss all the time." I reminded him that they didn't kiss all the time and he grudgingly agreed. Heart pounding, I asked him if he knew what it was called when men want to love men and women want to love women. "No." I explained the terms "lesbian" and "gay" and used examples of myself and my lover, as well as other important people in our lives to illustrate lesbian, gay, and heterosexual relationships. I also told him that some people didn't approve of lesbian and gay relationships. "Why?" I explained that some people were afraid of or threatened by things or people that were different from them. He said this sounded like his book, Follow the Drinking Gourd, which explains the story of the underground railroad and has led to some discussions of slavery and racism. He asked if the people who didn't want two women to be able to marry were the same ones who had owned slaves. I gave a complicated "yes and no" answer to that one. His final word on the subject was that moms do not get to decide for their kids who they marry when they grow up. I agreed emphatically and added that he also gets to decide with what friends, teachers...he wants to share this information.

It is difficult to explain time and history and the connections between oppressions to a five year old while trying to get home through rush-hour traffic and figure out what to do about dinner.

Jonathon has always seen so many caring, healthy relationships of all sorts without making distinctions between those that are same and those that are opposite-sex couples. That innocence has been refreshing; however, he has learned what the traditional family structure is and still tries to sort out how and where we fit. While I wish I could make everything easy and sweet for this boy of mine, I know I can't. I am heartened, though, by his ability to make connections between issues. Jonathon needs to know, and on some level seems to know, that while there will always be difficult issues for him and for others, difference does not have to lead to condemnation, fear, or violence. This comes up a lot in other areas — in teaching him not to tease his friend who is afraid of the water, in helping him to deal with being called names by an older kid in the neighborhood. At times, he does not see how all this is related, but then there are those moments when some of these issues do seem clear, and he holds his friend's hand tightly as he helps him ease his way into the shallow end of the pool.

March, 1989. At dinner tonight Jonathon asked me to explain again why we don't know who his seed daddy is. I first explained that I didn't know a man who wanted to be a seed daddy when I wanted to have him. I also told him that I didn't want anyone to ever try to take him away from me, so I thought it would be better to have an anonymous seed daddy. When I asked him, "Does that make you sad?" he said, "a little." I told him we could always talk about that; "I know."

Jonathon was shocked to learn that children sometimes get taken away from their parents, and was glad to know that he would have no such fate. However, he was a bit sad. I have to make an effort not to trivialize or simply push away the sadness. I want him to be able to share his concerns and feelings. When he does, he is at this best — most relaxed, least argumentative.

This conversation brought to mind some articles I've read about a group of women who were adopted or who gave up children for adoption being strongly against the use of anonymous sperm donors. The claim, I think, is that all children and adults have an inherent need and right to know their biological roots and their biological offspring. While I understand their concerns and respect the experiences that have informed their beliefs, my own situation — and by extension, Jonathon's — does not lend support to their conclusions regarding us.

In spite of Jonathon's occasional sadness about not having a dad, I have not seen in him an overriding sadness or an inherent need to know his genetic roots. Jonathon is a happy and confident child. He has a strong need to understand how and why he entered this world. He needs to know that he is wanted and loved by the people that truly make up his family. While I know that he, at times, wishes he had a dad like most of his friends, I doubt there is a biological base for a child's desire to know one's father. He certainly struggles to understand the complexities of his life and to appreciate its diversity. And for me, I do not think that I love and care for my child simply because he shares some of my genes. While I am happy to have experienced pregnancy, I've always seen my decision to raise a child, not my decision to have a baby, as the crucial one.

May, 1989. Jonathon and I took a walk tonight with my friend, Martha, and her seven year old daughter, Rachel. Martha and I were discussing an article on lesbian mothers that a student had asked us to comment on. When Jonathon heard us talking bout women choosing children, he said to Martha in his I'm-the-authority-on-such-matters voice, "Yeah, like my mom decided to have a kid, and you decided to have a kid, but my mom used a straw and you used a daddy!" She nodded in agreement and I hugged him and told him how happy I was that I had made that decision and that he was my special boy.

Jonathon seemed pleased with how well he remembered and could explain the situation, and I was proud of both him and myself for this clear and straightforward explanation.

I often get overwhelmed with the day-to-day issues of being a parent. Will the baby sitter be on time? What's the best way to teach sharing? How much TV is too much? But there I was, walking down a busy Chicago street listening to my son explain these different methods of conception, one of which most adults see as deviant, in simple and nonjudgmental terms.

June, 1989. Matthew, also five, and his parents moved into the building last week. Today Matt asked, "Does Jonathon have a dad?" When I said no, he asked why not. I told him that I had wanted a baby, not a husband. "Why?" "Because there are different kinds of relationships that people choose to have. Some women want husbands and some don't." (I thought it was better to bring in the word "lesbian" after I had come out to his parents.) "But you're still a wife, right?" Before I could answer, Jonathon jumped right in and said, "No, she's not a wife! She's a woman."

That's my boy!

Amy Blumenthal is an associate professor of English/ESL specialist at Oakton Community College in Des Plaines, IL. Jonathon is six years old and recently gave his kindergarten class a lesson on seed daddies.

B

American Sociological Association. 1991. "Sexual Harassment: A Sociological Perspective — Definitions, Myths, Realities, Contacts." Washington, D.C.: ASA.

SUMMARY, SEXUAL HARASSMENT GUIDELINES:
(Equal Employment Opportunity Commission)

Harassment on the basis of sex is a violation of Section 703 of Title VII: "Unwelcome sexual advances, requests for sexual favors and other verbal or physical conduct of a sexual nature constitute sexual harassment when (1) submission to such conduct is made either explicit or implicitly a term or condition of an individual's employment, (2) submission to or rejection of such conduct by an individual is used as the basis for employment decisions affecting such individual, or, (3) such conduct has the purpose or effect of unreasonably interfering with an individual's work performance or creating an intimidating, hostile or offensive working environment."

MYTH: Sexual harassment is not frequent or important.

REALITY: Sexual harassment is the most litigated workplace issue today. Social science research and public opinion polls indicate that over a third of American women have experienced some type of sexual harassment during their working lives.

A 1980 survey of federal employees revealed that 42 per cent of women had experienced some type of sexual harassment during the previous two years. Another study reveals that about 10 percent of all women in the workplace leave their positions because of sexual harassment.

Among undergaduate females, about 30 percent report being victims of sexual harassment in academic settings during their college years.

MYTH: If one woman is harassed in a particular workplace, others also will be harassed.

REALITY: It is often true that harassers have a pattern of victimizing several women in their workplace, either simultaneously or over time. That is why accusations of harassment from one victim often trigger complaints from other women as well.

However, sometimes a harasser chooses one victim for harassment while protecting his reputation through scrupulous behavior toward other women in the workplace. He may perceive his victim as especially vulnerable or desirable in some respect.

MYTH: Sexual harassment is simply or primarily an issue of sexuality.

REALITY: Sexual harassment is a matter of power that happens to be enacted in the area of sex and intimacy. Sexual harassment is an issue of power and interpersonal politics that usually involves misuse of superior power over a subordinate.

Sexual harassment occurs when a person is in a position of superior status compared to the victim. A boss or supervisor is defined as committing harassment not only because of his inappropriate acts, but because he is in a position of power over the victim. Sexual harassment is an interaction that centers on this power differential.

Sociological research indicates that women may be controlled by rewards and punishments that are not the same as those experienced by men. Norms and practices that govern the workplace are based at least in part by by sex stratification — that is, by different expectations regarding what is appropriate for women compared to men. Since, historically, men dominated most if not all occupational categories — even nursing and clerical work — the norms and rules governing the workplace have tended to favor male definitions of appropriateness.

This means that the power strategies available to women in the workplace may not be the same as those that are available for men. It is less acceptable for women, for example, to be assertive or to engage in open power plays.

This background affects the phenomenon of sexual harassment in the workplace.

MYTH: Women do not report or resist sexual harassment because they like it or they do not mind it.

REALITY: Women put up with harassment when they do not have the power to interrupt oppressive behavior. Women historically have been in subordinate positions in society. They have been taught, more than males, to be passive, submissive, and conforming. Historically, they have seen themselves as relatively powerless compared to men. Although this situation is changing, the changes are slow and the legacy of past definitions of male/female power relations still have enourmous impact.

AND, being a victim of sexual harassment can make a woman feel even more powerless, especially when the abuser is a male with superior reward power.

MYTH: Women who are being harassed are able to protect themselves and speak out about it.

REALITY: No more than seven percent of women who experience some form of sexual harassment ever file a formal complaint or grievance against their harasser.

Why? They fear loss of position, promotion, and opportunity. They fear that complaints will bring retaliation, retribution, or even further sexual harassment.

Women also fail to come forward with compaints because they lack support, even from other women, in challenging a powerful male figure. They may fear ridicule, harm to reputation, social isolation, being labeled a troublemaker, and — most importantly — being blamed for the harassment.

Like other types of assault against women (rape, battering), the victims are often blamed for the behavior of the attacker: her actions are perceived as inviting or causing the perpetrator's actions.

Women also may fear that people will not take their accusations seriously, or that people will label them as "sick" or "crazy."

MYTH: A woman who is harassed will confide in others in the workplace, or in her friends and family members.

REALITY: As with victims of rape, battery, and incest, many victims of sexual harassment decline to speak with anyone about their situation. They may feel humiliated and fear that others will blame them for the harasser's actions. They may have observed that other women who speak about their victimization end up being "put on trial" themselves.

Women who are in high-level professional positions, who are concerned with preserving their reputations and have a great deal to lose if their cases become public, may be the least likely to tell even one other person of the events.

MYTH: Sexual harassment is just a women's issue.

REALITY: Definitions of appropriate gender relations in the workplace are a matter of concern to both males and females. Further, women who are harassed may bring stress into other relationships with partners and families.

MYTH: It's all in her mind . . . a fantasy.

REALITY: Men and women may differ in their perceptions of what constitutes harassment, especially in the more subtle cases, but the law is clear. Many cases of sexual harassment do in fact occur — a woman is not necessarily imagining or fantasizing such acts. To accuse a woman of fantasizing may, in fact, further contribute to her power-lessness and unwillingness to pursue her case. She is then doubly victimized.

MYTH: Harassment is of minor importance to a woman's career or identity.

REALITY: Sociological research indicates that the effects of sexual harassment on victims include job loss, emotional stress, physical illness, poor work performance, derailed career or educational plans, lack of advancement, poor grades or evaluation, withdrawal from work or school, disrupted relationships, humiliation, self-doubt, and confusion.

MYTH: Sexual harassment is just between two people.

REALITY: Sexual harassment, especially if it persists, follows a pattern, or remains unchallenged, can affect the climate of the workplace and can make it uncomfortable for those who witness it.

That is why the Supreme Court in the late 1980s decided that an employer can be held liable for sex discrimination if sexual harassment creates a "hostile work environment" — even if job loss is not at issue.

MYTH: Women who are sexually harassed have asked for it by their demeanor, dress, or interaction.

REALITY: Women of all demeanors, dress, and appearance have been victims of sexual harassment. Regardless of how a person dresses or presents herself, she is a potential victim. Nor does her demeanor or appearance justify acts of sexual harassment.

CONTACTS:

The following sociologists may be able to shed light on the current discussions surrounding the Clarence Thomas/Anita Hill issue:

Pauline Bart, Sociology, University of Illinois-Chicago Circle. (312) 996-7376

Lee Bowker, Sociology, Humboldt University. (707) 826-3716 or 9764

Estelle Disch, Sociology, University of Massachusetts-Boston. (617) 287-6256 (w) or (617) 661-4667 (h)

Carla B. Howery, President, Sociologists for Women in Society. (202) 833-3410, ext. 323

Pamela Jenkins, University of New Orleans. (504) 286-6301

Felice J. Levine, Executive Officer, American Sociological Association. (202) 833-3410, ext. 316

Patricia Yancey Martin, Florida State University. (904) 644-1201

Tahi Lani Mottl, American Sociological Association. (202) 833-3410, ext. 318

Brenda Seals, Tulane University. (504) 865-5820

Ronnie Steinberg, Sociology, Temple University. (215) 787-1824

Barrie Thorne, Sociology, University of Southern California-L.A. (213) 740-3541 or (213) 254-7759

C

Roberta M. Feldman and Susan Stall. 1990. "(Grassroot) Resident Activism in Wentworth Gardens, a Chicago Public Housing Development: A Case Study of Building Community." Pp. 111-119 in *Coming of Age*.

The proceedings of the Environmental Design Research Association Annual Conference, edited by R.E. Selby, K.H. Anthony, J. Choi, and B. Orland: Urbana-Champaign, IL.

> This evening, Heavenly Father, as we come together in your name, we come thanking you today, Lord, for this meeting. We thank you for each and everyone that made it out here today. Whether thou will bless their home, Lord....And every meeting that we go to, Lord, let us get stronger and close together with love that you might be able to fight our battle, because the battle is not ours, it's yours, and we thank you for it, in Jesus' name we pray. Amen!
>
> (Mrs. Janie Dumas, Vice-Chair of Wentworth Gardens Residents for Survival, Closing Prayer, weekly meeting, December 15, 1989)

It was the threat to the physical survival of Wentworth Gardens and its surrounding neighborhood posed by the proposed construction of the new Chicago White Sox Stadium that brought Wentworth residents into the political arena to do "battle" to protect "their homes." The Wentworth residents' responses to this threat made public their struggles to build home and community in a 42 year old, 422 unit Chicago Housing Authority (CHA) lowrise development.

THE BATTLE

According to residents, a newspaper article showing the proposed stadium adjacent to the Wentworth Gardens development was the impetus to take action. A resident initiated on-site action committee had been meeting regularly over more than a year to assist the Local Advisory Council (LAC), the CHA designated site representative, in their on-going frustration with the non-responsiveness of CHA to attend to years of deferred building and site maintenance, and inadequate services to meet basic daily needs of the residents. This committee became the focal group moved to collective action by what they believed to be a "crisis", one with an immediate, tangible impact on their community. Through strong leadership, persistent organizing efforts, and the assistance they sought from a community organizer lent by a Chicago city-wide not-for-profit organization, in 1987, the committee was incorporated and named themselves the Wentworth Gardens Residents United for Survival (Wentworth United).[1]

Wentworth United is struggling to improve living conditions for all Wentworth residents. Most immediately, they have been working against resident displacement and for economic benefit from the new ball park. They have played a pivotal role in the formation of the South Armour Square Neighborhood Coalition, a not-for-profit community development corporation representing residents from neighborhoods directly impacted by the White Sox Stadium. It is to the credit of the organizational reputation and expertise of Wentworth United, that its members have provided local leadership among impacted home owners, renters, and CHA residents in the political and legal actions with the Illinois Sports Facility Authority, the White Sox Corporation, and the City of Chicago.

For policy makers and the public alike, the role that public housing women have been playing in the political battle over the new stadium might be unexpected. Their grassroot activism, as well as that of other women, especially low income women of color, all too often remains invisible. In the media, these women are typically depicted as helpless victims of despair, incapable of forming and participating in an active, productive community.[2]

It has been assumed by all social reform efforts that low income people lack social organization and community (Cloward, 1968; Fisher, 1984).

How is it then that Wentworth United activists representing 1,264 people, mostly low income female-headed Black families have been able to effectively challenge the interests of the city and state government and private developers? They came to this battle prepared!

This study seeks to begin to uncover the history of invisible work that Wentworth women engaged in to reproduce and change conditions in their communities to prepare them for visible action in the high stakes political arena.

There has been considerable research on citizen participation — "a process in which individuals take part in decision making in the institutions, programs, and environments that affect them." (Heller et al., 1984). In the analysis of particular instances of neighborhood participation, researchers have identified many influential variables, several of which allude to participation as a historical process (reviewed in Churchman, 1987; Heller et al., 1984). In explaining the likelihood of participation and the success of a particular participatory effort, researchers have reported on the contribution of existing neighborhoodresident groups and organizations; individual residents who had past participatory and leadership experiences; and the strength of the social fabric of the community, presumably developed over time — active involvement in informal neighborly relations and social interaction, and in formal groups and organizations, as well as frequent use of neighborhood facilities and services. In addition, individuals' participation in voluntary neighborhood organizations has been related to demographic variables indicative of rootedness in places such as older, female, residents who have lived in an area longer than non-participants.

This study will elaborate on the contribution of neighborhood residents' past collective actions and its outcomes to better understand present grassroot participatory efforts.[3]

It will illustrate the ways in which these past efforts provided a rich environment for nuturing individual residents, local leadership, and resident empowerment. This study reports on initial findings from an ongoing case study analysis of the history of resident activism among selected female residents at Wentworth Gardens. The case study method was chosen because of "what the case study does best is study process" (Stoecker, 1989a, p.11). It facilitates the explication of the historical causal process behind a particular event or variable. The case study attempts to inductively understand community life from the perspective of the actor(s) (Becker, 1966).

A CASE STUDY OF THE INVISIBLE WORK OF BUILDING COMMUNITY

Wentworth United members' readiness for visible public action in the stadium battle is rooted in an invisible history of on-site community building work that spans nearly three decades. Community-building has been defined as "actions engaged in by a group of people on their own initiative in order to increase social cohesiveness of unrelated persons or to enhance the opportunities or redress the injustices of persons with whom the group identifies beyond their own family" (Reinharz, 1984, p. 20). Since the 1950's, women in Wentworth Gardens have been gradually shaping, and in turn have been shaped by their efforts to build home and community in their public housing development. These invisible efforts have prepared the Wentworth Gardens residents in their "battle for survival."

Community building activities at Wentworth Gardens are rooted in a rich social life which has ranged from informal social gatherings with neighbors and neighborly support such as information sharing, errand running, child care, and spiritual development; to more formal resident initiated service programs and facilities including grounds clean-ups, garden planting, food and clothing distributions, youth and senior programs, crime prevention and education programs, organized sports activities and trips, and an on-site laundromat and grocery store; as well as celebrations and ritual events — the yearly summer Funfest, the Back to School Party, and the Christmas Party, and the awards banquet paying tribute to residents who have worked tirelessly in the community. And, it is through the efforts of individual residents that these on-going social service programs, events and rituals are sustained. One such resident is Mrs. Weatherbee.

Originally from the south, Mrs. Weatherbee, the mother of eight children and granmother of twenty grandchildren, has lived in Wentworth Gardens for fourteen years. In addition to her roles as Chair of the Senior Committee of Wentworth United, and volunteer in the LAC/Wentworth United office, she initiated the annual awards banquet at Wentworth Gardens, and has served as its coordinator for the past six years. She explained how it began:

I had a girl friend. Me and her were sitting down one day and talking about all of the contributions — the things that had been done in the area. And we knew Mrs, Amey (the first award recipient) had been volunteering in the community for like thirty years. And we had an active person, like eighty-five years old, and he was still active and volunteering in the community, and other older people — and it got started from that.

Mrs. Weatherbee has been motivated to participate in her community because, in her own words:

I've loved living here better than I have anyplace in my life!...I stayed home a few years before I got involved, and since I've come out to get involved I keep this (LAC/Wentworth United) office open most of the time...because I love working here. I love working with people. Anything that anybody wants to be done, if I can give any help, I will do it.

Mrs. Weatherbee, as did the other women activists who were interviewed, explained that their participation was not elicited by outside institutions or motivated by monetary reward; rather, it has been based on personal relationships among the involved residents, their sense of civic duty and dedication, and their feelings of attachment and commitment to the physical place they call home (their dwelling and the housing development).

Of all the activities and programs mentioned by Wentworth resident activists, there are two service programs in particular, both sustained efforts, that were of great signifi-cance to them: the organized youth programs in the field house and the laundromat. These also are particularly illustrative of the history of collective actions that are building community in Wentworth Gardens.

The Field House Youth Program, Modest Victories,

Resident organized activities at Wentworth Gardens are run by a core group of women (fluctuates between 10-20). Participation is further encouraged by "centerwomen", sustainers of neighborhood networks. These are women leaders who engage with people one-on-one, enlisting their skills and ensuring that obligations are fulfilled; through their enthusiasm, they ignite others to join with them (Sacks, 1988).[4] One such leader is Mrs. Hallie Amey, President of Wentworth United.

Mrs. Hallie Amey moved to Wentworth with her husband and daughters in 1951. But it was not until she was widowed in 1958 that she became active in her community. With three school-aged children and a small baby in tow she first became involved at the PTA of the local school. Her first "venture into the community" was an attempt, along with other residents, to reinstate an organized youth recreation program in an unused field house.

Mrs. Amey described the precipitating incident that mobilized this effort in the early 1960s:

One day I looked out the window, I think we were giving a small fish fry or something, and there was a group of boys marching through the area with picket signs on them, picketing CHA. And I told the ladies, "They're picketing the wrong group. They should be picketing us." I said, "If anything comes up in here for us, it's going to come through us....There just comes a point and a time when there's a need for something, and a group of people gather and decide that they are going to do this for the benefit of their community — they can do it.
When appeals to CHA and on-site management failed, these women chose an alternative strategy. Mrs. Amey:

So what we did, we sat down and decided, what could we start with nothing... we decided we'd start a small preschool program because one would bring a ball and different little things that we had at home, and that's how we began. And we carried that program on for about two years.

With the preschool program as their base of operations, a small core of volunteers expanded to fifteen stable volunteers. Over time they organized four out of the seven blocks in Wentworth. Then in turn, in 1964, it was this group of female residents that organized a development-wide elected Residents' Council. Despite a lack of support from CHA, the residents remained committed to "stick together." And this time, "sticking together" yielded results. They achieved their primary goal — the field house was finally reopened.

In the mid-1960's, the Residents' Council proposed to operate a youth program in the field house. To win CHA approval, the Resident's Council had to demonstrate their effec tiveness. Once again, the residents "had to get up and work on our own." The Residents' Council organized a program, attracted resident volunteers, and operated the center five days a week. When the program was well established, the CHA did officially grant the residents control of the facility. Ultimately, with technical assistance from Illinois Institute of Technology and other outside institutions, the Park District was pressured to assume responsibility for the recreation program. They are still there today. In setting up the preschool program and the youth program in the field house, the residents achieved modest victories, small, fragmented but positive changes their lives.[5] "

Although they are small, modest victories, they are not insignificant. These short-lived successful protests of daily life illustrate the possibilities for significant change from below. Modest victories allow residents to alter community in the here and now, and through their efforts gain self-confidence and skills.

Wentworth Gardens Laundromat, a "Social Space"

In their attention to community activism, Sara Evans and Harry Boyte (1981) have offered historical evidence that rootedness in communal settings and participation in communal structures "can serve as the arenas where people can distinguish themselves from elite (societal) definitions of who they are, (and) gain the skills and mutual regard necessary to act as a force for change" (1981, p. 56). Particularly for women, communal structures can serve as "social spaces" offering arenas outside of the family where women can develop "a growing sense that they had (have) the right to work—first in behalf of others, then in behalf of themselves" (p. 61).

One Wentworth Gardens' social space, a place for neighboring and a primary recruitment ground for community activists, is the resident run laundromat founded in 1968 by the Resident Council. Prior to 1968, Wentworth Gardens had no laundry facilities. The nearest retail laundromat was ten blocks away through the "unsafe turf" of other low income neighborhoods. It was Mrs. Taylor's who "instigated" the idea for the laundromat and organized volunteers to supervise the original five machines. It was Mrs. Amey, with the help of other residents who pressed the CHA for the space and funds for the initial leasing costs.

It has been the on-going volunteer work of female residents spanning two decades that has assured the laundromat's continued operation — women like Mrs. Elizabeth Thomas, one of the original laundromat volunteers, who for seventeen years has worked up to three hours per day, four days per week; and Mrs. Henrietta Shah, described as the "rock of Gibraltar" because in addition to her own shift (working up to four days per week), she often relieves other operators as the need arises, and she does simple washer repairs learned through years of volunteering.

It is in this social space that female volunteers have provided a necessary service as well as created a sense of solidarity and a sense of significance that are fundamental to the experience of community (Clark, 1973).[6] When interviewed the laundromat operators expressed intense attachment to this social space. One woman who had volunteered for nearly twenty years described the laundromat as "our community." Others mentioned the friends they've made through their work — Mary Rais explained that she loved her laundromat work because, in her words "I like meeting people, and you know everybody in the community." And there are the rituals created to reinforce solidarity such as birthdays celebrated "right down here." Perhaps the high degree of social cohesion and interdependence generated through participation in this social space can best be demonstrated by Lucille Burns, who although she and her husband moved out of Wentworth over a year ago, still returns three times a week to work in the laundromat.

A sense of significance is derived by being a part of this core of volunteers that provide this necessary service. Wentworth residents rely on this facility; it is cost efficient and convenient. One volunteer explained that the residents "had a fit" when it had to close for a month recently for painting. Moreover, "not just any resident can work in the laundromat." The operators must first be trustworthy — it is a cash business — and demonstrate commitment to other community work before being entrusted with a laundromat operator position. One Wentworth activist explained, "If they work around here with you long enough...then you ease them into the laundromat"; and once "here", operators learn the nuts and bolts of running a business. Finally, there is a shared sense of achievement in the laundromat's success and in its mission to return all profits (above maintenance, repair and replacement costs) to the community. A resident Service Committee meets monthly to resolve problems and to prioritize requests for laundromat monies which in the past have included financing yearly community festivals and a scholarship fund.

Social spaces can extend women's roles and their participation in the community. As one Wentworth activist explained, "Most of the people that started out working in the laundromat...came out to do other things...different people had to be found."

Invisible Work Becomes Visible:

Years of participation in the invisible work of building home and community have laid the foundation for current resident initiatives. Wentworth United members recognized that they needed a visible sign of their growing effectiveness for all of the Wentworth Gardens development, and CHA and municipal officials: Mrs. Amey: "We decided that we really needed something...to win so that we could get some attention." The field house, once again served as a focus for their efforts.

It was the spring of 1987. The field house roof was in such poor repair that the scheduled children's summer food program was at risk of being canceled. To pressure for the roof repair, the women of Wentworth United began to attend the weekly CHA Board of Commissioners' meetings. Time and persistence resulted in CHA approval, but no available funds "at the present time." Undaunted, Wentworth United women persevered and continued to press the CHA Regional Supervisor until repair monies were located and allocated, and the roof was repaired. For Wentworth United women, this was a proud time. Mrs. Amey: "...that was the first main victory for Wentworth Gardens Residents United for Survival, and we were ever, ever so grateful."

CONCLUSIONS

Becoming Empowered

Through nearly three decades of experiences of community building and some tangible victories, Wentworth United's members have gained the skills and the sense of self-efficacy to negotiate with powerful actors in the proposed White Sox Stadium deal. It is through these varied, ongoing experiences that Wentworth women are becoming empowered.

Charles Kieffer (1984) in his study of the developmental process of empowerment, stressed that experience is at the core — a "building up" of skills through repetitive cycles of action and reflection which evoke new skills and understandings, which in turn provoke new and more effective actions. Kieffer further described empowerment as the attainment of commitment and capabilities which he refers to as "participatory competence."

These competencies include the development of a more positive self-concept and self-confidence; a more critical world view; and the cultivation of individual and collective skills and resources for social and political action. According to this conceptualization Wentworth women in their community building and modest victories are developing and sustaining participatory competence.

Wentworth resident activists have created and maintained organizations which work to improve the lives of all Wentworth Gardens' residents. What began as a loosely structured core of concerned residents, today is a not-for-profit organization with attendant greater organizational structure and maintenance activities, and some political legitimacy in the local and municipal arenas.

Through their modest victories, Wentworth women have developed a critical world view.
In collective actions with others, "confronting institutions, many women have come to a better understanding of the power relations that affect their lives and of their own abilities — together with others — to have some influence on them" (Ackelsberg, 1988, p. 304). Wentworth activists have learned to be pragmatists, setting their goals and strategies to match their resources and if need be and when available, draw on outside resources. They acknowledged that modest victories cannot be accomplished alone; they require a "partnership" with outside professionals, corporations and institutions. They have come to know that all their endeavors will not necessarily be victorious and that sometimes their modest victories may be shortlived; but with time and persistence, they may achieve some successes. And indeed, Wentworth activists have gained better on-site services and improved management accountability.

The Elusive Gains of Building Community

The observations of Wentworth women's activism share many commonalities with research of other grassroot community activism among poor and working class women, particularly of color (e.g. Morgan & Bookman, 1988; Krauss, 1983; Leavitt & Saegert, 1988) Poor and working class women cannot rely on culturally normative routes of electoral politics to work in their best interests, nor do they have the financial resources to exercise economic power to achieve their interests. Limited political and economic resources constrains their residential alternatives and their actual power over the places in which they live. Poor women of color gain their power from individual dedication and persistence and their social relations that are embedded in the communities in which they live.

Furthermore, the skills they bring to collective actions are cultivated through everyday routine activities of maintaining households and communities — tasks necessary to the "social reproduction" of individual households as well as social arrangements they make to protect, enhance and preserve the cultural experiences of all members of the community [7] (Stall, 1982, 1984; Stoecker, 1989b;).

It is in the social spaces of Wentworth Gardens, spaces traditionally viewed as functioning solely for the maintenance of social reproduction, that social change has occurred. Wentworth women's experiences in the practical affairs of the household and community has had a substantial impact on their grassroot activism. As safe and decent shelter becomes increasingly difficult to obtain, these experiences provide alternative means for low income women of color to develop resources for collective power (Stoecker, 1989b).

The Future

The women interviewed at Wentworth Gardens do not see their efforts as extraordinary; rather they see their collective actions as a means to effect immediate necessary changes in their lives and in their community. According to Morgan and Bookman (1988):

For the (working class) women....empowerment is rarely experienced as upward mobility or personal advancement. Rather "feeling powerful" is constrained for them by the ways in which their gender, as well as their race and class, limit their access to economic resources and political power. For these women, empo-werment begins when they change their idea about the causes of their powerlessness when they recognize the systemic forces that oppress them, and when the act to change the conditions of their lives. (p. 4)

Ultimately, resident leaders have come to know that Wentworth women's ability to make substantial changes in their lives rests in changes in local and national housing policy. Their understanding is rooted in a vision of a better past, when public housing "was a good place to live," and their first-hand knowledge about the public housing policies that contributed to making this so. They also have aspirations for a future in which public housing will once again become a better place to live. To assist in achieving this goal, Wentworth women are ready to take on new challenges and to take advantage of any opportunity that presents itself to exert control in their lives.

The long-term goal of Wentworth United is to become a resident-managed development. Steps are being taken in this direction. Wentworth United has applied for and received HUD funds for resident rehabilitation of unoccupied units. In addition, they have applied for and are waiting for a response from HUD for a training grant to prepare residents for the development of a Public Housing Resident Management Corporation. There is much left to be accomplished, but the Wentworth residents we spoke to believe that they have established the core group of experienced volunteers that will in the not-too-distant future make Resident Management a reality at Wentworth Gardens. As Maggie Mahon, Chair of the Security Committee of Wentworth United so aptly said, "It can be done. Don't give up. Keep on fighting!"

BIBLIOGRAPHY

Ackelsberg, M. A. 1988. Communities, resistance and women's activism: some implications for a democratic polity. In *Women and the Politics of Empowerment*, edited by A. Bookman & S. Morgen. Philadelphia: Temple University Press, 297-313.

Bookman, A. & Morgen, S. 1988. *Women and the Politics of Empowerment*, edited by A. Bookman & S. Morgen. Philadelphia: Temple University Press.

Churchman, A. 1987. Can resident participation in neighborhood rehabilitation programs succeed? Israel's Project Renewal through a comparative perspective. In *Neighborhood and Community Environments,* edited by I. Altman & A. Wandersman. New York: Plenum, 113-162.

Clark, D. 1973. The concept of community: a re-examination. Sociological Review, 21,3:397-416.

Cloward, R. A. 1960. The war on poverty: Are the poor left out? In *Poverty: Power and Politics*, edited by C. I. Waxman . New York: Grosset & Dunlap, 159-179.

Evans, S. M. & Boyte, H. C. 1981. Schools for action: radical uses of social space. Democracy, Summer: 55-65.

Fischer, R. 1984. Let the People Decide: Neighborhood Organizations in America, Boston: Twayne.

Heller, K. Price, R., Reinharz, S., Rigers, S., & Wandersman, A. 1984. *Psychology and Community Change: Challenges of the Future*, second edition, Homewood, IL: Dorsey Press.

Kieffer, C. H. 1984. Citizen empowerment: a developmental perspective. In *Studies in Empowerment: Steps Toward Understanding and Action*, edited by J. Rappaport, C. Swift & R. Hess. New York: Haworth, 9-36.

Krauss, C. 1983. The elusive process of citizen activism. Social Policy, Fall: 50-55.

Morgan, S. & Bookman, A. 1988. Rethinking women and politics: an introductory essay.
In *Women and the Politics of Empowerment*, edited by A. Bookman & S. Morgen. Philadelphia: Temple University Press, 3-29.

Reinharz, S (1984) Women as competent community builders. In *Social and Psychological Problems of Women*, edited by A U Rickel, M Gerrard & I Iscoe. Washington: Hemisphere.

Stoecker, R (1989a) On the "N of 1" question: the need for case study research in sociology. Paper presented at the Midwest Sociological Society Annual Meeting.

Stoecker, R (1989b) Who takes out the garbage? Social reproduction as a neglected dimension of social movement theory. Paper presented at the Midwest Sociological Society Annual Meeting.

(1) Wentworth United is a unique organization within Chicago public housing, one of two resident initiated not-for-profit organizations located in the nineteen CHA developments. Most public housing residents are represented solely by the Local Advisory Council, the CHA designated site representative.

(2) For example, residential life in public housing was given considerable press in Chicago with a twelve part series, "The Chicago Wall" in the Chicago *Tribune*, December 1986 and the Public Broadcasting System documentary "Crisis on Federal Street" filmed in Robert Taylor Homes, a CHA development, and aired in Chicago on January 6, 1989.

(3) Grassroot participation is defined as organizations and social movements intitiated by citizens (Heller, et al., 1984).

(4) In her study of a University Hospital organizing effort, Sacks (1988) contrasted two aspects of leadership. Most generally recognized is the leader as public speaker and confrontational negotiator. Sacks argued that this is a limiting view of leadership, which is inadvertently a "class, gender, and perhaps racially biased one" (p. 120). In equating leadership with speaking we often miss "women's key leadership role as centerwomen" (p. 121), and equally importantly, we leave "the impression that people act as individuals following an articulate orator" (p. 214).

(5) The notion of modest victories was adapted from Celene Krauss's (1983) concept of "modest victories," "small, fragmented, and sometimes contradictory efforts by people to change their lives" (p. 54).

(6) Clark (1973) defined solidarity as a "we-feeling," all those sentiments which draw people together. Significance was defined as "the sense of place and stations, a sense of achievement and/or fulfillment, so that each person within a community feels that she or he has an important role to play" (p. 404).

(7) In interpreting the role of domestic life in women's grassroot organizing, feminist scholars have contested the notion that women's participation is motivated solely by their concerns as wives and mothers (reviewed by Morgan & Bookman, 1988). These scholars do not deny that women's domestic responsibilities contribute to their political consciousness and actions; rather they advocate an approach that gives due recognition to the ways in which race and class specify women's community based needs and the nature of their involvement in grassroots politics.

D1

The Chicago Coalition for the Homeless Women's Empowerment Project. 1992. *Illinois Women's Advocate*, Summer.

Editor's Note: Special thanks to Della Mitchell of the Chicago Coalition for the Homeless

For the last year, the Chicago Coalition for the Homeless (CCH) has been developing a project no one thought was possible. It's called the Women's Empowerment Project.

Della Mitchell, the Project's coordinator, began with the goal of empowering homeless women and creating a stable homeless women's advocacy organization. She began visiting shelters on the South Side, building relationships of trust with women in the shelters, asking about their lives, and listening. "I have not experienced what you have experienced," says Della, "but I care. I come to you not as a social worker, but as a sister."

One year later the Project has several active committees, has held five public actions and provided numerous training sessions in organizing skills. The Project's co-ordinating committee meets twice a month and is made up of representatives from ten shelters.

The women have identified five priorities: treatment at shelters; affordable housing; day care; jobs; and job training. In an effort to influence public policy on these issues, the group went to Springfield to protest budget cuts in social services and met and negotiated with HUD's regional administrator Gertrude Jordan. They also held a press conference and gave public testimony on the Presidential Towers scandal, and are working on how to develop grievance procedures to guide conflict resolution in shelters. Some of the women have become Deputy Registrars so they can register other homeless women to vote [see Legislative Watch homeless voting rights bill].

Long range plans include acquiring an abandoned building from the city, learning how to rehabilitate it, and building a co-operating living establishment with an in-house day care center which would serve not only the women living there, but the community in which they live. Some of the residents would enter training programs to become licensed day care providers.

These are some of the accomplishments of the Empowerment Project, but as important is the support the women in the group provide for each other. In providing a place where homeless women can share their experiences and work toward common goals, the Project allows women the opportunity to feel the power that comes from working together, and to feel hope.

"We have met women who are at their lowest point," says Della Mitchell. "[We try to] turn their anger into positive action." Everybody has a right to be angry, she affirms, because everybody has a right to affordable housing.

Two of the toughest problems the Project has faced are child care and transportation. Child care is a constant problem for women who are homeless. Living in shelters means women are with their children 24 hours a day. Most shelters will not allow the children to stay in the shelter without their mother, even if the mother has arranged for someone else to be there to take care of the children. The Empowerment Project has organized volunteers to help with child care during meetings, but the larger problem of lack of affordable day care remains a major barrier for homeless women.

There are several ways to get involved with the Empowerment Project — join a support group to provide child care during Project meetings and events; help with transportation to events and meetings; join the Empowerment Advisory Committee; or join the Chicago Coalition for the Homeless' Women's Issues Committee. The Empowerment Project will also be holding an Empowerment Dinner and Speakout on August 28, 1992. Tickets are $10 and guests are asked to sponsor a homeless woman. For more information, call 435-4348.

The Chicago Coalition for the Homeless estimates there are 50,000 homeless in Chicago. 40% are women and their children, who are the fastest growing segment of the homeless population. According to Sarah's Circle, a North Side shelter for women and children, 40% of women in Chicago shelters cite domestic violence as the primary reason for their lack of housing. A Chicago Institute on Urban Poverty survey showed that 45% of homeless women with work experience have never earned more than $5/hr. According to the Interfaith Council for the Homeless, nearly $50 billion less federal funds were spent in 1980-1990 than were spent in 1970-1980 on low-income housing.

D2

Bob Sperber. 1992. "Homeless Families in Chicago." *Chicago Coalition for the Homeless Newsletter.*

Desiree Maurer, a 30-year hold mother of four children, experienced a temporary but turbulent period of homelessness last year. Desiree quit high school and left home at 14, and moved out to find work, pay rent, and eventually raise a family. Today, 16 years later, she has 4 children. The oldest is 7 year old Alicia. Her three sons, Christopher, Nicholas, and Tory, are 6, 4, and 1 1/2 years old. The children's father lived with the family until their September eviction, a consequence of Public Aid sanctioning. Desiree was sanctioned (had her check cut off) because of failure to comply with one of the agency's requirements. She never received the notice in the mail. Says Desiree, "We didn't have much to begin with, but we lost everything."

The family's first stop was an overnight shelter. According to Desiree, "There was no structure, no privacy. The kids became totally wild. They told me they hated me. I couldn't take them anywhere because they just wouldn't behave," said Desiree.

After a month, the family found a place at a transitional shelter, where structure was enforced. "Mothers weren't allowed to leave the kids for one minute. Soon, they became too dependent; if I left the room, they'd cry out.

Now, 9 months after joining the Chicago Coalition for the Homeless Women's Empowerment Project, the family has moved back into a rental apartment. Desiree is earning her high school Graduation Equivalency Diploma, and her children are in day care. "I am very close with them. I can see them becoming more normal, more gentle, and they're learning to trust people again."

The situation of homeless families in Chicago mirrors the problem nationwide. Homeless families are the fastest growing segment of the homeless population, accounting for approximately 35 percent of the total. Every night, 2,032 beds in shelters throughout Chicago are occupied by women with their children. Unfortunately, approximately twice that number seek emergency assistance and cannot be helped. Many of these families sleep, doubled up with friends and relatives, in abandoned buildings or cars, and some sleep on the street.

A study on homeless families in Chicago found that 77 percent of the women with children staying in shelters are African-American, 12 percent are white, 10 percent are Hispanic-American, and 1 percent are American-Indian. One half of the women surveyed were between the ages of 25 and 34; over half of the women had not completed high school, and approximately one half had either dropped out of school or become homeless as a result of a pregnancy during their teen years.

The families surveyed had an average of 3.3 children, over half of whom were under age 5. Furthermore, almost half of the women surveyed did not have all their children with them.

Clearly, the, homelessness both causes and results in families coming apart during early formative years of children, and result in experiences that can and do cause medical, emotional, behavioral problems.

Prior to becoming homeless, family life for these mothers and their children was already unstable. Two-thirds of the women interviewed became homeless as a result of abuse or harassment by a partner or husband. Most of the other one third became homeless because of problems paying the rent, paying utility bills, or problems with late welfare checks.

Homeless families are often trapped in a cycle of homelessness. Forty-six percent of the women surveyed had been homeless at least once in the previous three years. Of all the families surveyed, the average number of moves before arriving at the shelter was almost 4; that is, families had been moving from place to place for some time before turning to the emergency shelter system.

Needless to say, this mobility has serious consequences for the stability of the lives of the children. Over half of the children surveyed in shelters had missed one or more weeks of schooling. Fifty-nine percent of the mothers surveyed stated that their children's behavior had changed, including children becoming more clingy, afraid of separation, and extensive crying and unruly behavior.

Chicago has an extensive network of shelters serving families, although the need far outstrips the number of shelter beds available.

Shelters: a primer

DROP-IN CENTER: offers a place to stay during the day. Meals, showers, clothing, and social services may be provided. The are 18 city-funded drop-in centers in Chicago.

WARMING CENTER: provides temporary shelter, often in church basements, often during the coldest months.

OVERNIGHT SHELTER: provides an overnight bed on a first come, first served basis. There are 16 in Chicago.

TRANSITIONAL SHELTER: provides three to six months of shelter for homeless individuals and families. Transitional shelters provide intensive services to assist homeless people in the transition back to housing and independent living. There are 34 city-funded transitional shelters.

SECOND STAGE HOUSING: provides up to 18 months of housing, primarily for families. Like transitional shelter, these programs provide extensive services to assist in the transition back to independent living. There are 26 second-stage housing programs in Chicago.

E.

"NCASA Guidelines for Choosing a Self-Defense Course." 1992. *Women in the Martial Arts.* National Women's Martial Arts Federation Newsletter.

Ideally, a good self-defense program should reflect these philosophical points in its outlook:

1) Women do not ask for, cause, invite, or deserve to be assaulted. Women and men sometimes exercise poor judgment about safety behavior, but that does not make them responsible for the attack. Attackers are responsible for their attacks and their use of violence to overpower, control and abuse another human being.

2) Whatever a woman's decision in a given self-defense situation, whatever action she does or does not take, she is not at fault. A woman's decision to survive the best way she can must be respected. Self-defense classes should not be used as judgment against a victim/survivor.

3) Good self-defense programs do not "tell" an individual what she "should" or "should not" do. A program should offer options, techniques, and a way of analyzing situations. A program may point out what USUALLY works best in MOST situations, but each situation is unique and the final decision rests with the person actually confronted by the situation.

4) Empowerment is the goal of a good self-defense program. The individual's right to make decisions about her participation must be respected. Pressure should not be brought to bear in any way to get a woman to participate in an activity if she's hesitant or unwilling.

Q: What is self-defense?

Self-defense is a set of awareness, assertiveness, verbal confrontation skills with safety strategies and physical techniques that enable someone to successfully escape, resist and survive violent attacks. A good self-defense course provides psychological awareness and verbal skills, not just physical training.

Q. Does self-defense work?

Yes. Self-defense training can increase your options and help you prepare responses to slow down, de-escalate, or interrupt an attack. Like any tool, the more you know about it, the more informed you are to make a decision and to use it.

Q: Is self-defense a guarantee?

No. There are no guarantees when it comes to self-protection. However, self-defense training can increase your choices/options and your preparedness.

Q: Is there a standard self-defense course?

No. There are many formats for training. They may be as short as two hours or as long as 8 weeks or a semester. Whatever the length of the program, it should be based on maximizing options, simple techniques, and respect for women's experience.

Q: Is there a course I should stay away from?

Only you can answer this question. Find out about the philosophy of the program and the background of the instructor. Observe a class session if you can, and talk to an instructor or a student. Is the instructor knowledgeable and respectful of your concerns? Is it a length that you can commit to and at a cost that you can afford? You deserve to have all your questions answered before taking a class.

Q: Who's better, a male or female instructor?

There is an advantage to having a female instructor as a role model and who has similar experiences surviving as a woman. All-woman classes tend to provide an easier atmosphere in which to discuss sensitive issues. On the other hand, some women feel having male partners to practice with can add to their experience. The quality of a class depends on the knowledge, attitude and philosophy of the instructor, not necessarily on gender. The most important aspect is that the instructor, male or female, conducts the training for the students geared to their individual strengths and abilities. Feeling safe and building trust comes before learning.

Q: Must I train for years to learn to defend myself?

No. A basic course can offer enough concepts and skills to help you develop self-protection strategies that you can continue to build upon. Self-defense is not karate or martial arts training. It does not require years of study to perfect. There are women who have successfully improvised and prevented an assault and never have taken a class. Women often practice successful self-defense strategies without knowing it!

Q: If I use physical self-defense could I get hurt worse?

The question to answer first is what does "hurt worse" mean? Rape survivors speak eloquently about emotional hurts lasting long after physical hurts heal. Studies show a physical self-defense response does not increase the level of physical injury, and sometimes decreases the likelihood. Also, women going along with the attacker have sometimes been brutally injured anyway. The point of using self-defense is to de-escalate a situation and get away as soon as possible. Knowing some physical techniques increases the range of possible self-defense options, but the decision to choose a physical option must remain with the person in the situation.

Q: What does realistic mean?

Words like "most realistic," "best," "guaranteed success," etc., are all advertising gimmicks. Choosing a self-defense class is a serious decision and is preferably based on some research. No program or instructor can replicate a "real" assault since there are so many different scenarios, and because a real attack would require a no-holds barred fight which would be irresponsible and extremely dangerous to enact. Responsible self-defense training requires control. It is important that each student in a class is able to control her own participation in the class and never feel forced to participate.

Q: What is the role of mace or other aggressive "devices" as self-defense aids in harming an attacker?

Any device is useless to you unless you understand how to use, and you have it in your hand ready to use at the time of the attempted assault. There is nothing "guaranteed" about any of these devices. None are foolproof. None of them can be counted on to work against all possible attackers (no matter what the labeling may state to the contrary). Realize that anything you can use against an attacker can also be taken away and used against you. While some of these devices have sometimes helped women escape to safety, it is important to be aware of their limitations and liabilities.

Q: How much should I pay?

Paying a lot of money for a course does not mean that you automatically get better instruction. On the other hand, don't assume that all programs are the same and just go for the cheapest. It is always beneficial to be an educated consumer. Shop around the same as for anything else you buy that is important to you.

Q: Where can I find a self-defense class?

Check with your local rape crisis center. Some centers provide self-protection classes or can refer you to one. YWCA's and Community Colleges sometimes offer classes. Some martial arts schools provide seminars and workshops. Check the phone book. If there isn't one in your community, get involved and try to organize one.

Q: Am I too old? Out of shape? What if I have some disabilities?

You don't have to be an athlete to learn how to defend yourself. A good program is designed to adapt to every age and ability and provides each student with the opportunity to learn. Each individual is unique and students should be able to discuss their own needs. Some programs have specialized classes for specific groups.

Q: How can I tell a "good" course from a "bad" one?

A good course covers critical thinking about self-defense strategies, assertiveness, powerful communication skills, and easy-to-remember physical techniques. The instructor respects and responds to your fears and concerns. Instruction is based on the belief that women can act competently, decisively, and take action for their own protection. Essentially, a good course is based on intelligence and not muscle. It offers tools for enabling a woman to connect with her own strength and power. These courses are out there. Good luck in your research. Taking a self-defense class is one of the most positive acts a woman can do for herself!

ORGANIZATIONS

Listed below are all the organizations mentioned on the videotape or in the Study Guide of "Women and Social Action." This list is by no means exhaustive for Chicago or other communities. This list is a beginning point for recognizing the extent to which women are engaged in diverse social actions on behalf of themselves and their communities.

Access Living of Metropolitan Chicago. 310 S. Peoria. Chicago, IL 60607. (312) 226-5900.

American Association of University Women. 1111 Sixteenth Street NW, Washington, D.C. 20036-4873. (202) 785-7700.

American College of Nurse Midwives (ACNM). 1522 K Street NW, Suite 1120, Washington, D.C. 20005. (202) 345-5445.

American Indian Economic Development Association (AIEDA). 4753 N. Broadway Ave. Chicago, IL 60640. (773) 784-0808.

American Jewish Congress Commission of Women's Equality. Midwest Region. 22 W. Monroe, #1900, Chicago IL 60603. (312) 332-7355.

American Sociological Association. 1722 N Street NW, Washington, D.C. 20036. (202) 833-3410.

Apna Ghar ["Our Home"]. 4753 N. Broadway, Suite 502, Chicago, IL 60640. (773) 334-4663;

Asian Human Services of Chicago, Inc. 4753 N. Broadway, Suite 632, Chicago, IL 60640. (773) 728-2235.

Boston Women's Health Book Collective. Women's Health Information Center. P.O.Box 192, West Somerville, MA 02144.

B.J.'s KIDS Day Care Home. 2473 N. Albany, Chicago, IL 60647. (773) 342-3054.

Catholics for a Free Choice. 1436 U Street NW, Suite 301, Washington, D.C. 20009. (202) 986-6093.

Chicago Abortion Fund. P.O. Box 578307 Chicago, IL 60657. Client Services: (773) 248-4541   Administration: (773) 248-4807.

Chicago Association for the Education of Young Children. 410 S. Michigan, Suite 525, Chicago, IL 60605. (312) 427-5399.

Chicago Coalition for the Homeless Empowerment Project for Homeless Women with Children. 1325 S. Wabash, Suite 205, Chicago, IL 60605-2504. (312) 435-4548.

Chicago Community Midwives. 2459 N. Berteau Ave., Chicago, IL 60618. (773) 588-3255.

Chicago Housing Authority Residents Taking Action (CHARTA). (now dissolved)

The Chicago Religious Network on Central America. (now dissolved)

Chicago Women in Trades. 37 S. Ashland Ave, Chicago, IL 60607. (312) 942-1444.

Chicago Women's Health Center. 3435 N. Sheffield Ave. Chicago IL 60657. (773) 935-6126.

Child Care Initiatives. 1300 W. Belmont Avenue. Suite L100. Chicago IL 60657.

Child Development Center, Chinese American Service League. 310 W. 24th Place, Chicago IL 60616. (312) 791-0454 or (312) 791-0418.

Chimera, Inc. 59 E. Van Buren, Chicago IL 60605. (312) 939-5341.

Cook County Child Care Resource and Referral. (773) 769-8000.

Council for Disability Rights. 208 South LaSalle, Suite 1330, Chicago, IL 60604.
(312) 444-9484. TDD (312) 444-1967.

Day Care Action Council of Illinois. 4753 N. Broadway, Suite 726, Chicago, IL 60640.

Ecumenical Program on Central America and the Carribean. 1470 Irving St. NW, Washington,
D.C. 20010. (202) 332-0292.

Emergency Clinic Defense Coalition. P.O. Box 1634, Evanston IL 60204. (847) 845-6838.

EMPATHY: Gay and Lesbian Advocacy Research Project. P.O. Box 5085, Columbia, SC
29250.

Environmental Design Research Association (EDRA). P.O. Box 24083, Oklahoma City, OK
73124.

Genesis House. 911 West Addison, Chicago IL 60613. (773) 281-3917.
                Satellite Drop-in Center, 743 S. Sacramento, Chicago, IL

Habitat for Humanity-Uptown. 3225 W. Foster Ave, Chicago IL 60625, (773) 509-6034.

Health Resource Center for Women with Disabilities. c/o Dr. Kristi Kirschner, Rehabilitation
Institute of Chicago. 345 E. Superior, Chicago, IL 60610. (312)908-4744.

The Hopi Tribe. P.O. Box 123. Kykotsmovi, Arizona, 86039. (602) 734-2441.

Illinois Birth Center Task Force. Health and Medicine Policy Research Group. Women's Health
Task Force. 332 S. Michigan Ave., Chicago, IL 60604. (312) 922-8057.

Illinois Clemency Project for Battered Women. P.O.Box 257292, Chicago IL 60625.

IMPACT International, Inc. 701 Richmond Avenue, Silver Spring MD 20910. (301) 589-1349.
        IMPACT self-defense courses are offered by
        BAMM IMPACT. 1561 Industrial Way, San Carlos CA 94070-4111. (415) 592-7300
        DC IMPACT. 701 Richmond Ave, Silver Spring, MD 20910. (301)589-1349
        IMPACT of Indianapolis. (317) 255-5881 or (317) 257-9527.
        IMPACT of Minnesota. P.O. Box 47052, Minneapolis, MN. (612)475-4008
        Self Empowerment Group. 6219 N. Sheridan Ave., Chicago, IL 60660. (773)338-4545.

Jane Addams Hull House Association. 118 N. Clinton St. Chicago, IL 60661. (312) 726-1526.

Korean Self-Help Center, Women's Program. 4934 N. Pulaski Rd. Chicago, IL 60630.
(773) 545-8348.

La Leche League International. P.O. Box 1209, Minneapolis Ave., Franklin Park, IL 60131.
(708) 455-7730.

Lesbian Community Cancer Project. 1902 W. Montrose Ave., Chicago, IL 60613.
(773) 561-4662.

Maria Shelter. 7320 S. Yale Ave., Chicago, IL 60621. (773) 994-5350.

Midwest Women's Center. 828 S. Wabash, Chicago, IL 60605. (312) 922-8530.

Midwives Alliance of North America (MANA). P.O. Box 1121, Bristol, VA 24202.
(615) 764-5561.

Mujeres Latinas En Acción (Latin Women in Action). 1823 West 17th St. Chicago, IL 60608.
(312) 226-1544.

National Assembly of Religious Women (NARW). 529 S. Wabash, Room 404, Chicago, IL
60605. (312) 663-1980.

National Association for the Education of Young Children. 1509 16th St NW, Washington, DC 20036-1426. (800) 424-2460 or (202) 232-8777.

National Black Women's Health Project. 1237 Ralph Abernathy Blvd., SW, Atlanta, GA 30310. (404) 758-9590.

National Coalition Against Sexual Assault (NCASA). P.O. Box 21378, Washington, D.C. 20009.

National College of Midwifery. Drawer SSS. Taos, NM 87571. (505) 758-1216.

National Latina Health Organization/Organización Nacional de la Salud de la Mujer Latina. P.O. Box 7567, Oakland, CA 94601. (415) 534-1362.

National Organization for Women (NOW), Chicago chapter. 53 West Jackson Boulevard, #924, Chicago, IL 60604. (312) 922-0025.

National Women's Health Network. 1325 G Street NW, Washington, DC 20005. (202) 347-1140.

National Women's Martial Arts Federation. c/o Melanie Fine. P.O. Box 4688, Corpus Christi, TX 78469-4688.

Native American Educational Service (NAES). 2838 West Peterson Ave. Chicago, IL 60659. (773) 761-5000.

Native American Women's Health Education Resource Center. P.O. Box 572. Lake Andes, SD 57356. (605) 487-7072.

Organization of the North East (O.N.E.). 5121 N. Clark St. Chicago, IL 60640. (773) 769-3232.

Orr Community Academy Infant and Family Development Center. 730 N. Pulaski Ave. Chicago, IL 60624. (773) 826-1090.

Planned Parenthood Information and Referral Hotline. 14 E. Jackson Blvd. Chicago Il 60604. (312) 427-2275.

Professional Development Program, University-Schools Collaborative Project, Chicago Teachers' Center. 770 N. Halsted, Suite 420, Chicago, IL 60622. (312) 733-7330.

Radical Feminist Organizing Committee (RFOC). 109 Ellerbee Street, Durham, NC 27704.

The Research Clearinghouse and Curriculum Integration Project on Women of Color and Southern Women. Center for Research on Women. Memphis State University. Memphis, TN 38152.

Seattle School of Midwifery. 2524 16th Ave, Seattle, WA 98144. (206) 322-8834.

Seeking Educational Equity and Diversity (S.E.E.D.). National S.E.E.D. Project on Inclusive Curriculum. Wellesley College for the Center for Research on Women. Wellesley, MA 02181. (617) 283-2522.

Self Empowerment Group. 6219 N. Sheridan Ave., Chicago IL 60660. (773) 338-4545.

Support Advocates for Women...Both Inside and Outside Prison (S.A.W.). 9453 S. Ashland Avenue, Suite 14, Chicago, IL 60620.

Telling Women's Lives Historical Encyclopedia of Chicago Women Project. Contact: Rima Schultz. 320 N. Ridgeland, Oak Park, IL 60302. (708) 383-7026.

Thousand Waves: Martial Arts and Self-Defense for Women and Children. 1220 W. Belmont, Chicago, IL 60657. (773) 472-7663

Traditional Childbearing Group. P.O. Box 638. Boston, MA 02118. (617) 541-0086.

Union of Palestinian Women's Association. 3148 W. 63rd Street. Chicago, IL 60629. (773) 436-6060.

Urban League. 4510 S. Michigan Ave. Chicago, IL 60653. (773) 285-5800.

U.S. Equal Employment Opportunities Commission (EEOC). Check your local phone book.

Wellesley College. Center for Research on Women. 106 Central St., Wellesley, MA 02181-8259.

Wentworth Resident Management Council. 252 W. 39th Street, Chicago, IL 60609. (773) 548-8453 or (773) 548-7512.

Women Employed. 22 W. Monroe Ave., Suite 1400, Chicago, IL 60603. (312) 782-3902.

Women for Economic Security. 200 S. Michigan Avenue, Suite 1400, Chicago, IL 60604. (312) 663-3574.

Women of All Red Nations (WARN). 4511 N. Hermitage Ave., Chicago, IL 60640. (773) 493-2791.

Women Organizers' Collective. c/o ECCO, Hunter College School of Social Work. 129 E. 79th Street, New York, NY 10021.

Women United for a Better Chicago. (now dissolved)

Women's Action Coalition (WAC). P.O. Box 1862, Chelsea Station, New York, NY 10011. (212) 967-7711, ext WACM (9226).

Women's Program, Howard Brown Health Center. 945 W. George, Chicago, IL 60657. (773) 871-5777.

Women's Studies Program, Northeastern Illinois University. 5500 N. St. Louis, Chicago, IL 60625. (773) 583-4050, Ext. 3308.

Woodlawn East Community and Neighbors (WE CAN). 1541 E. 65th Street, Chicago, IL 60649. (773) 288-3000. Greater Chicagoland: (800) 400-4010.

Y-Me National Organization for Breast Cancer Information and Support. 18220 Harwood Ave. Homewood, Il 60430. 24 hour Emergency Breast Cancer Hotline (708) 799-8228. Monday - Friday, 9 am - 5 pm CST, call 1-800-221-2141.

ACKNOWLEDGEMENTS

We wish to thank the following individuals and groups who made invaluable contributions to Women and Social Action.

Advisory committee members:

> Joan Hill, Department of Sociology, Chicago State University
> Harriet Gross, Division of Humanities and Social Sciences, Governors State University
> Gail Mason, Department of Speech Communication, Eastern Illinois University
> Polly Radosh, Department of Sociology, Anthropology, and Social Work, Western Illinois University
> Susan Stall, Department of Sociology, Northeastern Illinois University
> Carol Lanning, Office of the Vice Chancellor for Academic Affairs, Board of Governors of State Colleges and Universities

Teleclass students:

> Christine Baltzer
> Linda Daniels
> Felicia Davis
> Gail Donnelly
> Peg Donohue
> Janet Doran
> Virginia Eysenbach
> Deborah Forestal
> Judy Gustawson
> Mary Howes
> Helen Hughes
> Joan Johns
> Caryn Johnson
> Sharon Kroopkin
> Janet Ksiazek
> Phyllis McLaurin
> Ada Middleton
> Gunther Oberth
> Trenace Pyles
> Carlos Reyes
> Joe Talluto
> Laura Williams
> Claudia Zekas

Video Interviews and Studio Guests:
Unless otherwise mentioned, interviews and guests were from the Chicago area.
Betty Achinstein, Thurgood Marshall Middle School
Larry Alexander, Jane Addams Uptown Center
Dihya Al Kahina, National Assembly of Religious Women (NARW)
Margorie Altergott, Northeastern Illinois University
Alicia Amador, Mujeres Latinas En Acción
Hallie Amey, Wentworth Gardens
Brenda Chock Arksey, Chinese American Service League
Shelley Bannister, Northeastern Illinois University
Pauline Bart, co-author of *Stopping Rape: Successful Survival Strategies*
Patricia Beardon, Metcalf Elementary School
Rhanjana Bhargava, Apna Ghar
Amy Blumenthal, author of "Scrambled eggs and seed daddies: conversations with my son," *Empathy, Gay and Lesbian Advocacy Research Project*
Jonathon Blumenthal
Marca Bristo, Access Living, A Center for Service, Advocacy and Social Change for People

with Disabilities

Leslie Brown, Support Advocates for Women...Both Inside and Outside Prison (SAW)

Irene Campos Carr, Northeastern Illinois University

Ellen Cannon, Northeastern Illinois University

Chicago Coalition for the Homeless Empowerment Project for Homeless Women with Children Coordinating Committee

Joe Connelly, Self Empowerment Group

Regina Curry, Woodlawn East Community and Neighborhood (WE CAN)

Rabbi Ellen Dreyfus, Congregation Beth Sholom, Park Forest, Illinois

Emergency Clinic Defense Coalition at Cook County Hospital demonstration

Aida Giachello, University of Illinois in Chicago

Randy Gold, Lawrence, Kamin, Saunders, and Uhlenhop

Renny Golden, Northeastern Illinois University

Harriet Gross, Governors State University, University Park, Illinois

Beatrice Harris, Wentworth Gardens

Andrea Henley, Wentworth Gardens

The Hopi Tribe, Lynn Ables, Marla Dacawyma, Marlene Jackson, Carol James, Lynn Kalectaca, LuAnn Leonard, Nicole Marietta Leonard, Farron Lomakema, Grace Nejman, Beatrice Norton, Thelma Tewahaftewa, Ethelene Tootsie, and Ellen Wadsworth, Kykotsmovi AZ

Demetria Iazzetto, contributor to *Our Bodies, Ourselves, Updated and Expanded for the '90s.*

Maha Jarad, Union of Palestinian Women and Women United for a Better Chicago

Melissa Josephs, Women Employed

Eileen Kreutz, Chicago Women in Trades

Jean Lachowitz, Genesis House

Nancy Lanoue, Thousand Waves: Martial Arts and Self-Defense for Women and Children

Rachel Lucas-Thompson

Lee Maglaya, Apna Ghar

Mary McCauley II, Lesbian Community Cancer Project

Laura McAlpine, Chicago Women's Health Center

Della Mitchell, Chicago Coalition for the Homeless Empowerment Project for Homeless Women with Children

Mary Mittler, Oakton Community College, Skokie, Illinois

Catherine Moore, Orr Community Academy Infant Care Facility

Yvonne Murry-Ramos, American Indian Economic Development Association (AIEDA)

Orr Community Academy Infant Care Facility children, parents, teachers, and staff

Judy Panko Reis, Health Resource Center for Women with Disabilities

Charles Payne, Northwestern University, Evanston, Illinois

Paulette Patterson, Council for Disability Rights

Rev. Cheryl Pero, Crossings Ministry, Harold Washington College Campus Ministry

Theo Pintzuk, Women's Program, Howard Brown Health Center

Sharon Powell, Chicago Women's Health Center

Steve Rehrauer, Self Empowerment Group

B.J. Richards, B.J.'s KIDS

Stephanie Riger, co-author of *The Female Fear*

Sheila Rogers, Women Employed

Betty Sandifer, Orr Community Academy Infact Care Facility

Mary Ann Schwartz, Northeastern Illinois University
Barbara Scott, Northeastern Illinois University
Norma Seledon-Telez, Mujeres Latinas En Acción
Self Empowerment Group, sponsor of IMPACT Self-Defense
Geri Shangreaux, Native American Educational Services
Radhika Sharma, Apna Ghar
Yolanda Simmons, King High School
Andrea Smith, Women of All Red Nations
Spiritual Israel Church Shelter for Homeless Women with Children
Wendy Stack, Chicago Teacher's Center, Northeastern Illinois University
Susan Stall, Northeastern Illinois University
Robin Stein, Lesbian Community Cancer Project
Sandra Steingraber, Lesbian Community Cancer Project
Elaine Stocker, IMPACT Self-Defense
Doris Thompson, Orr Community Academy Infant Care Facility
Helen Um, Women's Program, Korean Self-Help Center
Judy Vaughn, National Assembly of Religious Women (NARW)
Pam Wilson, Apna Ghar
Women's Action Coalition (WAC) at Cook County Hospital demonstration
Carol Zimmerman, Lesbian Community Cancer Project

Suggestions for people to interview and readings to include:
Lynn Ables, Keams Canyon Public Health Service, Arizona
Margorie Altergott, Northeastern Illinois University
Hallie Amey, Wentworth Gardens
Shelley Bannister, Northeastern Illinois University
Amy Blumenthal, author "Scrambled eggs and seed daddies"
Irene Campos Carr, Northeastern Illinois University
Ellen Cannon, Northeastern Illinois University
CL Forshner, Southern Illinois University at Carbondale
Diane Haslett, Northeastern Ilinois University
Helen Hughes, Governors State University, University Park, Illinois
Demetria Iazzetto, Urban Education Program, Associated Colleges of the Midwest
Renny Golden, Northeastern Illinois University
Mary Grady, S.E.E.D. Project, Glenbard, Illinois
Harriet Gross, Governors State University, Unviversity Park, Illinois
Maha Jarad, Union of Palestinian Women and Women United for a Better Chicago
Arlene Kaplan Daniels, Northwestern University, Evanston IL
LuAnn Leonard, The Hopi Tribe, Kykotsmovi AZ
Mary Mittler, Oakton Community College, Skokie IL
Judy Panko Reis, Health Center for Women with Disabilities
Polly Radosh, Western Illinois University, Macomb, Illinois
Wendy Stack, Northeastern Illinois University
Susan Stall, Northeastern Illinois University
Jeanne Wirpsa, (at the time) Chicago Abortion Fund

Becky Yane, (at the time) Cambodian Association, Chicago

The Writing Group who commented on every chapter of the Study Guide:
Diane Haslett
Susan Stall

Others who read and commented upon sections of the Study Guide:
Marjorie Altergott
Shelley Bannister
Amy Blumenthal
Demetria Iazzetto
Renny Golden
Mary Mittler
Mary Ann Schwartz
BarBara Scott

Others who provided lots of support:
Jim Lucas
Rachel Lucas-Thompson
Theo Pintzuk
Bettie Clapp Thompson

And the faculty and staff of the:
      Division of Humanities and Social Sciences
      College of Arts and Sciences
      Governors State University
      Dr. Roger K. Oden, Chairperson

TELECLASS PRODUCTION

Instructional Developer ....David Ainsworth

Producer/Director ....Cheryl Lambert

Audio Supervisor .... Jack Mulder

Video Engineers .... Ed Flowers

Bob White

Tom Sauch

Larry Lewis

Electronic Paintbox and Study Guide Design .... Margo Witkowsky

Production Assistants .... Candice Aljundi

Greg Brown

Jonathan Horjus

Jane Hu

Karl Rademacher

Renard Thomas

Teresa Toune

Produced by Communications Services .... Gary Fisk, Director

A division of the Center for Extended Learning and Communications Services
Ralph Kruse, Executive Director

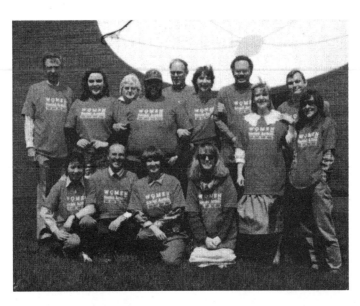